MW01222059

SLOW COOKER

THE COMPLETE COLLECTION

THE AUSTRALIAN
Women's Weekly

SLOW
COOKER

THE COMPLETE COLLECTION

CONTENTS

8 HOURS AND OVER

UNDER 8 HOURS

COOK IT SLOWLY

Slow cookers are available in a range of shapes and sizes and come with a variety of features. We tested the recipes in this cookbook using either a 4.5-litre (18-cup) slow cooker or a 5-litre (20-cup) slow cooker. If you have a smaller or larger cooker you will have to decrease or increase the quantity of food, and almost certainly the liquid content, in the recipes.

The first step when using your slow cooker is to read the manufacturer's instructions as each cooker will differ depending on its features. It will also outline appropriate safety measures, such as not leaving the appliance unattended at any time.

Some cookers heat from the base and side, while others heat just from the base; some have timers that cut off after the cooking time has expired, while others have timers that will keep the food warm by reducing the temperature until you're ready to eat.

SLOW COOKER SETTINGS

Generally, the longer meat takes to cook the more tender and more intense the flavours will be; so if you have the time, set your cooker to a low setting. However, if you're pressed for time, setting the slow cooker on high will halve the cooking time. No matter which setting you use, the food will reach simmering point. Some slow cookers have a warm setting; this is not used for cooking but rather to maintain the temperature of the food until it's time to eat. Over time you will find what works best for you and your slow cooking needs.

TEST KITCHEN TIP
* A general rule of thumb is that high heat settings on a slow cooker will cook twice as fast as the lower setting.

BEST CUTS FOR SLOW COOKING

Long, slow cooking will tenderise even the toughest cut of meat. Stewing or braising cuts are the best choices. Tough cuts are usually inexpensive, but cutting the meat off the bone yourself can usually save you more money, as you're not paying for the convenience of pre-cut meat. Cutting up the meat yourself also gives you the opportunity to trim off visible fat and make the pieces a uniform size.

The best cuts of meat to use are:

* **Beef** topside, oyster, blade, skirt, round, chuck, gravy beef.
* **Veal** osso buco, shanks, shoulder.
* **Lamb** neck chops, boneless shoulder, shanks, boneless forequarter.
* **Pork** forequarter chops, neck, belly, shoulder.
* **Chicken** any pieces on the bone, such as drumsticks, thighs, marylands.

Seafood is generally not suitable for slow cooking as it toughens quickly. However, there are many recipes for sauces that can be cooked in the slow cooker; add the seafood just before serving. Large octopus will cook and become tender in a slow cooker.

TEST KITCHEN TIP
* **Secondary cuts of goat, venison, rabbit, hare and kangaroo also work well in the slow cooker.**

BROWN THE MEAT FIRST

As straightforward as most slow cooking recipes are, it is best not to just throw all your ingredients in. Browning the meat first enhances the flavour and gives the meat a beautiful rich colour. Do this in a heated, oiled, large frying pan, adding the meat in batches, and turning it so that it browns evenly. Make sure there is a sufficient amount of oil in the pan so that the meat caramelises rather than scorches. Be sure to have the pan heated before adding the meat – it's also important to maintain the heat during the browning process; if the pan is not hot enough the meat will stew rather than brown.

TEST KITCHEN TIP
* If you're pushed for time, brown the meat or vegetables the night before. Once everything is browned, put it in a sealable container, along with any juices, and refrigerate until the next day.

THICKENING THE SAUCE

Coating the meat in flour before browning will result in a sauce that is thick enough to make a light coating gravy. If the recipe does not suggest coating the meat, then it is a good idea to thicken the sauce using plain flour or cornflour.

Blending the flour or cornflour with butter or a cold liquid such as water or some of the cooled juices from the cooker will help it combine with the cooking juices when stirred into the pan at the end of the cooking time. Put the lid back on and leave the sauce to thicken while the slow cooker is on the highest setting – this will take 10-20 minutes.

Another trick to thicken the sauce is to blend some of the cooked vegetables until smooth, and then stir them into the cooking juices.

TEST KITCHEN TIP
* The high setting comes in handy when you need to add ingredients or thicken the sauce at the end of the cooking time. Remove the lid and add the ingredients, or the mixture you are using to thicken the sauce, replace the lid and leave it on high for 10-20 minutes.

9

TIPS FOR FREEZING

Throughout this book we've suggested whether or not recipes are suitable to freeze. We've chosen to say 'not suitable' when coconut milk or large quantities of mushrooms and potatoes are used, and often when large pieces of meat are an ingredient. However, if you don't mind the food looking a bit sad after it's thawed, almost anything will tolerate freezing.

Slow-cooked meals will freeze for up to three months. There is usually a large quantity of liquid, so transfer the meat and vegetables to appropriate-sized freezer-friendly containers, then pour in enough of the liquid to cover the meat etc. Leave a 2.5cm (1-inch) space between the food and the lid to allow for expansion then seal the container. Label and date the container before placing in the freezer.

A NOTE ON DRIED BEANS

Some dried beans need to be cooked before adding to a slow cooker because of a certain chemical they contain. Kidney-shaped beans of all colours and sizes are related to each other and MUST be washed, drained and boiled in fresh water until tender. Add the cooked beans to the slow-cooked dish, just like canned beans.

Dried, unsoaked chickpeas and soya beans are fine to use in the slow cooker, just rinse them well first; there's no need for overnight soaking before cooking.

TEST KITCHEN TIP
* The condensation on the lid of your slow cooker is evaporation of moisture from the food being cooked. As the liquid evaporates it hits the lid, gently drips down onto the food and slowly bastes the meat as it cooks, ensuring tender meat and a rich sauce.

FOUR THINGS
YOU NEED TO KNOW

1

The recipes in this chapter have a minimum of 8 hours cooking time; if you need to reduce the cooking time, leave the cooker on the high setting for the duration. This will halve the cooking time specified. This works particularly well for recipes based on beef and lamb.

2

Be smart about choosing cuts of meat to use in the slow cooker. Don't buy expensive, lean cuts as they'll toughen and dry out during the long cooking time. Trim obvious fat from the meat, if you like. There will be some marbled fat left in the meat; the taste of the meal will benefit from this.

3

If in doubt about which cuts of meat to use in your slow cooker, the key words to look for at the butcher are casserole, stew and braise. Any cuts labelled with these methods will be perfect. Ask the butcher's advice if all else fails.

4

If you don't have the same-sized slow cooker as the ones we used for testing, don't worry. Read the manual that came with the cooker and it will advise you about the depth of liquid and how much food the cooker will hold. It is easy to adjust our recipes to suit the size of your own cooker – it's usually a case of simply adjusting the liquid content.

HOURS
AND OVER

8
HOURS AND OVER

BEEF

SECONDARY CUTS OF BEEF TOLERATE LONGER
COOKING TIMES THAN ANY OTHER MEAT

Short ribs are sections of beef ribs usually taken from the second to the tenth rib. Each 'slab' can contain from two to eight ribs. The meat is full of flavour but very tough so it is best braised slowly over low heat.

BOURBON-GLAZED
BEEF RIBS

prep + cook time 8 hours 30 minutes ✳ serves 4

* 1 medium brown onion (150g), chopped finely
* 5 cloves garlic, chopped coarsely
* ½ cup (140g) tomato sauce (ketchup)
* ½ cup (140g) sweet chilli sauce
* ⅓ cup (80ml) light soy sauce
* ½ cup (125ml) bourbon
* ½ cup (175g) honey
* 8 beef short ribs (2kg)

1   Combine onion, garlic, sauces, bourbon and honey in a 4.5-litre (18-cup) slow cooker. Add beef; turn to coat in mixture. Cook, covered, on low, about 8 hours. Carefully remove beef from cooker; cover to keep warm.

2   Transfer sauce to a large frying pan; bring to the boil. Boil, skimming fat from surface, for 10 minutes or until sauce reduces to 2 cups.

3   Spoon sauce over beef to serve.

Suitable to freeze
at the end of step 1.

Serving suggestion
Thinly sliced fried potatoes.

Nutritional count per serving *20.7g total fat (7.8g saturated fat); 3087kJ (738 cal); 47g carbohydrate; 75.5g protein; 0.1g fibre*

ITALIAN BEEF CASSEROLE

prep + cook time 8 hours 30 minutes ✳ serves 6

* 1.2kg (2½ pounds) beef blade steak, chopped coarsely
* ¼ cup (35g) plain (all-purpose) flour
* 1 tablespoon olive oil
* 1 large brown onion (200g), chopped coarsely
* 2 cloves garlic, crushed
* ½ teaspoon dried chilli flakes
* ½ cup (125ml) dry red wine
* 400g (12½ ounces) canned diced tomatoes
* ¼ cup (70g) tomato paste
* 2½ cups (625ml) beef stock
* 2 dried bay leaves
* 1 large red capsicum (bell pepper) (350g), chopped coarsely
* 1 tablespoon finely chopped fresh oregano
* ⅓ cup coarsely chopped fresh basil
* 1 large zucchini (150g), halved lengthways, sliced thickly
* 185g (6 ounces) swiss brown mushrooms, halved
* ⅓ cup loosely packed fresh basil leaves

1 Toss beef in flour to coat, shake off excess. Heat half the oil in a large frying pan; cook beef, in batches, until browned. Transfer to a 4.5-litre (18-cup) slow cooker.

2 Heat remaining oil in same pan; cook onion, garlic and chilli, stirring, until onion softens. Add wine; bring to the boil. Boil, uncovered, until liquid reduces by half.

3 Stir onion mixture into cooker with tomatoes, paste, stock, bay leaves, capsicum, oregano and chopped basil. Cook, covered, on low, about 7½ hours.

4 Add zucchini and mushrooms to cooker. Cook, covered, on low, a further 30 minutes. Discard bay leaves. Season to taste.

5 Sprinkle casserole with basil leaves to serve.

Suitable to freeze
at the end of step 3.

Serving suggestion
Creamy polenta, mashed potato or pasta.

Nutritional count per serving *16.8g total fat (6.2g saturated fat); 1731kJ (414 cal); 12.5g carbohydrate; 47.6g protein; 4g fibre*

BEEF CASSEROLE
WITH CHEESY HERB DUMPLINGS

prep + cook time 8 hours 30 minutes ✱ serves 6

* 1kg (2 pounds) gravy beef
* 1 tablespoon olive oil
* 1 large brown onion (200g), chopped coarsely
* 2 cloves garlic, crushed
* 2 tablespoons tomato paste
* 400g (12½ ounces) canned whole peeled tomatoes
* 1 cup (250ml) beef stock
* ½ cup (125ml) dry red wine
* 4 sprigs fresh thyme
* 250g (8 ounces) button mushrooms, halved
* 1 cup (150g) self-raising flour
* 50g (1½ ounces) cold butter, chopped finely
* 2 tablespoons finely chopped fresh flat-leaf parsley
* ⅔ cup (80g) coarsely grated vintage cheddar
* ½ cup (125ml) buttermilk, approximately

1 Cut beef into 3cm (1¼-inch) pieces. Heat oil in a large frying pan over medium-high heat. Cook beef, in batches, until browned. Transfer to a 4.5-litre (18-cup) slow cooker.

2 Add onion and garlic to same pan; cook, stirring, for 5 minutes or until onion softens. Add paste, tomatoes, stock, wine and thyme to pan; bring to the boil. Transfer mixture to slow cooker; add mushrooms.

3 Cook, covered, on low, about 7 hours. Remove and discard thyme sprigs. Season to taste.

4 Meanwhile, place flour in a medium bowl; rub in butter. Add half the parsley and half the cheddar; stir to combine. Stir in enough buttermilk to make a soft, sticky dough. Drop rounded tablespoons of the dumpling mixture, 2cm (¾-inch) apart, on top of casserole in cooker; scatter with remaining cheddar. Cook, covered, for 1 hour or until dumplings are cooked through. Scatter with remaining parsley to serve.

Suitable to freeze *at the end of step 3.*

Serving suggestion *Steamed green beans or spinach.*

Tip *We used a cabernet-style wine in this recipe.*

Nutritional count per serving *25.1g total fat (12g saturated fat); 2071kJ (495 cal); 24.7g carbohydrate; 38g protein; 4.4g fibre*

BALSAMIC AND PORT
BEEF SHANKS

prep + cook time 8 hours 20 minutes * serves 6

* 1 tablespoon olive oil
* 1.8kg (3¾-pound) piece beef shank, cut into 6 pieces
* 1 large red onion (300g), sliced thickly
* 1 stalk celery (150g), trimmed, sliced thickly
* ½ cup (125ml) beef stock
* ½ cup (125ml) port
* ¼ cup (60ml) balsamic vinegar
* 400g (12½ ounces) canned diced tomatoes
* 2 sprigs fresh thyme
* 1 tablespoon light brown sugar
* ⅓ cup coarsely chopped fresh basil
* 2 teaspoons finely grated lemon rind
* ½ cup (60g) seeded black olives

1 Heat oil in a large frying pan; cook beef, in batches, until browned. Transfer to a 4.5-litre (18-cup) slow cooker. Add onion, celery, stock, port, vinegar, tomatoes, thyme and sugar to slow cooker; cook, covered, on low, about 8 hours.

2 Stir in basil, rind and olives; season to taste.

3 Serve beef with sauce.

Suitable to freeze *at the end of step 1.*

Serving suggestion *Risotto, mashed potato or soft polenta.*

Tips *Ask the butcher to cut the beef shank into pieces for you, or use six 300g (10-ounce) pieces of beef osso buco. Dry red wine can be used instead of port.*

Nutritional count per serving *16.3g total fat (5.9g saturated fat); 1726kJ (413 cal); 12.1g carbohydrate; 48.2g protein; 1.9g fibre*

VEAL AND
ROSEMARY CASSEROLE

prep + cook time 8 hours 35 minutes ✳ serves 6

* 1.2kg (2½ pounds) boneless veal shoulder, chopped coarsely
* ¼ cup (35g) plain (all-purpose) flour
* 1 tablespoon olive oil
* 1 medium brown onion (150g), chopped coarsely
* 2 cloves garlic, crushed
* ½ cup (125ml) dry red wine
* 2 medium carrots (240g), chopped coarsely
* 2 stalks celery (300g), trimmed, chopped coarsely
* 2 medium parsnips (500g), chopped coarsely
* 2½ cups (625ml) beef stock
* 3 sprigs fresh rosemary
* ⅓ cup coarsely chopped fresh flat-leaf parsley

1 Toss veal in flour to coat, shake off excess. Heat half the oil in a large frying pan; cook veal, in batches, until browned. Transfer to a 4.5-litre (18-cup) slow cooker.

2 Heat remaining oil in same pan; cook onion and garlic, stirring, until onion softens. Add wine; bring to the boil. Boil, uncovered, until liquid reduces by half.

3 Stir onion mixture into cooker with carrot, celery, parsnip, stock and rosemary. Cook, covered, on low, about 8 hours. Season to taste.

4 Serve casserole sprinkled with parsley.

Suitable to freeze *at the end of step 3.*

Serving suggestion *Crusty bread or soft creamy polenta.*

Tip *If the butcher has some good stewing veal available, it's fine to use in this recipe.*

Nutritional count per serving *8.6g total fat (2g saturated fat); 1513kJ (362 cal); 15.6g carbohydrate; 49.5g protein; 4.2g fibre*

CHILLI CON CARNE

prep + cook time 8 hours 45 minutes ✱ serves 6

✱ 1 tablespoon olive oil
✱ 1 large brown onion (200g), chopped finely
✱ 2 cloves garlic, crushed
✱ 750g (1½ pounds) minced (ground) beef
✱ 1 teaspoon ground cumin
✱ 1½ teaspoons dried chilli flakes
✱ 1 cup (250ml) beef stock
✱ ⅓ cup (95g) tomato paste
✱ 820g (28 ounces) canned crushed tomatoes
✱ 1 tablespoon finely chopped fresh oregano
✱ 800g (1½ pounds) canned kidney beans, rinsed, drained
✱ ½ cup loosely packed fresh coriander (cilantro) leaves
✱ 6 flour tortillas, warmed

1   Heat oil in a large frying pan; cook onion and garlic, stirring, until onion softens. Add beef, cumin and chilli; cook, stirring, until browned. Transfer to a 4.5-litre (18-cup) slow cooker. Stir in stock, paste, tomatoes and oregano. Cook, covered, on low, about 8 hours.
2   Add beans; cook, covered, on high, for 30 minutes or until hot. Season to taste.
3   Sprinkle chilli con carne with coriander; serve with tortillas.

Suitable to freeze
at the end of step 1.

Serving suggestion
Steamed rice and a dollop of sour cream, plus a green leafy salad.

Nutritional count per serving *14.8g total fat (5.4g saturated fat); 1743kJ (417 cal); 30.9g carbohydrate; 35.1g protein; 9.5g fibre*

BEEF, DATE
AND SPINACH TAGINE

prep + cook time 8 hours 35 minutes ✳ serves 6

* 1.2kg (2½ pounds) beef blade steak, chopped coarsely
* ¼ cup (35g) plain (all-purpose) flour
* 1 tablespoon olive oil
* 1 large red onion (300g), chopped finely
* 2 cloves garlic, crushed
* 1 teaspoon ground cinnamon
* 1 teaspoon ground cumin
* ½ teaspoon ground ginger
* ½ teaspoon ground turmeric
* ¼ teaspoon saffron threads
* 1 cup (250ml) beef stock
* 400g (12½ ounces) canned diced tomatoes
* ¾ cup (100g) seeded dried dates
* 315g (10 ounces) spinach, shredded coarsely
* 1 tablespoon thinly sliced preserved lemon rind
* ⅓ cup (45g) coarsely chopped roasted unsalted pistachios

1 Toss beef in flour to coat, shake off excess. Heat half the oil in a large frying pan; cook beef, in batches, until browned. Transfer to a 4.5-litre (18-cup) slow cooker.
2 Heat remaining oil in same pan; cook onion and garlic, stirring, until onion softens. Add spices; cook, stirring, until fragrant. Add ½ cup of the stock; cook, stirring, until mixture boils.
3 Transfer onion mixture to cooker with remaining stock and tomatoes; stir to combine. Cook, covered, on low, about 8 hours.
4 Add dates, spinach and half the preserved lemon rind; cook, covered, on high, for 10 minutes or until spinach wilts. Season to taste.
5 Sprinkle tagine with nuts and remaining preserved lemon rind.

Suitable to freeze *at the end of step 3.*

Serving suggestion *Steamed couscous or rice.*

Tips *Beef shin or chuck steak could also be used. Preserved lemon is available at delis and some supermarkets. Remove and discard the flesh, wash the rind, then use it as the recipe directs.*

Nutritional count per serving *20.4g total fat (6.5g saturated fat); 1977kJ (473 cal); 22g carbohydrate; 47.5g protein; 5.6g fibre*

BEEF RIBS WITH STOUT
AND CARAMELISED ONION

prep + cook time 8 hours 45 minutes ✳ serves 6

* 1 tablespoon olive oil
* 2.5kg (5¼ pounds) racks beef short ribs
* 2 large brown onions (400g), sliced thinly
* 1 tablespoon light brown sugar
* 1 tablespoon balsamic vinegar
* ¼ cup (60ml) water
* 3 medium carrots (360g), sliced thickly
* 400g (12½ ounces) canned diced tomatoes
* 5 sprigs fresh thyme
* 1 tablespoon dijon mustard
* 1 cup (250ml) beef stock
* 1 cup (250ml) stout

1 Heat half the oil in a large frying pan; cook beef, in batches, until browned. Remove from pan.
2 Heat remaining oil in a large frying pan; cook onion, stirring, until soft. Add sugar, vinegar and the water; cook, stirring occasionally, for 10 minutes or until onion caramelises.
3 Transfer onion mixture to a 4.5-litre (18-cup) slow cooker; stir in carrot, tomatoes, thyme, mustard, stock and stout. Add beef, turn to coat in sauce mixture. Cook, covered, on low, about 8 hours. Season to taste.
4 Cut beef into ribs; serve with the sauce.

Suitable to freeze
at the end of step 3.

Serving suggestion
Steamed rice and a green leafy salad.

Tips *For best results, ask the butcher to cut the ribs into individual pieces. They will become more tender and fit more easily into the slow cooker. Stout is a strong-flavoured, dark-coloured beer originally from Britain. It is made with roasted barley, giving it its characteristic dark colour and bitter-sweet, almost coffee, flavour.*

Nutritional count per serving *21.4g total fat (8.1g saturated fat); 2228kJ (533 cal); 12g carbohydrate; 67.2g protein; 3.5g fibre*

SIMPLE BEEF AND
VEGETABLE CASSEROLE

prep + cook time 8 hours 30 minutes ✳ serves 6

* 1.2kg (2½ pounds) beef chuck steak, chopped coarsely
* ⅓ cup (50g) plain (all-purpose) flour
* ¼ cup (60ml) olive oil
* 2 medium brown onions (300g), cut into thick wedges
* 2 medium carrots (240g), chopped coarsely
* 2 stalks celery (300g), trimmed, chopped coarsely
* 1 medium parsnip (250g), chopped coarsely
* 1 medium swede (rutabaga) (225g), chopped coarsely
* 3 cloves garlic, crushed
* ¼ cup (70g) tomato paste
* 400g (12½ ounces) canned crushed tomatoes
* 1 cup (250ml) beef stock
* 2 dried bay leaves
* 10 sprigs fresh thyme
* ⅓ cup coarsely chopped fresh flat-leaf parsley

1 Coat beef in flour; shake off excess. Heat 2 tablespoons of the oil in a large frying pan; cook beef, in batches, until browned all over. Transfer beef to a 4.5-litre (18-cup) slow cooker.

2 Heat remaining oil in same pan; cook onion, carrot, celery, parsnip, swede and garlic; stirring, until onion softens. Add paste; cook, stirring, about 1 minute. Remove from heat; stir in tomatoes and stock.

3 Stir vegetable mixture and bay leaves into cooker; add thyme. Cook, covered, on low, about 8 hours. Discard thyme and bay leaves; season to taste.

4 Serve casserole sprinkled with parsley.

Suitable to freeze
at the end of step 3.

Serving suggestion
Crusty bread.

Tips *Gravy beef can be used instead of chuck steak. Use whatever vegetables you like: turnip, celeriac and jerusalem artichokes are all good choices. Swede is also known as swedish turnip.*

Nutritional count per serving *18.7g total fat (5.2g saturated fat); 1827kJ (437 cal); 19.3g carbohydrate; 44.9g protein; 5.9g fibre*

OSSO BUCO
WITH MIXED MUSHROOMS

prep + cook time 8 hours 50 minutes ✳ serves 6

* 6 large pieces beef osso buco (1.7kg)
* ¼ cup (35g) plain (all-purpose) flour
* 2 tablespoons olive oil
* 1 large brown onion (200g),
chopped coarsely
* 1 cup (250ml) marsala
* 1½ cups (375ml) beef stock
* ¼ cup (60ml) worcestershire sauce
* 2 tablespoons wholegrain mustard
* 2 sprigs fresh rosemary
* 185g (6 ounces) swiss brown mushrooms,
sliced thickly
* 155g (5 ounces) portabello mushrooms,
cut into 8 wedges
* 155g (5 ounces) oyster mushrooms,
chopped coarsely
* ½ cup (125ml) pouring cream
* ¼ cup (35g) gravy powder
* 2 tablespoons water
* ½ cup coarsely chopped fresh
flat-leaf parsley

1 Coat beef in flour, shake off excess. Heat half the oil in a large frying pan; cook beef, in batches, until browned all over. Remove from pan.

2 Heat remaining oil in same pan; cook onion, stirring, until onion softens. Add marsala; bring to the boil. Add onion mixture to a 4.5-litre (18-cup) slow cooker; stir in stock, sauce, mustard and rosemary. Place beef in cooker, fitting pieces upright and tightly packed in a single layer. Add mushrooms to cooker. Cook, covered, on low, about 8 hours.

3 Carefully remove beef from cooker; cover to keep warm. Add cream and combined gravy powder and the water to cooker; cook, covered, on high, for 10 minutes or until mixture thickens slightly. Stir in parsley; season to taste.

4 Serve beef with mushroom sauce.

Not suitable to freeze.

Serving suggestion *Kumara, potato or celeriac mash and a green leafy salad.*

Tips *Ask the butcher for either veal or beef shin (osso buco) – veal will be smaller than beef, in which case you will need about 12 pieces to serve six people. You can use a mixture of mushrooms as we have, or just one variety with a good robust flavour – you will need a total of 500g (1 pound).*

Nutritional count per serving *16.5g total fat (7.1g saturated fat); 1902kJ (455 cal); 17.4g carbohydrate; 45.5g protein; 3.7g fibre*

RED WINE, BEEF
AND MUSHROOM STEW

prep + cook time 8 hours 25 minutes ✳ serves 6

* 16 spring onions (400g)
* 2 tablespoons olive oil
* 375g (12 ounces) button mushrooms
* 4 rindless bacon slices (260g), chopped coarsely
* 3 cloves garlic, crushed
* 1 cup (250ml) dry red wine
* ¼ cup (70g) tomato paste
* ½ teaspoon caster (superfine) sugar
* 1.2kg (2½ pounds) gravy beef, chopped coarsely
* 2 medium fennel bulbs (600g), sliced thickly
* ⅓ cup coarsely chopped fresh flat-leaf parsley

1   Trim green ends from onions, leaving about 8cm (3 inches) of stems attached; trim roots. Heat oil in a large frying pan; cook onions, mushrooms, bacon and garlic, stirring, until onion softens. Stir in wine, paste and sugar; bring to the boil, boil, uncovered, about 2 minutes.

2   Place beef, fennel and onion mixture in a 4.5-litre (18-cup) slow cooker. Cook, covered, on low, about 8 hours.

3   Stir in parsley; season to taste.

Not suitable to freeze.

Serving suggestion
Mashed potato or creamy polenta and steamed green beans.

Tip *Use chuck steak or any stewing steak instead of gravy beef.*

Nutritional count per serving *21.3g total fat (6.8g saturated fat); 1952kJ (467 cal); 6.3g carbohydrate; 53.1g protein; 5.2g fibre*

BRAISED BEEF
CHEEKS IN STOUT

prep + cook time 9 hours 45 minutes ✳ serves 6

* ✱ 2 tablespoons olive oil
* ✱ 6 beef cheeks (1.5kg)
* ✱ 12 shallots (300g)
* ✱ 2 cloves garlic, crushed
* ✱ 1 cup (250ml) beef stock
* ✱ 2 medium carrots (240g), chopped coarsely
* ✱ 250g portabello mushrooms, chopped coarsely
* ✱ 3 cups (750ml) stout
* ✱ 2 tablespoons dark brown sugar
* ✱ 2 sprigs fresh rosemary
* ✱ ¼ cup (35g) cornflour (cornstarch)
* ✱ 2 tablespoons water
* ✱ ⅓ cup coarsely chopped fresh flat-leaf parsley

1 Heat half the oil in a large frying pan; cook beef, in batches, until browned all over. Transfer to a 4.5-litre (18-cup) slow cooker.

2 Meanwhile, peel shallots, trim roots; halve shallots lengthways.

3 Heat remaining oil in same pan; cook shallots and garlic, stirring, until shallots are browned lightly. Add stock; bring to the boil. Stir shallot mixture into cooker with carrot, mushrooms, stout, sugar and rosemary. Cook, covered, on low, about 9 hours.

4 Carefully remove beef from cooker; cover to keep warm. Stir blended cornflour and the water into cooker; cook, covered, on high, for 15 minutes or until sauce has thickened slightly. Season to taste.

5 Serve beef with the sauce, sprinkled with parsley.

Not suitable to freeze.

Serving suggestion
Creamy mashed potato or colcannon (mashed potato with cabbage).

Tip *Beef cheeks are available from most butchers, but you might need to order them in advance. Substitute with beef shin, chuck or blade steak if cheeks are unavailable.*

Nutritional count per serving *26.2g total fat (9.4g saturated fat); 2424kJ (580 cal); 16.8g carbohydrate; 55.7g protein; 2.8g fibre*

BORSCHT

prep + cook time 8 hours 50 minutes ✳ serves 6

* 60g (2 ounces) butter
* 2 medium brown onions (300g), chopped finely
* 500g (1 pound) beef chuck steak, cut into large chunks
* 1 cup (250ml) water
* 750g (1½ pounds) beetroot (beets), peeled, chopped finely
* 2 medium potatoes (400g), chopped finely
* 2 medium carrots (240g), chopped finely
* 4 small (360g) finely chopped tomatoes
* 1 litre (4 cups) beef stock
* ⅓ cup (80ml) red wine vinegar
* 3 dried bay leaves
* 4 cups (320g) finely shredded cabbage
* 2 tablespoons coarsely chopped fresh flat-leaf parsley
* ½ cup (120g) sour cream

1 Melt half the butter in a large frying pan; cook onion, stirring, until soft. Place onion in a 4.5-litre (18-cup) slow cooker. Melt remaining butter in same pan; cook beef, stirring, until browned all over. Place beef in cooker. Add the water to the same pan; bring to the boil, then add to slow cooker with beetroot, potato, carrot, tomato, stock, vinegar and bay leaves. Cook, covered, on low, about 8 hours.
2 Discard bay leaves. Remove beef from soup; shred using two forks. Return beef to soup with cabbage; cook, covered, on high, for 20 minutes or until cabbage is wilted. Stir in parsley.
3 Serve soup topped with sour cream.

Suitable to freeze
at the end of step 1.

Nutritional count per serving 20.6g total fat (12.4g saturated fat); 1689kJ (404 cal); 25.3g carbohydrate; 25.3g protein; 8.8g fibre

CORNED BEEF
WITH HORSERADISH SAUCE

prep + cook time 8 hours 10 minutes ✳ serves 6

* 1.5kg (3-pound) piece corned silverside
* 1 medium brown onion (150g), chopped coarsely
* 1 medium carrot (120g), chopped coarsely
* 1 stalk celery (150g), trimmed, chopped coarsely
* 10 black peppercorns
* 1 tablespoon brown malt vinegar
* 1 teaspoon light brown sugar
* 2.5 litres (10 cups) water, approximately

HORSERADISH SAUCE
* 45g (1½ ounces) butter
* 2 tablespoons plain (all-purpose) flour
* 2 cups (500ml) hot milk
* 1 tablespoon horseradish cream
* 1 tablespoon coarsely chopped fresh flat-leaf parsley

1 Rinse beef under cold water; pat dry with paper towel. Place beef, onion, carrot, celery, peppercorns, vinegar and sugar in a 4.5-litre (18-cup) slow cooker. Add enough of the water to barely cover beef. Cook, covered, on low, about 8 hours.
2 Make horseradish sauce just before serving.
3 Remove beef from cooker; discard liquid and vegetables.
4 Slice beef thickly; serve with horseradish sauce.

HORSERADISH SAUCE Melt butter in a medium saucepan, add flour; cook, stirring, about 1 minute. Gradually add milk, stirring, until sauce boils and thickens. Stir in horseradish cream and parsley. Season to taste.

Not suitable to freeze.

Serving suggestion *Steamed seasonal vegetables such as baby potatoes and beans, or carrots, peas, squash and zucchini.*

Nutritional count per serving *26.1g total fat (13.9g saturated fat); 2266kJ (542 cal); 10.2g carbohydrate; 65.7g protein; 1.4g fibre*

BEEF POT ROAST

prep + cook time 8 hours 30 minutes ✳ serves 4

* ¼ cup (60ml) olive oil
* 4 small potatoes (180g), unpeeled, halved
* 375g (12-ounce) piece unpeeled pumpkin, cut into 4 wedges
* 8 baby onions (200g), halved
* 375g (12 ounces) baby carrots
* 250g (8 ounces) jerusalem artichokes (sunchokes)
* 750g (1½-pound) piece beef blade steak
* 1 tablespoon wholegrain mustard
* 2 teaspoons smoked paprika
* 2 teaspoons finely chopped fresh rosemary
* 1 garlic clove, crushed
* 1½ cups (375ml) beef stock
* ½ cup (125ml) dry red wine
* 2 tablespoons balsamic vinegar
* ¼ cup (35g) gravy powder
* 2 tablespoons water

1 Heat 2 tablespoons of the oil in a large frying pan; cook potato, pumpkin and onion, in batches, until browned all over. Place vegetables in a 4.5-litre (18-cup) slow cooker with carrots and artichokes.

2 Heat 2 teaspoons of the remaining oil in same pan; cook beef until browned all over. Remove beef from pan; spread with combined mustard, paprika, rosemary, garlic and remaining oil.

3 Place beef on vegetables in slow cooker; pour over combined stock, wine and vinegar. Cook, covered, on low, about 8 hours.

4 Remove beef and vegetables from cooker; cover beef, stand 10 minutes before slicing thinly. Cover vegetables to keep warm.

5 Meanwhile, blend gravy powder with the water in a small bowl until smooth. Stir gravy mixture into liquid in slow cooker; cook, covered, on high, for 10 minutes or until gravy is thickened slightly. Season to taste. Strain gravy.

6 Serve beef with gravy and vegetables.

Not suitable to freeze.

Serving suggestion
Steamed green beans or broccoli.

Tips *We used nicola potatoes and jap pumpkin in this recipe. Jerusalem artichokes can be hard to find; add swede, parsnip or turnip to the pot roast instead. Gravy powder is an instant gravy mix made with browned flour. Plain flour can be used for thickening instead.*

Nutritional count per serving *26.8g total fat (7.5g saturated fat); 2353kJ (563 cal); 25g carbohydrate; 46.8g protein; 7.1g fibre*

OLD-FASHIONED
CURRIED SAUSAGES

prep + cook time 8 hours 20 minutes ✳ serves 6

* 12 thick beef sausages (1.8kg)
* 1 tablespoon vegetable oil
* 2 medium brown onions (300g), sliced thinly
* 2 tablespoons mild curry powder
* 400g (12½ ounces) canned diced tomatoes
* 1 cup (250ml) beef stock
* 1 cup (250ml) water
* 4 medium potatoes (800g), unpeeled, cut into thick wedges
* 1 cup (120g) frozen peas, thawed
* ½ cup (80g) sultanas

1 Place sausages in a large saucepan, add enough cold water to cover sausages; bring to the boil. Boil, uncovered, about 2 minutes; drain.
2 Heat oil in same pan; cook onion, stirring, until softened. Add curry powder; cook, stirring, until fragrant. Remove from heat; stir in tomatoes, stock and the water.
3 Place potatoes in a 4.5-litre (18-cup) slow cooker; top with sausages and onion mixture. Cook, covered, on low, about 8 hours.
4 Stir in peas and sultanas. Season to taste.

Not suitable to freeze.

Serving suggestion
Crusty bread.

Nutritional count per serving *79.8g total fat (37g saturated fat); 4435kJ (1061 cal); 40g carbohydrate; 41.3g protein; 13.7g fibre*

BRAISED
ASIAN-STYLE BEEF RIBS

prep + cook time 8 hours 30 minutes ✳ serves 6

* 2kg (4 pounds) racks beef short ribs
* ½ cup (190g) hoisin sauce
* ¼ cup (60ml) salt-reduced soy sauce
* ¼ cup (60ml) mirin
* 2 x 3cm (1¼-inch) strips orange rind
* ½ cup (90g) honey
* 5cm (2-inch) piece fresh ginger (25g), grated
* 3 cloves garlic, crushed
* 1 fresh long red chilli, sliced thinly
* 2 teaspoons sesame oil

1   Cut beef into pieces to fit into a 4.5-litre (18-cup) slow cooker; place beef in cooker. Combine remaining ingredients in a large jug; pour sauce over ribs. Cook, covered, on low, about 8 hours. Season to taste.
2   Cut beef into ribs; serve with the sauce.

Not suitable to freeze.

Tip *Ask the butcher to cut the ribs so that they will fit into your slow cooker.*

Nutritional count per serving *15g total fat (5.7g saturated fat); 1622kJ (388 cal); 25g carbohydrate; 35.1g protein; 3.8g fibre*

STEAK AND PEPPER
DUMPLING PIE

prep + cook time 8 hours 45 minutes * serves 6

* 2½ tablespoons olive oil
* 1.2kg (2½ pounds) beef chuck steak, cut into 3cm (1¼-inch) pieces
* 12 shallots (300g), peeled
* 2 cloves garlic, crushed
* 4 rindless bacon slices (250g), chopped coarsely
* 400g (12½ ounces) button mushrooms, halved
* 2 teaspoons cracked black pepper
* 1 tablespoon plain (all-purpose) flour
* 2 tablespoons tomato paste
* 1½ cups (225g) self-raising flour
* 75g (2½ ounces) cold butter, chopped finely
* ¼ cup finely chopped fresh flat-leaf parsley
* ½ cup (40g) finely grated parmesan
* ¾ cup (180ml) milk, approximately

1 Heat 1½ tablespoons of the oil in a large frying pan over medium-high heat. Cook beef, in three batches, until browned. Transfer to a 4.5-litre (18-cup) slow cooker.

2 Heat remaining oil in the same pan; cook shallots, garlic, bacon and mushrooms, stirring, for 10 minutes or until shallots soften. Add pepper and plain flour; cook, stirring, about 1 minute. Add paste; stir to combine. Transfer mixture to slow cooker. Cook, covered, on low, about 7 hours. Season with salt.

3 Meanwhile, place self-raising flour in a medium bowl; rub in butter. Add parsley and parmesan; stir to combine. Stir in enough milk to make a soft, sticky dough. Roll dough into a 30cm (12-inch) square on a lightly floured surface. Roll up to form a log shape; trim ends. Slice into 2cm (¾-inch) thick rounds. Place rounds, in a single layer, over beef mixture. Cook, covered, a further 1 hour or until dumplings are risen and cooked through.

Suitable to freeze
at the end of step 2.

Serving suggestion
Steamed green beans.

Nutritional count per serving *43.8g total fat (17.2g saturated fat); 3223kJ (770 cal); 29.4g carbohydrate; 64.3g protein; 6.5g fibre*

OXTAIL STEW
WITH RED WINE AND PORT

prep + cook time 9 hours 15 minutes ✳ serves 8

* 2kg (4 pounds) oxtails, cut into 5cm (2-inch) pieces
* 2 tablespoons plain (all-purpose) flour
* 2 tablespoons vegetable oil
* 12 brown pickling onions (480g)
* 2 medium carrots (240g), chopped coarsely
* 1 stalk celery (150g), trimmed, sliced thickly
* 8 cloves garlic, peeled
* 1½ cups (375ml) dry red wine
* 2 cups (500ml) port
* 2 cups (500ml) beef stock
* 4 sprigs fresh thyme
* 1 dried bay leaf
* ½ cup lightly packed fresh flat-leaf parsley leaves

1   Trim excess fat from oxtail; toss oxtail in flour to coat, shake off excess. Heat half the oil in a large frying pan; cook oxtail, in batches, until browned. Transfer to a 4.5-litre (18-cup) slow cooker.

2   Meanwhile, peel onions, leaving root ends intact.

3   Heat remaining oil in same pan; cook onions, carrot, celery and garlic, stirring, for 5 minutes or until vegetables are browned lightly. Transfer to cooker. Add wine and port to pan; bring to the boil. Boil, uncovered, until reduced to 1 cup. Transfer to cooker with stock, thyme and bay leaf. Cook, covered, on low, about 8 hours.

4   Discard thyme and bay leaf. Remove oxtail; cover to keep warm. Cook sauce, uncovered, on high, for 30 minutes or until thickened. Skim fat from surface. Season to taste. Return oxtail to sauce to heat through.

5   Serve stew sprinkled with parsley.

Suitable to freeze *at the end of step 4.*

Serving suggestion *Potato, celeriac or parsnip puree.*

Tip *Oxtails are often sold frozen or may need to be ordered from the butcher. Beef brisket, beef cheeks and chuck steak are all suitable to use instead.*

Nutritional count per serving *48.4g total fat (17.4g saturated fat); 2959kJ (708 cal); 14.5g carbohydrate; 30.9g protein; 2g fibre*

Pulled beef, or pork, comes from pulling extremely tender pieces of meat apart – rather than cutting it into slices – usually with two forks, which separates the meat into strands. Low, slow cooking is required to get meat tender enough to pull apart into pieces.

PULLED BEEF
WITH BARBECUE SAUCE

prep + cook time 8 hours 45 minutes ✳ serves 6

* 2 cloves garlic, crushed
* 1 fresh long red chilli, chopped finely
* 2 tablespoons dark brown sugar
* 1½ cups (420g) tomato sauce (ketchup)
* 1½ tablespoons worcestershire sauce
* 2 tablespoons cider vinegar
* 750g (1½-pound) piece beef rump
* 6 long crusty bread rolls

1 Place garlic, chilli, sugar, sauces and vinegar in a 4.5-litre (18-cup) slow cooker. Stir well to combine; add beef and turn to coat in mixture. Cook, covered, on low, about 8 hours.

2 Carefully remove beef from cooker; shred meat coarsely using two forks.

3 Transfer sauce mixture to a large saucepan, bring to the boil over medium heat. Boil, uncovered, for 10 minutes or until thickened. Stir in beef.

4 Split rolls in half lengthways, fill with beef and sauce mixture.

Suitable to freeze
at the end of step 3.

Serving suggestion
Fill rolls with beef mixture, lettuce, finely grated cheddar and pickled peppers.

Nutritional count per serving *8.9g total fat (2.6g saturated fat); 2159kJ (516 cal); 70.4g carbohydrate; 36g protein; 5.8g fibre*

CHINESE BRAISED
BEEF CHEEKS

prep + cook time 8 hours 30 minutes ✻ serves 8

✻ 1 large orange
✻ 4 green onions (scallions), trimmed,
cut into 6cm (2½-inch) lengths
✻ 6 cloves garlic, crushed
✻ 10cm (4-inch) piece fresh ginger (50g),
sliced thickly
✻ 1½ cups (375ml) chinese cooking wine
✻ 1 cup (250ml) soy sauce
✻ 1 cup (220g) brown sugar
✻ ½ teaspoon sesame oil
✻ 5 star anise
✻ 2 cinnamon sticks
✻ 8 beef cheeks (2.5kg)
✻ 1 fresh long red chilli, sliced thinly
✻ 2 green onions (scallions), extra,
trimmed, sliced thinly lengthways
✻ ½ cup firmly packed fresh coriander
(cilantro) leaves

1   Using a vegetable peeler, peel three wide strips of rind from orange.
2   Combine rind, onion, garlic, ginger, wine, sauce, sugar, oil, star anise and cinnamon in a 4.5-litre (18-cup) slow cooker. Stir until the sugar dissolves. Add beef; turn to coat in mixture. Cook, covered, on low, about 8 hours.
3   Serve beef with a little cooking liquid; sprinkle with chilli, extra onion and coriander.

Suitable to freeze
at the end of step 2.

Serving suggestion
Steamed rice.

Tip *You may need to order beef cheeks in advance from the butcher.*

Nutritional count per serving *12.7g total fat (5.4g saturated fat); 1521kJ (366 cal); 29g carbohydrate; 34.7g protein; 0.8g fibre*

MASSAMAN BEEF CURRY

prep + cook time 8 hours 45 minutes ✳ serves 6

* **2 tablespoons peanut oil**
* **2 large brown onions (400g),
cut into thin wedges**
* **1kg (2 pounds) gravy beef,
chopped coarsely**
* **⅔ cup (200g) massaman curry paste**
* **1 cup (250ml) coconut milk**
* **1 cup (250ml) chicken stock**
* **2 cinnamon sticks**
* **2 dried bay leaves**
* **3 medium potatoes (600g),
chopped coarsely**
* **½ cup (70g) roasted unsalted peanuts**
* **2 tablespoons light brown sugar**
* **1 tablespoon fish sauce**
* **⅓ cup lightly packed fresh coriander
(cilantro) leaves**
* **1 lime, cut into wedges**

1 Heat half the oil in a large frying pan; cook onion, stirring, for 10 minutes or until browned lightly. Transfer to a 4.5-litre (18-cup) slow cooker.
2 Heat remaining oil in same pan; cook beef, in batches, until browned. Add paste; cook, stirring, for 1 minute or until fragrant. Transfer to cooker.
3 Add coconut milk, stock, cinnamon, bay leaves, potato and nuts to cooker. Cook, covered, on low, about 8 hours.
4 Discard cinnamon sticks. Stir in sugar and sauce. Serve sprinkled with coriander; accompany with lime wedges.

Not suitable to freeze.   **Tip** *Chuck steak is also suitable for this recipe.*

Nutritional count per serving *48.3g total fat (16.6g saturated fat); 3051kJ (730 cal); 25.9g carbohydrate; 45.6g protein; 7.5g fibre*

CORIANDER BEEF CURRY

prep + cook time 8 hours 30 minutes ✳ serves 6

* 6 fresh long green chillies
* 7.5cm (3-inch) piece fresh ginger (35g), chopped coarsely
* 4 cloves garlic, chopped coarsely
* 2 medium tomatoes (300g), chopped coarsely
* 1 tablespoon tomato paste
* 2 teaspoons sea salt flakes
* 2½ cups firmly packed fresh coriander (cilantro) leaves
* 1½ tablespoons vegetable oil
* 1.5kg (3 pounds) chuck steak or gravy beef, cut into 5cm (2-inch) pieces
* 400ml (14 ounces) canned coconut cream

1   Coarsely chop four of the chillies. Thinly slice remaining chillies, reserve.
2   Blend or process chopped chilli, ginger, garlic, tomato, paste, salt and 2 cups of the coriander until smooth. Reserve ½ cup of the coriander paste; cover, then refrigerate.
3   Heat 1 tablespoon of the oil in a large frying pan over medium-high heat; cook beef, in batches, until browned. Transfer beef to a 4.5-litre (18-cup) slow cooker.
4   Add remaining coriander paste and 1 cup of the coconut cream to cooker; stir to combine. (Refrigerate remaining coconut cream.) Cook, covered, on low, about 8 hours. Season to taste.
5   Heat remaining oil in a small frying pan; cook sliced chilli, stirring, for 2 minutes or until softened. Drizzle curry with remaining coconut cream; top with the reserved coriander paste, chilli and remaining coriander.

Suitable to freeze *at the end of step 4.*

Serving suggestion *Steamed jasmine rice.*

Tip *You will need about 2 large bunches of coriander.*

Nutritional count per serving *36.4g total fat (18.4g saturated fat); 2424kJ (579 cal); 4.9g carbohydrate; 57.6g protein; 2.3g fibre*

MEXICAN BEEF CHILLI MOLE

prep + cook time 8 hours 45 minutes ✳ serves 4

* 1kg (2 pounds) beef chuck steak,
cut into 3cm (1¼-inch) cubes
* 2 cups (500ml) beef stock
* 2 cups (500ml) water
* 3 chipotle peppers in adobo sauce,
chopped finely
* 4 rindless bacon slices (260g),
chopped coarsely
* 1 medium brown onion (150g),
chopped finely
* 4 cloves garlic, crushed
* 2 tablespoons tomato paste
* 439g (14 ounces) canned black beans,
rinsed, drained
* 410g (13 ounces) canned tomato puree
* 2 teaspoons each ground cumin, ground
coriander and sweet smoked paprika
* ¼ teaspoon chilli powder
* ½ teaspoon ground cinnamon
* 2 tablespoons finely grated
mexican chocolate
* ⅔ cup (80g) grated manchego cheese
* 1 fresh jalapeño chilli, sliced thinly
* 2 green onions (scallions), sliced thinly

1 Combine beef, stock, the water, chipotle, bacon, brown onion, garlic, paste, beans, puree and spices in a 4.5-litre (18-cup) slow cooker. Cook, covered, on low, about 8 hours. Season to taste.
2 Stir chocolate into cooker; season to taste.
3 Serve beef topped with cheese, jalapeño and green onion.

Suitable to freeze *at the end of step 2.*

Tips *Chipotle in adobo sauce and mexican chocolate are available from specialist delicatessens and grocers. If chipotle in adobo sauce is unavailable use 2-3 tablespoons hot Mexican-style chilli sauce (adding enough to suit your taste).*

If mexican chocolate is unavailable use dark (semi-sweet) chocolate. Manchego is an aged, hard, intensely flavoured Spanish cheese. It is available from Spanish delicatessens and specialist cheese shops; substitute haloumi or fetta if not available. If fresh jalapeño chillies are unavailable, use slices of bottled pickled jalapeño.

Nutritional count per serving *42.7g total fat (17g saturated fat); 3503kJ (838 cal); 30.3g carbohydrate; 78.9g protein; 9.6g fibre*

BEER AND THYME
BEEF CHEEKS

prep + cook time 10 hours 30 minutes ✱ serves 6

* 16 baby onions (400g)
* 3 stalks celery (450g), trimmed, chopped coarsely
* 400g (12½ ounces) baby carrots, trimmed
* 4 sprigs fresh thyme
* 1½ cups (375ml) beer
* 1 cup (250ml) beef stock
* ¼ cup (70g) tomato paste
* 2 tablespoons worcestershire sauce
* 1 tablespoon brown sugar
* 1 tablespoon wholegrain mustard
* 2kg (4 pounds) trimmed beef cheeks
* 150g (4½ ounces) green beans, trimmed

1 Peel onions, leaving root end intact. Combine onions with celery, carrots, thyme, beer, stock, paste, sauce, sugar and mustard in a 5-litre (20-cup) slow cooker. Add beef; turn to coat in mixture. Cook, covered, on low, about 9½ hours.

2 Discard thyme. Add beans to cooker; cook, covered, on low, for 30 minutes. Season to taste.

3 Serve beef sprinkled with extra fresh thyme, if you like.

Suitable to freeze *at the end of step 2.*

Serving suggestion *Creamy mashed potato or cheesy polenta.*

Tip *You will need 1 bunch of baby carrots. They may also be sold as 'dutch' carrots.*

Nutritional count per serving *25.8g total fat (8.1g saturated fat); 3244kJ (776 cal); 42.6g carbohydrate; 80.7g protein; 16.5g fibre*

VIETNAMESE BEEF BRISKET

prep + cook time 9 hours 45 minutes ✳ serves 4

* 1.5kg (3 pounds) beef brisket, trimmed, cut into 5cm (2-inch) pieces
* 1 large brown onion (200g), sliced thinly
* 3 cloves garlic, crushed
* 4 teaspoons finely grated fresh ginger
* 1 fresh long red chilli, sliced thinly
* 2 x 10cm (4-inch) sticks fresh lemon grass (40g), halved lengthways
* 2 fresh kaffir lime leaves, bruised
* 2 star anise
* 1 cinnamon stick
* 2 tablespoons grated palm sugar
* ¼ cup (60ml) fish sauce
* ¼ cup (60ml) dark soy sauce
* 3 cups (750ml) beef stock
* 1 large red capsicum (bell pepper) (350g), chopped coarsely
* 125g (4 ounces) baby corn, halved
* 150g (4½ ounces) snake beans, chopped coarsely
* ⅓ cup coarsely chopped roasted unsalted peanuts
* ⅓ cup loosely packed fresh coriander (cilantro) leaves
* 1 lime, cut into wedges

1 Combine beef, onion, garlic, ginger, chilli, lemon grass, lime leaves, star anise, cinnamon, sugar, sauces, stock, capsicum and corn in a 5-litre (20-cup) slow cooker. Cook, covered, on low, about 9 hours.

2 Add beans to cooker; cook, covered, a further 30 minutes.

3 Discard lemon grass, lime leaves, star anise and cinnamon; season to taste.

4 Sprinkle beef with nuts and coriander; accompany with lime wedges.

Suitable to freeze
at the end of step 3.

Serving suggestion
Steamed rice.

Nutritional count per serving *36.9g total fat (10.6g saturated fat); 3319kJ (794 cal); 24.8g carbohydrate; 88g protein; 6.9g fibre*

CHILLI AND BRANDY BEEF
WITH WHITE BEANS

prep + cook time 8 hours 25 minutes ✳ serves 6

* 6 shallots (150g)
* 1.2kg (2½ pounds) beef brisket, chopped coarsely
* 1 fresh long red chilli, chopped finely
* 2 cloves garlic, crushed
* 3 medium roma (egg) tomatoes (225g), chopped coarsely
* 2 tablespoons tomato paste
* 1 cup (250ml) beef stock
* ¼ cup (60ml) brandy
* 400g (12½ ounces) canned cannellini beans, rinsed, drained
* ⅓ cup coarsely chopped fresh flat-leaf parsley

1 Peel shallots, leaving root ends intact; cut shallots in half lengthways.

2 Combine shallots, beef, chilli, garlic, tomato, paste, stock and brandy in a 4.5-litre (18-cup) slow cooker; cook, covered, on low, about 8 hours.

3 Add beans; cook, covered, on high, for 20 minutes or until hot. Stir in parsley; season to taste.

Suitable to freeze *at the end of step 2.*

Serving suggestion *A simple green salad or crusty bread.*

Tips *Beef brisket is an economical cut of meat; ask the butcher to trim the fat away and to chop the meat for you. For a slightly richer colour and flavour, brown the beef before adding it to the cooker.*

Nutritional count per serving *12.1g total fat (5.1g saturated fat); 1375kJ (329 cal); 3.6g carbohydrate; 45g protein; 2.2g fibre*

BEEF AND VEGETABLE SOUP

prep + cook time 9 hours 45 minutes ✳ serves 4

* 1kg (2 pounds) gravy beef, trimmed,
cut into 2.5cm (1-inch) pieces
* 1 garlic clove, crushed
* 1 medium brown onion (150g),
cut into 1cm (½-inch) pieces
* 2 stalks celery (300g), trimmed,
cut into 1cm (½-inch) pieces
* 2 medium carrots (240g),
cut into 1cm (½-inch) pieces
* 2 medium potatoes (400g),
cut into 1cm (½-inch) pieces
* 400g (12½ ounces) canned diced tomatoes
* 1 litre (4 cups) water
* 2 cups (500ml) beef stock
* 2 dried bay leaves
* 1 cup (120g) frozen peas
* ⅓ cup coarsely chopped fresh
flat-leaf parsley

1 Combine beef, garlic, onion, celery, carrot, potato, tomatoes, the water, stock and bay leaves in a 5-litre (20-cup) slow cooker. Cook, covered, on low, about 9 hours.
2 Add peas to cooker; cook, covered, a further 30 minutes.
3 Discard bay leaves. Season to taste.
4 Serve soup sprinkled with parsley.

Suitable to freeze
at the end of step 3.

Serving suggestion
*Thick slices of
crusty bread.*

Nutritional count per serving *14.5g total fat (5.4g saturated fat); 1940kJ (464 cal); 20.9g carbohydrate; 57.4g protein; 8.9g fibre*

BEEF RIB BOURGUIGNON

prep + cook time 8 hours 30 minutes ✳ serves 4

* 12 shallots (300g)
* 200g (6½ ounces) button mushrooms
* 200g (6½ ounces) swiss brown mushrooms
* 4 rindless bacon slices (260g),
cut into 5cm (2-inch) lengths
* 3 cloves garlic, sliced thinly
* 2 fresh thyme sprigs
* 2 fresh bay leaves
* 1½ cups (375ml) dry red wine
* 3 cups (750ml) beef stock
* 2 tablespoons tomato paste
* 1.2kg (2½ pounds) beef short ribs
* ½ cup finely chopped fresh flat-leaf parsley

1 Place shallots, mushrooms, bacon, garlic, thyme, bay leaves, wine, stock, paste and beef in a 4.5-litre (18-cup) slow cooker. Cook, covered, on low, about 8 hours. Season to taste.
2 Discard thyme and bay leaves. Stir in half the parsley; season to taste. Serve topped with remaining parsley and accompany with crusty bread, if you like.

Not suitable to freeze.

Serving suggestion *Mashed potato or steamed baby new potatoes.*

Tip *Cut the shallots in half if they are large.*

Nutritional count per serving *47.8g total fat (16.2g saturated fat); 3106kJ (743 cal); 6g carbohydrate; 60.9g protein; 4.3g fibre*

COCONUT CURRIED BEEF

prep + cook time 10 hours 45 minutes ✳ serves 4

* 1kg (2 pounds) diced beef
* 2 tablespoons thai yellow curry paste
* 1⅔ cups (410ml) coconut milk
* 2 cups (500ml) beef stock
* 4 teaspoons finely grated fresh ginger
* 3 cloves garlic, crushed
* 2 medium brown onions (300g), cut into thin wedges
* 2 fresh kaffir lime leaves
* 8 fresh curry leaves
* 2 tablespoons fish sauce
* 2 tablespoons grated palm sugar
* 150g (4½ ounces) snow peas
* 2 tablespoons finely chopped peanuts, toasted
* ¼ cup firmly packed fresh thai basil leaves
* 1 fresh long red chilli, sliced thinly

1 Place beef, paste and coconut milk in a 4.5-litre (18-cup) slow cooker; stir until paste dissolves.
2 Add stock, ginger, garlic, onion, lime leaves, curry leaves, sauce and sugar to cooker. Cook, covered, on high, about 2 hours. Reduce to low; cook a further 8 hours. Season to taste.
3 Discard lime leaves. Stir in snow peas; cook, covered, on low, for 10 minutes or until peas are tender. Season to taste. Serve beef topped with nuts, basil and chilli.

Not suitable to freeze.

Serving suggestion
Steamed jasmine rice or fresh rice noodles accompanied with lime wedges.

Nutritional count per serving *46.5g total fat (22.5g saturated fat); 3043kJ (728 cal); 17.3g carbohydrate; 59.2g protein; 5g fibre*

HOISIN AND
STAR ANISE OXTAIL

prep + cook time 9 hours 30 minutes * serves 4

* 2kg (4 pounds) oxtails, cut into 5cm (2-inch) pieces
* ⅔ cup (160ml) hoisin sauce
* 1 cup (250ml) beef stock
* ¼ cup (60ml) dry sherry
* 1 tablespoon finely grated orange rind
* ⅔ cup (80ml) orange juice
* 3 cloves garlic, crushed
* 2 tablespoons brown sugar
* ½ teaspoon cracked black pepper
* 2 star anise
* 500g (1 pound) buk choy, trimmed, quartered lengthways
* 1 fresh long red chilli, sliced thinly
* 3 green onions (scallions), sliced thinly

1   Trim excess fat from oxtail. Pack oxtail tightly, in a single layer, in the base of a 5-litre (20-cup) slow cooker. Whisk sauce, stock, sherry, rind, juice, garlic, sugar and pepper in a medium jug until combined; add star anise. Pour mixture over oxtail in cooker. Cook, covered, on low, about 8 hours.

2   Discard star anise. Remove oxtail; cover to keep warm. Skim fat from surface of liquid in cooker.

3   Add buk choy to cooker; cook, uncovered, on high, for 5 minutes or until wilted.

4   Return oxtail to cooker; cook, uncovered, on high, until oxtail is heated through. Season to taste.

5   Serve oxtail with buk choy and cooking liquid. Sprinkle with chilli and onion.

Suitable to freeze *at the end of step 2.*

Serving suggestion *Steamed rice.*

Tip *To reduce the liquid, uncover the cooker for the last hour of cooking time in step 1.*

Nutritional count per serving *59.8g total fat (22.5g saturated fat); 3850kJ (921 cal); 40.5g carbohydrate; 50.3g protein; 5.1g fibre*

HUNGARIAN
VEAL GOULASH

prep + cook time 8 hours 30 minutes ✳ serves 6

* 1kg (2 pounds) boneless veal shoulder, chopped coarsely
* ¼ cup (35g) plain (all-purpose) flour
* 1 tablespoon sweet paprika
* 2 teaspoons caraway seeds
* ½ teaspoon cayenne pepper
* 2 tablespoons olive oil
* 15g (½ ounce) butter
* 1 large brown onion (200g), chopped coarsely
* 2 cloves garlic, crushed
* 2 tablespoons tomato paste
* 1½ cups (375ml) beef stock
* 400g (12½ ounces) canned crushed tomatoes
* 3 small potatoes (360g), quartered
* 2 medium carrots (240g), chopped coarsely
* ½ cup (120g) sour cream
* ½ cup coarsely chopped fresh flat-leaf parsley

1   Toss veal in combined flour and spices to coat; shake away excess flour. Heat half the oil and half the butter in a large frying pan; cook veal, in batches, until browned all over. Transfer to a 4.5-litre (18-cup) slow cooker.
2   Heat remaining oil and butter in same pan; cook onion and garlic, stirring, until onion is soft. Stir in paste and stock; bring to the boil. Stir into cooker with tomatoes, potato and carrot; cook, covered, on low, about 8 hours.
3   Season to taste; dollop with sour cream and sprinkle with parsley to serve.

Suitable to freeze *at the end of step 2.*

Serving suggestion *Crusty bread, rice or pasta.*

Tip *If the butcher has some good stewing veal available, it's fine to use in this recipe.*

Nutritional count per serving *20.7g total fat (8.7g saturated fat); 1835kJ (439 cal); 18.4g carbohydrate; 42.6g protein; 4.1g fibre*

SPANISH OXTAIL
AND CHICKPEA SOUP

prep + cook time 8 hours 45 minutes ✻ serves 6

* 1.5kg (3 pounds) oxtails, cut into 5cm (2-inch) pieces
* 400g (12½ ounces) canned chickpeas (garbanzo beans), rinsed, drained
* 400g (12½ ounces) canned diced tomatoes
* 2 small leeks (400g), sliced thinly
* 2 medium carrots (240g), halved, sliced thickly
* ½ cup (100g) thinly sliced roasted red capsicum (bell pepper)
* 3 cloves garlic, crushed
* 2 dried bay leaves
* 2 teaspoons smoked paprika
* 1 teaspoon dried chilli flakes
* ½ cup (125ml) dry sherry
* 1 litre (4 cups) water
* 2 cups (500ml) beef stock
* 250g (8 ounces) packaged microwave white long grain rice
* 1 cured chorizo sausage (130g), sliced thinly
* ⅓ cup loosely packed fresh flat-leaf parsley leaves
* 1 lemon, cut into wedges

1 Trim excess fat from oxtail. Combine oxtail, chickpeas, tomatoes, leek, carrot, capsicum, garlic, bay leaves, paprika, chilli flakes, sherry, the water and stock in a 5-litre (20-cup) slow cooker. Cook, covered, on low, about 8 hours.

2 Heat rice according to directions on packet.

3 Meanwhile, discard bay leaves from cooker. Skim fat from surface. Add rice to cooker; cook, uncovered, on high, for 5 minutes or until mixture is thickened slightly. Season to taste.

4 Cook chorizo in a heated small frying pan until browned and crisp; drain on paper towel. Divide oxtail into serving bowls; ladle hot soup into bowls. Serve soup topped with chorizo and parsley; accompany with lemon wedges.

Suitable to freeze *at the end of step 1.*

Serving suggestion *Warm crusty bread.*

Tip *If the soup is a little thick, add a little more water or stock.*

Nutritional count per serving *34.8g total fat (12.7g saturated fat); 2500kJ (598 cal); 28.7g carbohydrate; 33.9g protein; 4.7g fibre*

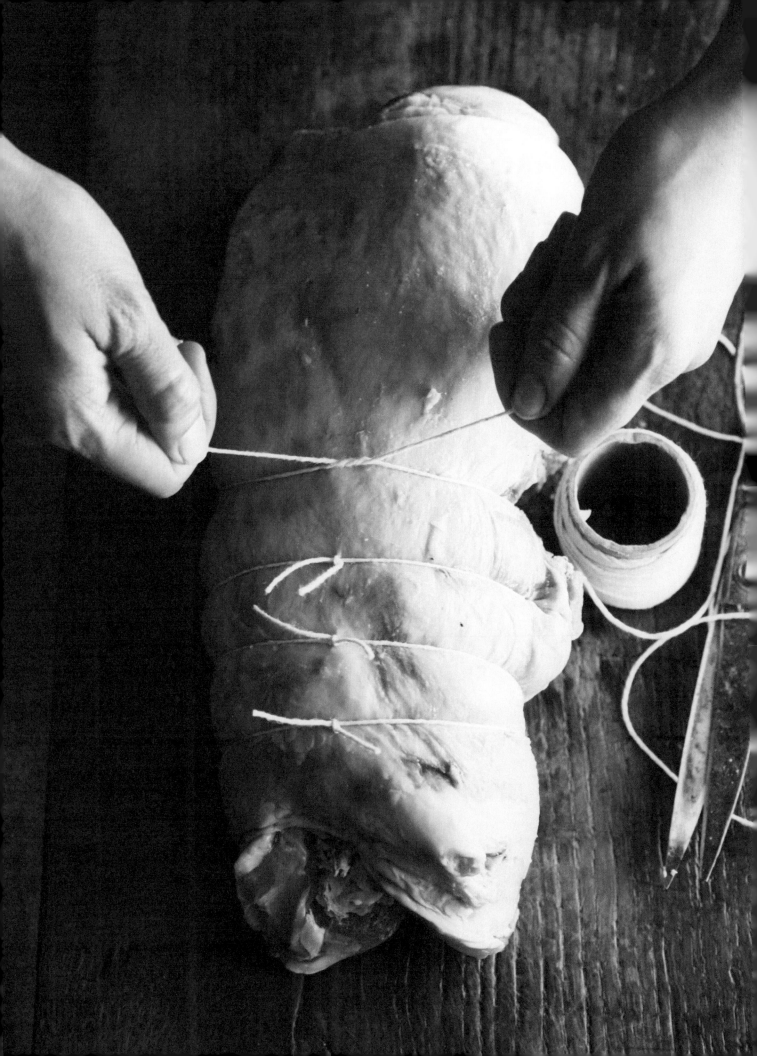

8
HOURS
AND OVER

LAMB

LAMB BECOMES EVEN MORE FLAVOURSOME
DURING LONG SLOW COOKING TIMES

LAMB WITH SAGE
AND PROSCIUTTO

prep + cook time 8 hours 45 minutes ✳ serves 6

* 1 large brown onion (200g), chopped coarsely
* 2 stalks celery (300g), trimmed, chopped coarsely
* 1 large carrot (180g), chopped coarsely
* ½ cup (125ml) dry red wine
* 1.5kg (3-pound) lamb shoulder, bone in
* ¼ cup loosely packed fresh sage leaves
* 4 cloves garlic, sliced thinly
* 12 thin slices prosciutto (180g)

1   Place onion, celery, carrot and wine in a 4.5-litre (18-cup) slow cooker.

2   Open out the lamb and place on a board, fat-side down. Slice through the thickest part of the lamb horizontally, without cutting all the way through. Open out the flap to form one large even piece; season, then scatter over sage and garlic. Roll lamb up to enclose seasoning. Wrap prosciutto around lamb, securing with kitchen string at 2cm (¾-inch) intervals. Add lamb to slow cooker. Cook, covered, on low, about 8 hours.

3   Carefully remove lamb from cooker; cover to keep warm. Strain sauce into a medium saucepan. Discard solids. Bring to the boil over medium heat; boil, uncovered, for 5 minutes or until sauce has reduced to ¾ cup. Drizzle lamb with sauce.

Not suitable to freeze.

Serving suggestion
Roasted root vegetables.

Tips *We used a shiraz-style wine in this recipe. Ask the butcher to butterfly the lamb for you.*

Nutritional count per serving *19.6g total fat (8.3g saturated fat); 1875kJ (448 cal); 5.4g carbohydrate; 58.7g protein; 2.3g fibre*

LAMB BIRYANI-STYLE

prep + cook time 9 hours ✳ serves 8

* **40g (1½ ounces) ghee**
* **½ cup (40g) flaked almonds**
* **2 large brown onions (400g), sliced thinly**
* **1 tablespoon vegetable oil**
* **1.2kg (2½ pounds) boneless lamb shoulder, chopped coarsely**
* **20g (¾ ounce) ghee, extra**
* **4 cloves garlic, crushed**
* **5cm (2-inch) piece fresh ginger (25g), grated**
* **2 fresh long green chillies, sliced thinly**
* **2 teaspoons each ground cumin and ground coriander**
* **3 teaspoons garam masala**
* **¾ cup (200g) Greek-style yoghurt**
* **½ cup coarsely chopped fresh coriander (cilantro)**
* **¼ cup coarsely chopped fresh mint**
* **1 litre (4 cups) water**
* **pinch saffron threads**
* **2 tablespoons hot milk**
* **2 cups (400g) basmati rice**
* **1 lime, cut into wedges**
* **½ cup loosely packed fresh coriander (cilantro) leaves**

1 Heat half the ghee in a large frying pan; cook nuts, stirring, until browned lightly. Remove from pan. Heat remaining ghee in same pan; cook onion, stirring, for 10 minutes or until soft and browned lightly. Remove from pan.

2 Heat oil in same pan; cook lamb, in batches, until browned. Transfer to a 4.5-litre (18-cup) slow cooker. Heat extra ghee in same pan; cook garlic, ginger, chilli and spices, stirring, until fragrant. Remove from heat; stir in yoghurt, chopped herbs and half the onion mixture. Transfer to cooker with half the water. Cook, covered, on low, about 8 hours. Season to taste.

3 Meanwhile, sprinkle saffron over hot milk in a small bowl; stand 15 minutes.

4 Wash rice under cold water until water runs clear; drain. Combine rice and the remaining water in a medium saucepan, cover; bring to the boil. Reduce heat; simmer, covered, for 8 minutes or until rice is tender. Season to taste.

5 Spoon rice over lamb in cooker; drizzle with milk mixture. Top with nuts and remaining onion mixture; cook, covered, for 30 minutes or until heated through.

6 Serve with lime wedges; sprinkle with coriander leaves.

Not suitable to freeze.

Serving suggestion
Raita (minted yoghurt and cucumber).

Tip *Biryani is a rice dish made with spices and meat, chicken, fish or vegetables. There are many versions as this delicious recipe is a favourite across the Middle-East and India.*

Nutritional count per serving *24.2g total fat (11.2g saturated fat); 2307kJ (552 cal); 45.2g carbohydrate; 36.8g protein; 2.1g fibre*

LAMB SHANK, FENNEL
AND VEGETABLE SOUP

prep + cook time 10 hours 30 minutes ✳ serves 6

* 1 tablespoon olive oil
* 4 french-trimmed lamb shanks (1kg)
* 1 medium brown onion (150g),
chopped coarsely
* 2 baby fennel bulbs (260g), sliced thinly
* 2 medium carrots (240g), chopped coarsely
* 4 cloves garlic, crushed
* 2 fresh small red thai (serrano) chillies,
chopped finely
* 2 teaspoons each ground cumin and
ground coriander
* 1 teaspoon each ground cinnamon and
caraway seeds
* pinch saffron threads
* 1.5 litres (6 cups) water
* 2 cups (500ml) beef stock
* 400g (12½ ounces) canned diced tomatoes
* 400g (12½ ounces) canned chickpeas
(garbanzo beans), rinsed, drained
* ¾ cup (90g) frozen baby peas
* 1 cup loosely packed fresh coriander
(cilantro) leaves

1   Heat half the oil in a large frying pan; cook lamb, until browned all over, then place in a 4.5-litre (18-cup) slow cooker.

2   Heat remaining oil in same pan; cook onion, fennel, carrot, garlic and chilli, stirring, until onion softens. Add spices; cook, stirring, until fragrant. Place vegetable mixture into cooker. Stir in the water, stock, tomatoes and chickpeas. Cook, covered, on low, about 10 hours.

3   Remove lamb from cooker. When cool enough to handle, remove meat from bones, shred meat; discard bones. Stir meat and peas into cooker. Season to taste.

4   Serve soup sprinkled with coriander leaves.

Suitable to freeze
at the end of step 3.

Serving suggestion
*Lemon wedges,
Greek-style yoghurt
and crusty bread.*

Nutritional count per serving *6.1g total fat (1.4g saturated fat); 953kJ (228 cal); 13.6g carbohydrate; 26.3g protein; 6.7g fibre*

MEXICAN SLOW-ROASTED
LAMB SHANKS

prep + cook time 8 hours 30 minutes ✳ serves 4

* 2 medium tomatoes (300g), chopped coarsely
* 1 medium red capsicum (bell pepper) (200g), chopped coarsely
* 1 medium yellow capsicum (bell pepper) (200g), chopped coarsely
* 2 tablespoons olive oil
* 2 teaspoons each sweet paprika and ground cumin
* 1 teaspoon ground coriander
* 2 cloves garlic, crushed
* 1 fresh long red chilli, chopped finely
* 2 tablespoons finely chopped fresh oregano
* 8 french-trimmed lamb shanks (2kg)

1   Combine tomato and capsicums in a 4.5-litre (18-cup) slow cooker.
2   Combine oil, spices, garlic, chilli and oregano in a large bowl; add lamb, turn to coat in marinade. Cook lamb in a heated large frying pan, in batches, until browned. Transfer to cooker. Cook, covered, on low, about 8 hours. Season to taste.
3   Serve lamb shanks drizzled with sauce; sprinkle with extra oregano leaves, if you like.

Suitable to freeze *at the end of step 2.*

Serving suggestion *Flour tortillas, lime wedges and a green salad.*

Tip *Lamb can be marinated in the spice mixture overnight.*

Nutritional count per serving *14.1g total fat (3.5g saturated fat); 1659kJ (397 cal); 4.2g carbohydrate; 61.9g protein; 2g fibre*

RED CURRY LAMB SHANKS

prep + cook time 8 hours 40 minutes ✳ serves 6

* 2 tablespoons vegetable oil
* 6 french-trimmed lamb shanks (2kg)
* 1 large kumara (orange sweet potato) (500g), chopped coarsely
* 3 fresh kaffir lime leaves, shredded thinly
* 1 large brown onion (200g), chopped finely
* 2 tablespoons red curry paste
* 1⅔ cups (400ml) canned coconut cream
* 2 cups (500ml) chicken stock
* 2 tablespoons fish sauce
* 375g (12 ounces) snake beans, chopped coarsely
* 1 cup loosely packed fresh coriander (cilantro) leaves
* 2 tablespoons lime juice

1   Heat half the oil in a large frying pan; cook lamb, in batches, until browned all over. Place lamb in a 4.5-litre (18-cup) slow cooker, add kumara and lime leaves.

2   Heat remaining oil in same pan; cook onion, stirring, until soft. Add paste; cook, stirring, until fragrant. Add coconut cream; bring to the boil. Remove pan from heat; stir in stock and sauce, pour over lamb. Cook, covered, on low, about 8 hours.

3   Add beans to cooker; cook, covered, on high, about 15 minutes. Stir in coriander and juice; season to taste.

Suitable to freeze *at the end of step 2.*

Serving suggestion *Steamed rice.*

Tips *Red curry paste is available in various strengths. Use whichever one suits your spice-level tolerance best. If you can't find snake beans, use regular green beans instead.*

Nutritional count per serving *33.2g total fat (18g saturated fat); 2337kJ (559 cal); 17g carbohydrate; 45.6g protein; 6g fibre*

GREEK-STYLE
DILL AND LEMON LAMB SHOULDER

prep + cook time 8 hours 45 minutes ✳ serves 6

* ✳ 1 tablespoon olive oil
* ✳ 2kg (4-pound) lamb shoulder, bone in
* ✳ 1 medium lemon (140g)
* ✳ 4 cloves garlic, crushed
* ✳ 2 teaspoons dried greek oregano
* ✳ 1 tablespoon coarsely chopped fresh dill
* ✳ 800g (1½ pounds) potatoes, cut into thick wedges
* ✳ 1 cup (280g) bottled passata
* ✳ 2 cups (500ml) salt-reduced chicken stock
* ✳ 50g (1½ ounces) seeded black olives
* ✳ 2 tablespoons fresh dill sprigs, extra

1 Heat oil in a large frying pan over medium heat; cook lamb until browned all over. Remove from pan.

2 Meanwhile, finely grate rind from lemon; reserve lemon. Combine garlic, rind, oregano and chopped dill in a small bowl. Rub mixture over lamb.

3 Place potato over the base of a 4.5-litre (18-cup) slow cooker. Pour passata and stock over potatoes. Top with lamb. Cook, covered, on low, about 8 hours.

4 Carefully remove lamb and potato from cooker; shred lamb coarsely using two forks. Cover to keep warm.

5 Pour cooking liquid into a medium saucepan; bring to the boil. Boil, uncovered, for 10 minutes or until liquid is reduced by half. Add olives; cook until heated through. Season to taste.

6 Cut reserved lemon into wedges. Serve lamb with potato, pan juices and lemon wedges; sprinkle with extra dill.

Not suitable to freeze.

Serving suggestion
Steamed broad beans.

Tips *Ask the butcher to separate the shank from the shoulder, leaving it attached; this will help it fit into the cooker. We used dutch cream potatoes in this recipe, as they hold their shape well. Passata is strained tomato puree available from supermarkets.*

Nutritional count per serving *20g total fat (7.5g saturated fat); 2035kJ (486 cal); 20.3g carbohydrate; 53.8g protein; 3g fibre*

LAMB ROGAN JOSH

prep + cook time 8 hours 20 minutes ✳ serves 6

* 1.5kg (3 pounds) boneless lamb shoulder, chopped coarsely
* 2 large brown onions (400g), sliced thinly
* 5cm (2-inch) piece fresh ginger (25g), grated
* 3 cloves garlic, crushed
* ½ cup (150g) rogan josh paste
* 2 tablespoons tomato paste
* 400g (12½ ounces) canned diced tomatoes
* ½ cup (125ml) beef stock
* 1 cinnamon stick
* 4 cardamom pods, bruised
* 2 dried bay leaves
* ½ cup loosely packed fresh coriander (cilantro) leaves

1   Combine lamb, onion, ginger, garlic, pastes, tomatoes, stock, cinnamon, cardamom and bay leaves in a 4.5-litre (18-cup) slow cooker. Cook, covered, on low, about 8 hours. Season to taste.
2   Serve curry sprinkled with coriander.

Suitable to freeze
at the end of step 1.

Serving suggestion
Steamed rice, naan bread and yoghurt.

Nutritional count per serving *30.1g total fat (10.8g saturated fat); 2249kJ (538 cal); 8.8g carbohydrate; 55.7g protein; 5.1g fibre*

LAMB SHANK
AND SPINACH KORMA CURRY

prep + cook time 8 hours 30 minutes ✻ serves 6

✻ 6 french-trimmed lamb shanks (1.5kg)
✻ 400g (12½ ounces) canned
crushed tomatoes
✻ 1 large brown onion (200g), sliced thickly
✻ 300ml pouring cream
✻ 100g (3 ounces) baby spinach leaves
✻ 1 cup (120g) frozen peas

KORMA PASTE
✻ 1 tablespoon cumin seeds
✻ 3 cloves garlic, quartered
✻ 5cm (2-inch) piece fresh ginger (25g),
grated finely
✻ ⅓ cup (50g) toasted cashew nuts
✻ ¼ cup (60ml) tomato sauce (ketchup)
✻ ¼ cup coarsely chopped coriander
(cilantro) root and stem mixture
✻ 2 tablespoons desiccated coconut
✻ 1 tablespoon garam masala
✻ 2 teaspoons each ground coriander,
ground turmeric and sea salt flakes
✻ ¼ cup (60ml) vegetable oil

1   Make korma paste.
2   Combine lamb, tomatoes, onion, cream and paste in a 4.5-litre (18-cup) slow cooker. Cook, covered, on low, about 8 hours.
3   Add spinach and peas to cooker; cook, covered, for 10 minutes or until heated through.

KORMA PASTE Place cumin in a small frying pan; cook, stirring, for 1 minute or until fragrant. Remove from heat. Blend or process cumin with remaining ingredients until smooth.

Suitable to freeze
at the end of step 2. Korma paste can be frozen separately.

Serving suggestion
Steamed basmati rice, yoghurt and naan bread.

Nutritional count per serving *44.3g total fat (19.3g saturated fat); 2473kJ (591 cal); 12.9g carbohydrate; 34g protein; 4.6g fibre*

98

8 HOURS AND OVER

Lamb

GREEK-STYLE ROAST LAMB
WITH POTATOES

prep + cook time 8 hours 40 minutes ✳ serves 4

* 2 tablespoons olive oil
* 1kg (2 pounds) baby new potatoes
* 2kg (4-pound) lamb leg
* 2 sprigs fresh rosemary, chopped coarsely
* 2 tablespoons finely chopped fresh flat-leaf parsley
* 2 tablespoons finely chopped fresh oregano
* 3 cloves garlic, crushed
* 1 tablespoon finely grated lemon rind
* 2 tablespoons lemon juice
* ½ cup (125ml) beef stock

1 Heat half the oil in a large frying pan; cook potatoes until browned. Transfer to a 4.5-litre (18-cup) slow cooker.
2 Make small cuts in lamb at 2.5cm (1-inch) intervals; press rosemary into cuts. Combine remaining oil, parsley, oregano, garlic, rind and juice in a small bowl; rub mixture over lamb, season.
3 Cook lamb in same heated pan until browned all over. Place lamb on top of potatoes; add stock. Cook, covered, on low, about 8 hours.
4 Remove lamb and potatoes; cover lamb, stand 10 minutes before slicing.
5 Serve lamb with potatoes and sauce.

Not suitable to freeze.

Serving suggestion *Greek salad or steamed spinach.*

Tip *Lamb can be refrigerated overnight at the end of step 2.*

Nutritional count per serving *29.5g total fat (10.2g saturated fat); 3206kJ (767 cal); 33.5g carbohydrate; 88.4g protein; 5.6g fibre*

LAMB AND BABY EGGPLANT
CURRY WITH CASHEW AND COCONUT

prep + cook time 8 hours 45 minutes ✳ serves 6

* ¼ cup (60ml) vegetable oil
* 6 baby eggplants (360g), cut into 3cm (1¼-inch) thick slices.
* 6 french-trimmed lamb shanks (1.5kg)
* 1 large brown onion (200g), chopped finely
* 3 cloves garlic, grated
* 5cm (2-inch) piece fresh ginger (25g), grated
* 3 fresh long red chillies, sliced thinly
* 2 teaspoons each ground cumin, ground coriander and garam masala
* 400g (12½ ounces) canned diced tomatoes
* 2 cups (500ml) beef stock
* 1 tablespoon sesame seeds
* ¼ cup (50g) toasted salted cashews
* 1 tablespoon desiccated coconut
* ¾ cup (200g) Greek-style yoghurt
* ¼ cup lightly packed fresh coriander (cilantro) leaves

1 Heat 1 tablespoon of the oil in a large frying pan over medium heat; cook eggplant, in batches, until browned. Transfer to a 4.5-litre (18-cup) slow cooker.

2 Heat 1 tablespoon of the oil in the same pan over medium heat; cook lamb, in batches, until browned. Transfer to cooker.

3 Heat remaining oil in same pan over medium heat; cook onion, stirring, for 5 minutes or until softened. Add garlic, ginger, chilli and spices; cook, stirring, for 1 minute or until fragrant. Stir in tomatoes and stock; bring to the boil. Transfer to cooker. Cook, covered, on low, about 8 hours.

4 Meanwhile, dry-fry seeds, nuts and coconut together until fragrant but not coloured; cool. Blend or process until finely ground. Stir nut mixture into curry. Season to taste.

5 Serve curry topped with yoghurt and coriander.

Suitable to freeze *at the end of step 3.*

Serving suggestion *Steamed basmati rice and asian greens.*

Tip *Sprinkle curry with fried chillies before serving, if you like. Thinly slice 2 fresh long red chillies, heat 2 teaspoons oil in a small frying pan, cook chilli, stirring, until softened.*

Nutritional count per serving *31g total fat (10g saturated fat); 1968kJ (470 cal); 12.1g carbohydrate; 34.1g protein; 4.2g fibre*

LAMB AND
ROSEMARY STEW

prep + cook time 8 hours 45 minutes ✳ serves 4

* 1.2kg (2½ pounds) lamb neck chops
* ⅓ cup (50g) plain (all-purpose) flour
* 2 tablespoons olive oil
* 1 cup (250ml) dry red wine
* 3 small brown onions (240g), sliced thickly
* 3 medium potatoes (600g), sliced thickly
* 2 medium carrots (240g), sliced thickly
* 2 tablespoons tomato paste
* 2 tablespoons finely chopped rosemary
* 1 cup (250ml) beef stock

1 Toss lamb in flour to coat; shake off excess. Heat half the oil in a large frying pan over medium-high heat; cook lamb, in batches, until browned. Transfer to a 4.5-litre (18-cup) slow cooker.
2 Add wine to same pan; bring to the boil. Boil, stirring occasionally, for 5 minutes or until liquid is reduced by half. Transfer to cooker. Add onion, potato, carrot, paste, rosemary and stock. Cook, covered, on low, about 8 hours.
3 Divide lamb and vegetables among plates. Spoon over a little cooking liquid to serve.

Suitable to freeze *at the end of step 2.*

Serving suggestion *Peas or green beans.*

Tip *We used a shiraz-style wine in this recipe.*

Nutritional count per serving *44.5g total fat (17.5g saturated fat); 3072kJ (734 cal); 32.3g carbohydrate; 41.8g protein; 5.9g fibre*

LAMB, KUMARA
AND ALMOND CURRY

prep + cook time 8 hours 45 minutes ✱ serves 4

✱ 1.2kg (2½-pound) boneless lamb leg,
cut into 5cm (2-inch) pieces
✱ 800g (1½ pounds) kumara (orange sweet
potato), cut into 5cm (2-inch) pieces
✱ 1 large brown onion (200g), sliced thinly
✱ 3 cloves garlic, crushed
✱ 1 fresh long red chilli, chopped finely
✱ 2 teaspoons each garam masala and
ground cumin
✱ 400g (12½ ounces) canned diced tomatoes
✱ 400ml canned coconut milk; reserve
2 tablespoons
✱ 250g (8 ounces) spinach, trimmed,
shredded coarsely
✱ ½ cup (60g) ground almonds
✱ ⅓ cup (45g) toasted slivered almonds
✱ ⅓ cup loosely packed fresh coriander
(cilantro) leaves

1 Combine lamb, kumara, onion, garlic, chilli,
spices, tomatoes and coconut milk in a 5-litre
(20-cup) slow cooker. Cook, covered, on low,
about 8 hours.
2 Add spinach and ground almonds to cooker;
cook, uncovered, on high, for 5 minutes or until
spinach wilts. Season to taste.
3 Drizzle curry with reserved coconut milk and
sprinkle with slivered almonds and coriander.

Suitable to freeze
at the end of step 1.

Serving suggestion
Steamed basmati rice.

Nutritional count per serving *71g total fat (31.9g saturated fat); 4443kJ (1063 cal); 31.8g carbohydrate; 72.2g protein; 7.2g fibre*

LAMB SHANKS
WITH LENTILS AND PANCETTA

prep + cook time 8 hours 45 minutes ✳ serves 4

* 1½ cups (300g) French-style green lentils
* 4 french-trimmed lamb shanks (800g)
* 200g (6½ ounces) bottled caramelised onions
* 2 medium carrots (240g), cut into 1cm (½-inch) pieces
* 2 stalks celery (300g), cut into 1cm (½-inch) pieces
* 2 cloves garlic, crushed
* 100g (3 ounces) thinly sliced pancetta, chopped coarsely
* ¼ cup (70g) tomato paste
* 3 cups (750ml) chicken stock
* ½ cup (125ml) dry white wine
* ½ cup (60g) frozen peas
* ⅓ cup coarsely chopped fresh flat-leaf parsley

1   Rinse lentils under cold water; drain.
2   Combine lentils, lamb, caramelised onion, carrot, celery, garlic, pancetta, paste, stock and wine in a 5-litre (20-cup) slow cooker. Cook, covered, on low, about 8 hours.
3   Add peas to cooker; cook, covered, a further 10 minutes. Season to taste.
4   Serve lamb sprinkled with parsley.

Suitable to freeze
at the end of step 3.

Nutritional count per serving   *22.4g total fat (6.2g saturated fat); 2370kJ (567 cal); 46.2g carbohydrate; 39.4g protein; 5.3g fibre*

FETTA, LEMON
AND HERB ROLLED LAMB

prep + cook time 8 hours 45 minutes ✳ serves 6

* 180g (5½ ounces) persian fetta in oil
* ¼ cup coarsely chopped fresh oregano
* ¼ cup coarsely chopped fresh mint
* ¼ cup coarsely chopped fresh basil
* 2 teaspoons finely grated lemon rind
* 2 tablespoons balsamic vinegar
* 1.5kg (3-pound) boneless lamb leg

1 Drain fetta reserving 2 tablespoons of the oil.
2 Combine fetta, herbs, rind and half the vinegar in a medium bowl. Season to taste.
3 Open out lamb and place on a board, fat-side down. Slice through the thickest part of the lamb horizontally, without cutting all the way through. Open out the flap to form one large even piece; spread fetta mixture over lamb. Roll lamb up to enclose the stuffing, securing with kitchen string at 2cm (¾-inch) intervals.
4 Heat half the reserved oil in a large frying pan over medium-high heat; cook lamb, turning, until browned. Transfer to a 4.5-litre (18-cup) slow cooker.
5 Combine remaining reserved oil and vinegar in a small bowl; brush over lamb. Cook, covered, on low, about 8 hours.

Not suitable to freeze.

Serving suggestion
Roasted wedges of pumpkin and fresh garden peas sprinkled with extra herbs.

Tips *Persian fetta is a soft, creamy cheese marinated in a blend of olive oil, garlic, herbs and spices. Ask the butcher to butterfly the lamb for you.*

Nutritional count per serving *24.3g total fat (11.1g saturated fat); 1957kJ (467 cal); 35g carbohydrate; 58.2g protein; 0.3g fibre*

CASSOULET

prep + cook time 8 hours 45 minutes ✳ serves 6

✳ 2 tablespoons olive oil

✳ 3 thick pork sausages (360g)

✳ 100g (3-ounce) piece speck, rind removed, cut into 3cm (1¼-inch) pieces

✳ 900g (1¾ pounds) boneless lamb shoulder, cut into 3cm (1¼-inch) pieces

✳ 1 large brown onion (200g), chopped finely

✳ 1 bay leaf

✳ 5 cloves garlic, chopped finely

✳ 800g (1½ pounds) canned diced tomatoes

✳ 1 cup (250ml) water

✳ 2 tablespoons tomato paste

✳ 4 x 400g (12½ ounces) canned white beans, rinsed, drained

✳ 2 tablespoons finely chopped fresh flat-leaf parsley

1 Heat half the oil in a large frying pan over medium-high heat; cook sausages and speck, turning, until browned. Transfer to a 4.5-litre (18-cup) slow cooker.

2 Heat same pan over medium-high heat; cook lamb, in batches, until browned. Transfer to cooker. Drain fat from pan.

3 Heat remaining oil in same pan over medium heat; cook onion and bay leaf, stirring, for 5 minutes or until onion softens. Add garlic; cook, stirring, for 1 minute or until fragrant. Transfer to cooker.

4 Add tomatoes, the water, paste and beans to cooker. Cook, covered, on low, about 8 hours.

5 Serve cassoulet sprinkled with parsley.

Suitable to freeze
at the end of step 4.

Serving suggestion
Lightly toast some breadcrumbs and combine with chopped parsley; sprinkle over cassoulet to serve.

Tip *There are many regional variations of cassoulet in France. For special occasions, add two confit duck marylands. Pan fry them until hot and browned, place on top of hot cassoulet before sprinkling with parsley.*

Nutritional count per serving *35.7g total fat (13.4g saturated fat); 2575kJ (615 cal); 19.3g carbohydrate; 50.8g protein; 9.8g fibre*

LANCASHIRE HOT POT

prep + cook time 8 hours 30 minutes ✳ serves 4

✳ **800g (1½ pounds) boneless lamb shoulder, cut into 3cm (1¼-inch) pieces**
✳ **⅓ cup (50g) plain (all-purpose) flour**
✳ **2 tablespoons olive oil**
✳ **2 medium brown onions (300g), chopped coarsely**
✳ **2 cloves garlic, chopped coarsely**
✳ **½ cup (125ml) dry red wine**
✳ **2 medium carrots (240g), chopped coarsely**
✳ **200g (6½ ounces) button mushrooms, halved**
✳ **1 tablespoon fresh thyme leaves**
✳ **1 tablespoon worcestershire sauce**
✳ **500g (1 pound) potatoes**

1 Toss lamb in flour to coat, shake off excess. Heat half the oil in a large frying pan over medium-high heat; cook lamb, in batches, until browned. Transfer to a 4.5-litre (18-cup) slow cooker.

2 Heat remaining oil in same pan; cook onion and garlic, stirring, for 5 minutes or until onion softens. Transfer to cooker.

3 Heat same pan; add wine, bring to the boil. Transfer to cooker with carrot, mushrooms, thyme and sauce; stir to combine.

4 Thinly slice potatoes. Arrange potato slices, slightly overlapping, over lamb mixture. Cook, covered, on low, about 8 hours. Season to taste.

Not suitable to freeze.

Serving suggestion
Buttered peas.

Tips *We used a merlot-style wine in this recipe. If you have a mandoline, use it to cut the potatoes into paper-thin slices, otherwise, use a very sharp knife.*

Nutritional count per serving *21.1g total fat (6.9g saturated fat); 2225kJ (532 cal); 30.4g carbohydrate; 47.5g protein; 6.8g fibre*

MOROCCAN LAMB
WITH HONEY

prep + cook time 8 hours 45 minutes ✳ serves 4

* 400g (12½ ounces) baby carrots, trimmed
* 600g (1¼ pounds) baby new potatoes
* 8 spring onions (200g), trimmed
* 1 cup (250ml) chicken stock
* 1.5kg (3-pound) lamb shoulder
* 2 tablespoons honey
* 2 tablespoons vegetable oil
* 3 cloves garlic, crushed
* 2 teaspoons fennel seeds
* 1 teaspoon each ground cinnamon, ginger and cumin
* ¼ teaspoon cayenne pepper

1 Combine carrots, potatoes, onions and stock in a 5-litre (20-cup) slow cooker.
2 Score lamb at 2.5cm (1-inch) intervals. Combine honey, oil, garlic, seeds and spices in a small bowl. Rub honey mixture over lamb. Place lamb on top of vegetables in cooker. Cook, covered, on low, about 8 hours.
3 Coarsely shred or slice lamb; serve with vegetables and some of the cooking liquid.

Not suitable to freeze.

Serving suggestion
Steamed green beans, peas, spinach or silver beet.

Nutritional count per serving *25.6g total fat (8.7g saturated fat); 2663kJ (637 cal); 37.1g carbohydrate; 60.7g protein; 7g fibre*

LAMB SHANKS
AND EGGPLANT STEW

prep + cook time 10 hours 45 minutes ✳ serves 4

✱ 4 french-trimmed lamb shanks (1kg)
✱ 2 medium eggplants (600g),
chopped coarsely
✱ 1 medium red onion (170g), sliced thinly
✱ 2 stalks celery (300g), trimmed,
sliced thinly
✱ 3 cloves garlic, sliced thinly
✱ 700g (1½ pounds) bottled passata
✱ 2 cups (500ml) beef stock
✱ 1 cup (250ml) water
✱ ⅔ cup (80g) seeded green olives
✱ 2 tablespoons rinsed, drained baby capers
✱ 2 tablespoons dried currants
✱ 1½ tablespoons red wine vinegar
✱ ½ cup loosely packed fresh
basil leaves, torn

1 Place lamb in a 4.5-litre (18-cup) slow cooker. Top with eggplant, onion, celery, garlic and passata. Pour over stock and the water. Cook, covered, on low, about 10 hours. Season to taste.
2 Carefully remove lamb. Skim excess fat from stew. Stir in olives, capers, currants, vinegar and basil.
3 Serve lamb with olive mixture; sprinkle with extra basil leaves, if you like.

Suitable to freeze *at the end of step 1.*

Serving suggestion *Creamy polenta and wilted greens; accompany with garlic and herb-rubbed bread.*

Tips *Make sure the lamb is on the base of the slow cooker as this prevents the vegetables from becoming too soft. Passata is strained tomato puree and is available from most supermarkets.*

Nutritional count per serving *26.4g total fat (7.7g saturated fat); 1956kJ (468 cal); 18.6g carbohydrate; 34g protein; 9.5g fibre*

Shawarma usually refers to meat cooked on a turning spit, but it also refers to a pitta bread sandwich. This is our slow cooker take on the shawarma.

TURKISH LAMB SHAWARMA

prep + cook time 8 hours 30 minutes ✳ serves 8

* 8 cloves garlic, crushed
* 3 teaspoons each ground cumin, ground cinnamon, ground coriander and paprika
* 1½ teaspoons each ground cardamom, nutmeg and allspice
* 1 teaspoon ground white pepper
* 2kg (4-pound) boneless lamb shoulder
* 1 cup (250ml) chicken stock
* 2 baby cos (romaine) lettuce (360g)
* 1 large red onion (300g)
* 4 medium tomatoes (600g)
* 16 pocket pitta breads

1   Combine garlic and spices in a small bowl. Rub spice mixture over lamb. Transfer lamb to a 4.5-litre (18-cup) slow cooker; pour over stock. Cook, covered, on low, about 8 hours.
2   Meanwhile, trim and finely shred lettuce. Peel and thinly slice onion; thinly slice tomatoes. Place lettuce, onion and tomato in separate serving bowls. Warm pitta bread under a preheated grill or in a microwave.
3   Using two forks, shred lamb coarsely; spoon over a little of the cooking liquid. Serve lamb with lettuce, onion, tomato and pitta bread.

Suitable to freeze
at the end of step 1.

Serving suggestion
Greek-style yoghurt and harissa, a fiery Moroccan paste. Or sliced cucumber, fresh mint or parsley leaves, and hummus.

Tip *Place the serving bowls on the table and let everyone make their own wrap.*

Nutritional count per serving *18.4g total fat (8.4g saturated fat); 2425kJ (579 cal); 40.3g carbohydrate; 59g protein; 4.3g fibre*

LAMB WITH
QUINCE AND HONEY

prep + cook time 8 hours 25 minutes (+ refrigeration) ✳ serves 4

✳ 1kg (2-pound) boneless lamb shoulder
✳ 6 cloves garlic, peeled, halved
✳ 2 tablespoons finely chopped coriander (cilantro) root and stem mixture
✳ 2 teaspoons ground cumin
✳ 1 teaspoon each ground coriander and sweet paprika
✳ 2 tablespoons olive oil
✳ 1 medium brown onion (150g), sliced thickly
✳ 1 cup (250ml) chicken stock
✳ 1 cinnamon stick
✳ 2 tablespoons honey
✳ 1 tablespoon quince paste
✳ ⅓ cup coarsely chopped fresh coriander (cilantro) leaves

1 Roll and tie lamb with kitchen string at 5cm (2-inch) intervals. Using a mortar and pestle, crush garlic, coriander root and stem mixture, spices and half the oil until almost smooth. Rub garlic mixture over lamb; cover, refrigerate 2 hours.

2 Heat remaining oil in a large frying pan; cook lamb until browned all over. Remove from pan. Add onion to same pan; cook, stirring, until onion softens.

3 Place stock, cinnamon and onion mixture in a 4.5-litre (18-cup) slow cooker; top with lamb, drizzle with honey. Season with salt and pepper. Cook, covered, on low, about 8 hours. Stand 10 minutes; stir quince paste into sauce.

4 Thickly slice lamb, serve with sauce; sprinkle with chopped coriander.

Not suitable to freeze.

Serving suggestion *Couscous.*

Tip *Cover and refrigerate lamb overnight at the end of step 1.*

Nutritional count per serving *31.5g total fat (11.4g saturated fat); 2366kJ (566 cal); 15.8g carbohydrate; 54g protein; 1.9g fibre*

SUN-DRIED TOMATO
AND BALSAMIC LAMB STEW

prep + cook time 8 hours 45 minutes * serves 4

* 8 lamb neck chops (1.4kg)
* 400g (12½ ounces) canned diced tomatoes
* 1 medium red onion (170g), sliced thinly
* 2 cloves garlic, crushed
* 1 cup (250ml) beef stock
* ½ cup (125ml) dry red wine
* ⅓ cup (80ml) balsamic vinegar
* ½ cup (75g) coarsely chopped sun-dried tomatoes
* ¼ cup loosely packed fresh basil leaves
* 2 sprigs fresh thyme
* 340g (11-ounce) jar marinated artichoke hearts, drained
* 2 teaspoons cornflour (cornstarch)
* 1 tablespoon water
* ¼ cup loosely packed fresh baby basil leaves, extra

1 Combine lamb, tomatoes, onion, garlic, stock, wine, vinegar, sun-dried tomatoes and herbs in a 5-litre (20-cup) slow cooker. Cook, covered, on low, about 8 hours.
2 Discard thyme from cooker; stir in artichokes. Combine cornflour with the water in a small cup; stir into cooker. Cook, covered, on high, for 10 minutes or until thickened slightly. Season to taste.
3 Serve stew sprinkled with extra basil.

Suitable to freeze *at the end of step 1.*

Serving suggestion *Mashed potato or creamy polenta.*

Tip *We used red wine but you can use white wine if you prefer.*

Nutritional count per serving *71.1g total fat (29.7g saturated fat); 3958kJ (947 cal); 18g carbohydrate; 52.2g protein; 7.2g fibre*

LAMB BIRRIA
(SPICY MEXICAN LAMB STEW)

prep + cook time 10 hours 45 minutes ✱ serves 4

* ✱ 3 teaspoons mexican chilli powder
* ✱ 1 teaspoon each dried oregano and ground cumin
* ✱ ¼ teaspoon each ground cloves and ground cinnamon
* ✱ 4 teaspoons finely grated fresh ginger
* ✱ 3 cloves garlic, sliced thinly
* ✱ 700g (1½ pounds) trimmed lamb rump steaks, cut into 3cm (1¼-inch) cubes
* ✱ 2 sprigs fresh thyme
* ✱ 2 fresh bay leaves
* ✱ 2 cups (500ml) salt-reduced chicken stock
* ✱ 1 cup (250ml) water
* ✱ 1 medium brown onion (150g), chopped coarsely
* ✱ 285g (9-ounce) jar whole roasted piquillo peppers, drained, chopped coarsely
* ✱ 410g (13 ounces) canned crushed tomatoes
* ✱ ½ cup (85g) seeded prunes, halved
* ✱ ½ cup loosely packed fresh coriander (cilantro) leaves

1 Place chilli powder, oregano, cumin, cloves, cinnamon, ginger and garlic in a 4.5-litre (18-cup) slow cooker. Add lamb; toss to coat in mixture.
2 Add thyme, bay leaves, stock, the water, onion, peppers and tomatoes. Cook, covered, on low, about 10 hours. Season to taste.
3 Remove and discard thyme and bay leaves. Stir in prunes. Cook, covered, on low, for 10 minutes or until prunes soften. Serve topped with coriander.

Suitable to freeze
at the end of step 2.

Serving suggestion
Grilled corn tortillas and lime wedges.

Nutritional count per serving *17.6g total fat (4.1g saturated fat); 1722kJ (412 cal); 18.2g carbohydrate; 42.6g protein; 4.4g fibre*

SICILIAN MEATBALLS
IN SPICY TOMATO SAUCE

prep + cook time 8 hours 45 minutes ✳ serves 4

* 700g (1½ pounds) bottled passata
* 410g (13 ounces) canned crushed tomatoes
* 1 medium brown onion (150g), chopped finely
* 45g (1½ ounces) canned anchovies, drained
* ¼ teaspoon dried chilli flakes
* 3 cloves garlic, sliced thinly
* 1 cup (250ml) chicken stock
* 2 cups (500ml) water
* ⅓ cup fresh oregano leaves, torn
* 600g (1¼ pounds) minced (ground) lamb
* 1 cup (70g) stale breadcrumbs
* 2 tablespoons pine nuts, chopped coarsely
* 1 tablespoon finely grated lemon rind
* ¼ cup (40g) sultanas, chopped coarsely
* ¼ cup (20g) finely grated parmesan
* ⅓ cup loosely packed small fresh basil leaves

1 Place passata, tomatoes, onion, anchovies, chilli, garlic, stock, the water and half the oregano in a 4.5-litre (18-cup) slow cooker. Stir to combine.
2 Using your hands, combine lamb, breadcrumbs, pine nuts, rind, sultanas, parmesan and remaining oregano in a large bowl; roll level tablespoons of mixture into balls. Transfer to cooker. Cook, covered, on low, about 8 hours. Season to taste.
3 Serve meatballs sprinkled with basil.

Suitable to freeze *at the end of step 2.*

Serving suggestion *Pasta, creamy polenta or mashed potato.*

Tip *Uncooked meatballs and sauce can be frozen separately, then cooked at a later stage.*

Nutritional count per serving *34.4g total fat (10.8g saturated fat); 2642kJ (632 cal); 33.4g carbohydrate; 44g protein; 4.3g fibre*

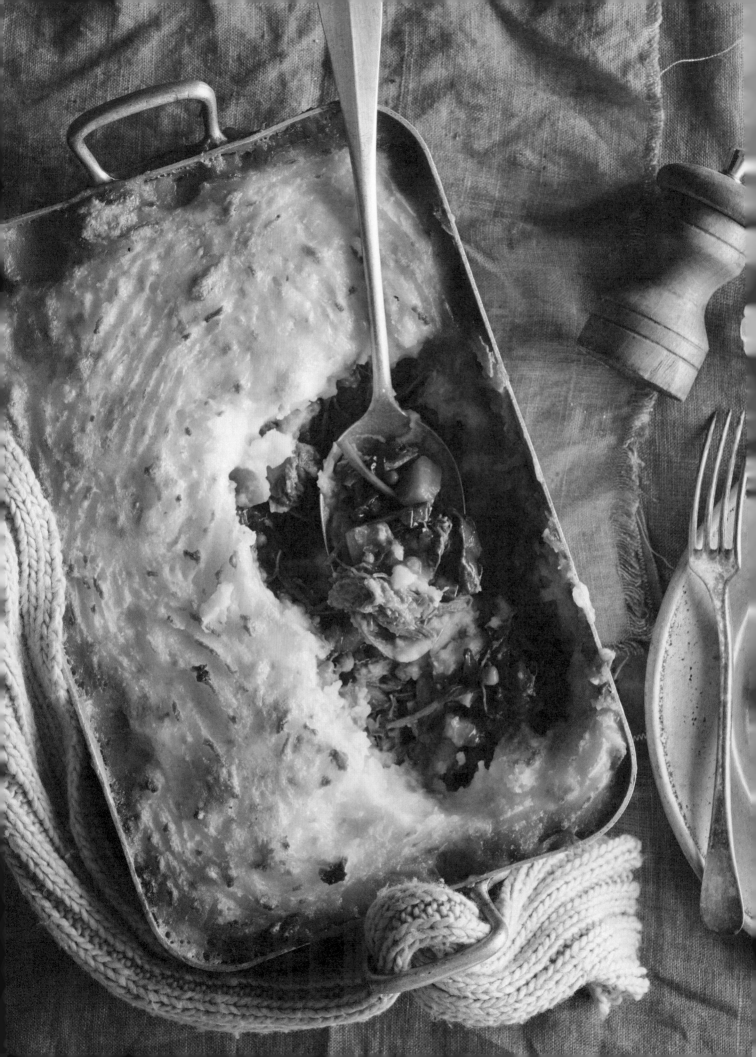

SHEPHERD'S PIE

prep + cook time 11 hours * serves 4

* 3 medium carrots (360g), chopped coarsely
* 3 stalks celery (450g), trimmed,
chopped coarsely
* 1 large brown onion (200g),
chopped coarsely
* 2 cloves garlic, crushed
* 4 sprigs fresh thyme
* 2 sprigs fresh rosemary
* ¼ cup (70g) tomato paste
* 2 tablespoons worcestershire sauce
* 2½ cups (625ml) beef stock
* 1.5kg (3-pound) lamb shoulder
* ½ cup (60g) frozen peas
* 150g (4½ ounces) baby spinach leaves
* 1 tablespoon cornflour (cornstarch)
* 1 tablespoon water
* 800g (1½ pounds) potatoes,
chopped coarsely
* 40g (1½ ounces) butter
* ½ cup (125ml) hot milk
* ½ cup (60g) coarsely grated cheddar

1   Combine carrot, celery, onion, garlic, herbs, paste, sauce and stock in a 5-litre (20-cup) slow cooker. Add lamb, turn to coat in mixture. Cook, covered, on high about 2 hours. Reduce to low; cook about 8 hours.
2   Remove lamb from cooker; shred meat coarsely, discard fat and bones. Discard herbs from cooker. Return lamb to cooker with peas and spinach. Blend cornflour and the water in a small cup, stir into cooker; cook, uncovered, on high, for 20 minutes or until thickened. Season to taste.
3   Meanwhile, boil, steam or microwave potato until tender; drain. Mash potato with butter and milk until smooth; season to taste.
4   Preheat grill (broiler).
5   Transfer lamb to a 2.5-litre (10-cup) ovenproof dish. Spoon potato over lamb mixture; sprinkle with cheddar. Grill for 5 minutes or until top is browned lightly.

Suitable to freeze.

Serving suggestion
*Green leafy salad
or coleslaw.*

Tip *Filling can
be frozen at the
end of step 2.*

Nutritional count per serving *40.1g total fat (18.8g saturated fat); 3160kJ (756 cal); 26g carbohydrate; 68.6g protein; 8.7g fibre*

LAMB, SPINACH AND
CHICKPEA RICE PILAF

prep + cook time 8 hours 30 minutes ✳ serves 6

✳ 2 tablespoons olive oil
✳ 1kg (2 pounds) boneless lamb shoulder, cut into 2cm (¾-inch) pieces
✳ 1 large brown onion (200g), sliced thinly
✳ 4 cloves garlic, crushed
✳ 1 tablespoon each ground cumin and ground coriander
✳ 2 teaspoons each ground allspice and chilli powder
✳ 3 cups (750ml) chicken stock
✳ 2 cups (400g) basmati rice
✳ 1 bunch silver beet (1kg), trimmed, chopped coarsely
✳ 400g (12½ ounces) canned chickpeas (garbanzo beans), rinsed, drained
✳ ⅔ cup (100g) raisins
✳ ½ cup (80g) pine nuts, toasted
✳ ½ cup coarsely chopped fresh coriander (cilantro)

1   Heat half the oil in a large frying pan over medium heat; cook lamb, in batches, until browned. Transfer to a 4.5-litre (18-cup) slow cooker.
2   Heat remaining oil in the same pan; cook onion and garlic, stirring, for 5 minutes or until onion softens. Add spices; cook, stirring, for 1 minute or until fragrant. Stir in stock; bring to the boil. Transfer mixture to cooker. Cook, covered, on low, about 7 hours.
3   Stir in rice; top with silver beet and chickpeas. Cook, covered, on high, about 50 minutes. Season to taste.
4   Stir in raisins, pine nuts and coriander to serve.

Suitable to freeze
at the end of step 2.

Serving suggestion
Greek-style yoghurt and lemon wedges.

Nutritional count per serving *27.7g total fat (6.5g saturated fat); 2507kJ (599 cal); 41.7g carbohydrate; 43.9g protein; 5.9g fibre*

8

HOURS
AND OVER

PORK

THE CHEAPEST CUTS OF PORK AND HAM WILL
PERFORM THE BEST WHEN COOKED SLOWLY

PORK WITH PRUNES

prep + cook time 9 hours ✳ serves 8

* **2kg (4-pound) boneless pork shoulder**
* **1½ tablespoons olive oil**
* **500g (1 pound) seeded prunes**
* **2 medium brown onions (300g), chopped finely**
* **3 sprigs fresh thyme**
* **3 cloves garlic, chopped finely**
* **½ cup (125ml) port**
* **½ cup (125ml) chicken stock**

1 Season pork generously with salt and pepper.

2 Heat 2 teaspoons of oil in a large frying pan over medium-high heat; cook pork, turning, until browned all over. Transfer to a 4.5-litre (18-cup) slow cooker, then add prunes.

3 Heat remaining oil in the same pan over medium heat; cook onion and thyme, stirring, for 5 minutes or until onion softens. Stir in garlic; cook, stirring, for 1 minute or until fragrant.

4 Add port and stock to pan, stir to combine. Bring to the boil, then pour over pork. Cook, covered, on low, about 8 hours.

5 Carefully remove pork and half the prunes (preferably the whole ones); cover to keep warm. Strain cooking liquid into a large bowl; reserve solids, but discard thyme. Blend or process solids until smooth. Stir pureed onion mixture into cooking liquid until sauce thickens (you may not need to use all the onion mixture).

6 Slice pork; drizzle sauce over pork, serve with prunes.

Not suitable to freeze.
Serving suggestion
Steamed broccoli and mashed potato or parsnip.

Tips *Sprinkle prunes over the pork when adding to the cooker; they will have a better chance of staying whole if they're not squashed under the pork. You can use either a tawny or ruby port for this recipe. Sherry will add a different flavour, but would also work well.*

Nutritional count per serving *6.6g total fat (1.6g saturated fat); 1823kJ (435 cal); 31.4g carbohydrate; 57g protein; 1.1g fibre*

HAM AND GREEN LENTIL
SOUP WITH GREMOLATA

prep + cook time 8 hours 30 minutes ✳ serves 6

* 1.8kg (3½-pounds) meaty ham hocks
* ½ cup (100g) French-style green lentils
* 1 tablespoon vegetable oil
* 2 medium brown onions (300g), chopped finely
* 2 medium carrots (240g), chopped finely
* 2 stalks celery (300g), trimmed, chopped finely
* 1 teaspoon fresh thyme leaves
* 2 cups (500ml) salt-reduced chicken stock
* 1.5 litres (6 cups) water

GREMOLATA
* 2 cloves garlic, crushed
* ¼ cup finely chopped fresh flat-leaf parsley
* 2 teaspoons finely grated lemon rind

1 Rinse ham hocks. Place in a 4.5-litre (18-cup) slow cooker.

2 Rinse lentils; drain well.

3 Heat oil in a medium frying pan over medium heat; cook onion, stirring, for 5 minutes or until softened. Transfer onion to cooker with carrot, celery, thyme, lentils, stock and the water. Cook, covered, on low, about 8 hours.

4 Carefully remove ham hocks from cooker. When cool enough to handle, remove and discard skin and bones. Shred meat finely using two forks. Return meat to cooker. Season to taste.

5 When almost ready to serve, make gremolata; sprinkle over soup.

GREMOLATA Combine ingredients in a small bowl.

Suitable to freeze *at the end of step 4.*

Serving suggestion *Crusty bread.*

Tip *Make sure the ham hocks are not too large to fit in the slow cooker. Ask the butcher to cut them, if necessary.*

Nutritional count per serving *10.3g total fat (2.8g saturated fat); 1108kJ (265 cal); 12g carbohydrate; 28.6g protein; 5.4g fibre*

SWEET AND SOUR
ITALIAN PORK WITH CAPSICUM

prep + cook time 8 hours 45 minutes ✳ serves 6

* 1.5kg (3-pound) piece pork scotch fillet (neck)
* 2 tablespoons olive oil
* 2 medium red capsicums (bell peppers) (400g)
* 2 medium brown onions (300g), chopped finely
* 1 stalk celery (150g), trimmed, chopped coarsely
* 2 cloves garlic, chopped finely
* ¼ cup (55g) caster (superfine) sugar
* ½ cup (125ml) red wine vinegar
* 2 tablespoons tomato paste
* ½ cup (125ml) chicken stock
* ¼ cup (40g) sultanas
* 2 tablespoons pine nuts
* 2 tablespoons chopped fresh flat-leaf parsley

1 Tie pork with kitchen string at 2cm (¾-inch) intervals. Heat half the oil in a large frying pan over medium-high heat; cook pork until browned. Transfer to a 4.5-litre (18-cup) slow cooker.

2 Meanwhile, cut capsicums lengthways into eighths; discard seeds and membranes.

3 Heat remaining oil in same pan over medium heat; cook onion, celery and garlic, stirring occasionally, for 5 minutes or until softened. Add sugar; cook, stirring occasionally, for 10 minutes or until golden and caramelised. Add vinegar; bring to the boil. Stir in paste and stock; bring to the boil, then pour over pork. Add sultanas and capsicum to cooker. Cook, covered, on low, about 8 hours.

4 Carefully remove pork from cooker; transfer to serving plate, cover to keep warm.

5 Meanwhile, toast pine nuts in a dry frying pan, stirring continuously over medium heat until just golden. Remove immediately from pan. Spoon sauce over pork. Serve sprinkled with pine nuts and parsley.

Not suitable to freeze.

Serving suggestion
Mashed potato or polenta.

Tip *'Agrodolce' is the Italian word used to describe the flavours in this dish. It means 'sour sweet'.*

Nutritional count per serving *10.7g total fat (2.2g saturated fat); 1789kJ (427 cal); 19.3g carbohydrate; 61.1g protein; 3.2g fibre*

PORK VINDALOO

prep + cook time 8 hours 30 minutes ✳ serves 6

* 1.2kg (2½-pound) pork scotch fillet (neck)
* 2 large brown onions (400g), sliced thinly
* 5cm (2-inch) piece fresh ginger (25g), grated
* 2 cloves garlic, grated
* 400g (12½ ounces) canned diced tomatoes
* ½ cup (150g) vindaloo paste
* 2 tablespoons tomato paste
* ¾ cup (180ml) beef stock
* ½ cup loosely packed fresh coriander (cilantro) leaves

1 Cut pork into 3cm (1¼-inch) pieces; discard any excess fat.
2 Place pork, onion, ginger, garlic, tomatoes, pastes and stock in a 4.5-litre (18-cup) slow cooker. Cook, covered, on low, about 8 hours.
3 Sprinkle vindaloo with coriander.

Suitable to freeze *at the end of step 2.*

Serving suggestion *Steamed basmati rice and pappadums.*

Tip *The king of curries, the fiery Indian vindaloo, is from the former Portuguese colony of Goa. The name is derived from the Portuguese words for vinegar and garlic, the dish's primary ingredients, which give the dish its sweet/sour taste. Jars of vindaloo paste are available from supermarkets.*

Nutritional count per serving *10.8g total fat (1.9g saturated fat); 1406kJ (336 cal); 7.7g carbohydrate; 49.1g protein; 2.6g fibre*

CUBAN BLACK BEAN SOUP

prep + cook time 8 hours 55 minutes (+ standing) * serves 6

You need to soak the beans overnight, so start the recipe the day before.

* 1½ cups (300g) dried black turtle beans
* 1 ham hock (1kg)
* 2 tablespoons olive oil
* 1 large brown onion (200g), chopped finely
* 1 medium red capsicum (bell pepper) (200g), chopped finely
* 3 garlic cloves, crushed
* 3 teaspoons ground cumin
* 1 teaspoon dried chilli flakes
* 400g (12½ ounces) canned crushed tomatoes
* 2 litres (8 cups) water
* 3 teaspoons dried oregano leaves
* 1 teaspoon ground black pepper
* 2 tablespoons lime juice
* 1 large tomato (220g), chopped finely
* ¼ cup coarsely chopped fresh coriander (cilantro)

1   Place beans in a medium bowl, cover with cold water; stand overnight.
2   Drain and rinse beans, place in a medium saucepan, cover with cold water; bring to the boil. Boil, uncovered, about 15 minutes; drain.
3   Meanwhile, preheat oven to 220°C/425°F.
4   Roast ham hock on an oven tray about 30 minutes.
5   Heat oil in a large frying pan; cook onion, capsicum and garlic, stirring, until onion is soft. Add cumin and chilli; cook, stirring, until fragrant.
6   Combine beans, ham hock, onion mixture, tomatoes, the water, oregano and pepper in a 4.5-litre (18-cup) slow cooker. Cook, covered, on low, about 8 hours.
7   Remove ham hock from cooker. When cool enough to handle, remove meat from bone; shred coarsely. Discard skin, fat and bone. Blend or process 2 cups soup mixture until smooth. Return meat to cooker with pureed soup, stir in juice and tomato. Season to taste.
8   Serve soup sprinkled with coriander.

Suitable to freeze
at the end of step 7.

Serving suggestion
Crusty bread, sour cream or yoghurt.

Nutritional count per serving *18.1g total fat (2.9g saturated fat); 1350kJ (323 cal); 9.6g carbohydrate; 24.7g protein; 12.4g fibre*

RED PORK
AND LYCHEE CURRY

prep + cook time 8 hours 30 minutes ✳ serves 4

✳ 565g (1¼ pounds) canned seeded lychees in syrup
✳ 1.5kg (3 pounds) pork belly ribs (spare ribs), rind removed, halved
✳ 1 large brown onion (200g), sliced thinly
✳ 2 cloves garlic, crushed
✳ ⅓ cup (100g) red curry paste
✳ 400ml canned coconut milk
✳ ½ cup (125ml) chicken stock
✳ 2 fresh kaffir lime leaves
✳ 2 tablespoons fish sauce
✳ 227g (7 ounces) canned water chestnut slices, rinsed, drained
✳ 125g (4 ounces) baby corn, halved
✳ 400g (12½ ounces) baby carrots, trimmed
✳ 200g (6½ ounces) snow peas, trimmed
✳ ⅓ cup (25g) fried shallots
✳ ⅓ cup loosely packed fresh coriander (cilantro) leaves
✳ 2 limes, cut into wedges

1 Drain lychees over a medium bowl; reserve ⅓ cup syrup. Refrigerate lychees.
2 Combine reserved syrup, pork, onion, garlic, paste, coconut milk, stock, lime leaves, sauce, water chestnut, corn and carrots in a 5-litre (20-cup) slow cooker. Cook, covered, on low, about 8 hours.
3 Discard lime leaves. Add lychees and snow peas to cooker; cook, uncovered, on high, for 5 minutes or until snow peas are tender. Season to taste. Serve curry sprinkled with shallots and coriander; accompany with lime wedges.

Not suitable to freeze.

Serving suggestion
Steamed jasmine rice.

Tip *Fried shallots are available, canned or in cellophane bags, at Asian grocery stores; once opened, they will keep for months if tightly sealed. Make your own by thinly slicing shallots and shallow-frying in vegetable oil until crisp and golden-brown; drain on paper towel.*

Nutritional count per serving *66.4g total fat (31.4g saturated fat); 4523kJ (1082 cal); 39.8g carbohydrate; 76.6g protein; 14.6g fibre*

PICKLED PORK

prep + cook time 8 hours 10 minutes ✻ serves 6

* 3kg (6½-pound) hand of pickled pork
* 2 tablespoons brown malt vinegar
* 2 dried bay leaves
* 1 teaspoon black peppercorns
* 2 tablespoons dark brown sugar
* 1.5 litres (6 cups) water, approximately

1   Place pork, vinegar, bay leaves, peppercorns, and sugar in a 4.5-litre (18-cup) slow cooker; add enough of the water to barely cover pork. Cook, covered, on low, about 8 hours.
2   Carefully remove pork from cooking liquid; cover, stand 10 minutes before slicing. Discard cooking liquid.

Not suitable to freeze.

Serving suggestion
Hot with mashed potato, wilted cabbage and mustard or cold (like ham) with potato salad or coleslaw.

Tip *The 'hand' of pickled pork is a portion of leg and breast. You might need to order it in advance from the butcher.*

Nutritional count per serving *27.8g total fat (10.7g saturated fat); 2801kJ (670 cal); 4.2g carbohydrate; 100.7g protein; 0g fibre*

RIBOLLITA

prep + cook time 8 hours 45 minutes ✳ serves 6

* 1 ham hock (1kg)
* 1 medium brown onion (150g), chopped finely
* 2 stalks celery (300g), trimmed, sliced thinly
* 1 large carrot (180g), chopped finely
* 1 small fennel bulb (200g), sliced thinly
* 3 cloves garlic, crushed
* 400g (12½ ounces) canned diced tomatoes
* 2 sprigs fresh rosemary
* ½ teaspoon dried chilli flakes
* 2 litres (8 cups) water
* 375g (12 ounces) cavolo nero, shredded coarsely
* 400g (12½ ounces) canned cannellini beans, rinsed, drained
* ½ cup coarsely chopped fresh basil
* 250g (½ pound) sourdough bread, crust removed
* ½ cup (40g) flaked parmesan

1 Combine ham hock, onion, celery, carrot, fennel, garlic, tomatoes, rosemary, chilli and the water in a 4.5-litre (18-cup) slow cooker. Cook, covered, on low, about 8 hours.

2 Remove ham hock from cooker; add cavolo nero and beans to soup. Cook, covered, on high, for 20 minutes or until cavolo nero is wilted.

3 Meanwhile, when ham hock is cool enough to handle, remove meat from bone; shred coarsely. Discard skin, fat and bone. Add meat and basil to soup; season to taste.

4 Break chunks of bread into serving bowls; top with soup and parmesan.

Not suitable to freeze.

Tip *Ribollita [ree-boh-lee-tah] literally means 'reboiled'. This Tuscan soup was originally made by reheating leftover minestrone or vegetable soup and adding bread, white beans and vegetables such as carrot, zucchini, spinach and cavolo nero.*

Nutritional count per serving *4.9g total fat (2.1g saturated fat); 798kJ (191 cal); 18g carbohydrate; 15.1g protein; 7g fibre*

PORK AND CHILLI STEW

prep + cook time 8 hours 45 minutes ✳ serves 4

* 1 tablespoon olive oil
* 750g (1½ pounds) diced pork
* 1 medium red onion (170g), chopped finely
* 2 cloves garlic, chopped finely
* 1 medium red capsicum (bell pepper) (200g), chopped coarsely
* 500g (1 pound) baby new potatoes, quartered
* 35g (1-ounce) sachet chilli spice mix
* 400g (12½ ounces) canned corn kernels, rinsed, drained
* 800g (1½ pounds) canned diced tomatoes
* 2 limes
* ½ cup (140g) sour cream
* 2 fresh long green chillies, sliced thinly
* ¼ cup chopped fresh coriander (cilantro)

1 Heat oil in a large frying pan over medium-high heat; cook pork, turning, until browned. Transfer to a 4.5-litre (18-cup) slow cooker.
2 Place onion, garlic, capsicum, potato, spice mix, corn and tomatoes in cooker. Cook, covered, on low, about 8 hours.
3 Cut cheeks from limes. Divide pork mixture into serving bowls. Top with sour cream, chilli and coriander; accompany with lime cheeks.

Suitable to freeze *at the end of step 2.*

Serving suggestion *Tortilla chips.*

Tips *If the potatoes are very small, halve them rather than cutting them into quarters. Most chilli spice mixes come as hot or mild; choose the heat level that you can tolerate.*

Nutritional count per serving *25.1g total fat (12.2g saturated fat); 2579kJ (616 cal); 42.8g carbohydrate; 49.1g protein; 8.5g fibre*

HONEY AND
BALSAMIC BRAISED PORK

prep + cook time 8 hours * serves 6

* 2 tablespoons olive oil
* 1.2kg (2½-pound) piece pork neck
* 9 shallots (225g), halved
* 1½ cups (375ml) chicken stock
* ⅓ cup (80ml) white balsamic vinegar
* ¼ cup (90g) honey
* 6 cloves garlic, peeled
* 2 sprigs fresh rosemary
* 1 cup (160g) seeded green olives

1   Heat oil in a large frying pan; cook pork until browned all over. Remove from pan.
2   Add shallots to same pan; cook, stirring, until browned all over. Add stock, vinegar and honey; bring to the boil.
3   Place garlic and rosemary in a 4.5-litre (18-cup) slow cooker; top with pork. Pour over shallot mixture; cook, covered, on low, about 7 hours.
4   Add olives; cook, covered, on low, about 30 minutes. Season to taste.
5   Remove pork; stand, covered, 10 minutes before slicing. Serve pork drizzled with sauce.

Suitable to freeze
at the end of step 3.

Serving suggestion
Soft creamy polenta or mashed potato and wilted shredded cabbage.

Nutritional count per serving *23.6g total fat (6.5g saturated fat); 1969kJ (471 cal); 20g carbohydrate; 44g protein; 1.1g fibre*

BOSTON BAKED BEANS

prep + cook time 10 hours 30 minutes ✳ serves 4

* 1 large brown onion (200g), chopped finely
* 300g (9½-ounce) piece speck, rind removed, chopped finely
* ¼ cup (90g) golden syrup
* ⅓ cup (75g) firmly packed brown sugar
* 2 tablespoons dijon mustard
* 1 tablespoon worcestershire sauce
* 1 tablespoon hot chilli sauce
* 410g (13 ounces) canned crushed tomatoes
* 400g (12½ ounces) canned cannellini beans, rinsed, drained
* 400g (12½ ounces) canned butter beans, rinsed, drained
* 400g (12½ ounces) canned borlotti beans, rinsed, drained
* 3 cups (750ml) salt-reduced chicken stock
* ½ cup finely chopped fresh flat-leaf parsley

1   Place onion, speck, syrup, sugar, mustard, sauces, tomatoes, beans and stock in a 4.5-litre (18-cup) slow cooker. Cook, covered, on low, about 9 hours. Uncover, cook, on low, for 1 hour or until thickened slightly. Season to taste.
2   Serve beans sprinkled with parsley.

Suitable to freeze *at the end of step 1.*

Serving suggestion *Baby spinach leaves and crusty bread.*

Tip *Substitute golden syrup with treacle for a darker, richer mixture.*

Nutritional count per serving *17.2g total fat (5.2g saturated fat); 2291kJ (548 cal); 63.7g carbohydrate; 30.3g protein; 9.7g fibre*

BEST-EVER
BOLOGNESE SAUCE

prep + cook time 10 hours 40 minutes ✳ serves 6

* 1 tablespoon olive oil
* 125g (4-ounce) piece prosciutto, chopped finely
* 2 medium brown onions (300g), chopped finely
* 1 large carrot (180g), chopped finely
* 2 stalks celery (300g), trimmed, chopped finely
* 2 cloves garlic, crushed
* 500g (1 pound) minced (ground) pork
* 500g (1 pound) minced (ground) veal
* 1 cup (250ml) dry red wine
* 1½ cups (375ml) beef stock
* ¼ cup (70g) tomato paste
* 1kg (2 pounds) ripe tomatoes, peeled, seeded, chopped coarsely
* ⅓ cup finely chopped fresh basil
* 2 tablespoons finely chopped fresh oregano

1 Heat half the oil in a large frying pan; cook prosciutto, stirring, until crisp. Add onion, carrot, celery and garlic; cook, stirring, until vegetables soften. Transfer to a 4.5-litre (18-cup) slow cooker.

2 Heat remaining oil in same pan; cook pork and veal, stirring, until browned. Add wine; bring to the boil. Stir mince mixture into cooker with stock, paste and tomato; cook, covered, on low, about 10 hours.

3 Stir in herbs; cook, covered, on high, about 10 minutes. Season to taste.

Suitable to freeze *at the end of step 2.*

Serving suggestion *Spaghetti or your favourite pasta; top with shaved parmesan.*

Tips *Prosciutto can be replaced with bacon. Fresh tomatoes can be replaced with 800g (1½ pounds) canned diced tomatoes.*

Nutritional count per serving *16.3g total fat (5.4g saturated fat); 1576kJ (377 cal); 7.4g carbohydrate; 41.7g protein; 3.5g fibre*

SOY PORK
WITH MUSHROOMS

prep + cook time 8 hours 30 minutes ✱ serves 4

* 1.2kg (2½-pound) boneless pork shoulder
* 2 cinnamon sticks
* 2 star anise
* ⅔ cup (160ml) soy sauce
* ½ cup (125ml) chinese cooking wine
* ¼ cup (55g) firmly packed brown sugar
* 1 fresh long red chilli, halved lengthways
* 5cm (2-inch) piece fresh ginger (25g), sliced thinly
* 6 cloves garlic, bruised
* 2½ cups (625ml) water
* 150g (4½ ounces) shiitake mushrooms, halved if large
* 150g (4½ ounces) oyster mushrooms, torn into large pieces
* 150g (4½ ounces) shimeji mushrooms
* 100g (3 ounces) enoki mushrooms
* 4 baby buk choy, halved or quartered

1 Place pork, cinnamon, star anise, sauce, cooking wine, sugar, chilli, ginger, garlic and the water in a 4.5-litre (18-cup) slow cooker. Cook, covered, on low, about 8 hours.

2 Carefully remove pork from cooker; stand, covered, 15 minutes. Using a slotted spoon, remove cinnamon, star anise, chilli, ginger and garlic from broth.

3 Add mushrooms and buk choy to cooker. Cook, covered, on high, for 15 minutes or until mushrooms are tender; season to taste. Serve slices of pork with vegetables and a little broth.

Not suitable to freeze.

Serving suggestion
Rice noodles.

Tip *When adding the mushrooms and buk choy, don't worry if they aren't covered by the broth. They will shrink slightly whilst cooking. Place the buk choy on top of the mushrooms as this will ensure it stays green.*

Nutritional count per serving *4.5g total fat (1.2g saturated fat); 2011kJ (481 cal); 17.8g carbohydrate; 78.5g protein; 12.3g fibre*

SPANISH COCIDO

prep + cook time 8 hours 30 minutes ✳ serves 4

* ✳ 2 medium leeks (700g), chopped coarsely
* ✳ 2 large carrots (360g), chopped coarsely
* ✳ pinch saffron threads
* ✳ 1 bay leaf
* ✳ 2 x 400g (12½ ounces) canned chickpeas (garbanzo beans), rinsed, drained
* ✳ 350g (11 ounces) beef chuck steak
* ✳ 1 raw chorizo sausage (170g)
* ✳ 1kg (2-pound) meaty ham hock
* ✳ 2 chicken thigh cutlets (400g)
* ✳ 1 litre (4 cups) water

1 Place leek, carrot, saffron, bay leaf, chickpeas, beef, chorizo, ham hock and chicken in a 4.5-litre (18-cup) slow cooker. Pour over the water. Cook, covered, on low, about 8 hours.
2 Remove ham hock and chicken from bones in large chunks; divide among bowls with chorizo, chunks of beef, vegetables and chickpeas.

Suitable to freeze.

Serving suggestion *Crusty bread.*

Tips *Pronounced 'co-see-do', this is a traditional Spanish chickpea and meat-based stew. The broth is often served first, as a starter, with rice and noodles, but you can serve the meat and vegetables with some broth in shallow bowls. Ask the butcher to chop the end off the ham hock where there's no meat.*

Nutritional count per serving *16.9g total fat (5.2g saturated fat); 2032kJ (485 cal); 26g carbohydrate; 52.2g protein; 11.7g fibre*

PEA AND HAM SOUP

prep + cook time 8 hours 20 minutes ✻ serves 6

* 500g (1 pound) green split peas
* 1 tablespoon olive oil
* 1 large brown onion (200g), chopped finely
* 3 cloves garlic, crushed
* 1 ham hock (1kg)
* 2 medium carrots (240g), chopped finely
* 2 stalks celery (300g), trimmed, chopped finely
* 4 fresh thyme sprigs
* 2 dried bay leaves
* 2 litres (8 cups) water

1   Rinse split peas under cold water until water runs clear; drain.

2   Heat oil in a large frying pan; cook onion and garlic, stirring, until onion softens. Place onion mixture into a 4.5-litre (18-cup) slow cooker; stir in peas and remaining ingredients. Cook, covered, on low, about 8 hours.

3   Remove ham hock from cooker. When cool enough to handle, remove meat from bone; discard skin, fat and bone.

4   Shred meat coarsely, return to cooker. Season to taste.

Suitable to freeze.

Serving suggestion
Top with coarsely chopped mint leaves, thinly sliced green onions (scallions) and Greek-style yoghurt.

Nutritional count per serving *6.4g total fat (1.2g saturated fat); 1517kJ (363 cal); 43g carbohydrate; 27.3g protein; 11g fibre*

CHOUCROUTE

prep + cook time 8 hours 30 minutes ✶ serves 8

* 1 tablespoon juniper berries
* 2 teaspoons caraway seeds
* 1 dried bay leaf
* 10 sprigs fresh flat-leaf parsley
* 800g (1½ pounds) canned sauerkraut, rinsed, drained
* 2 cups (500ml) salt-reduced chicken stock
* ½ cup (125ml) dry white wine
* 1 ham hock (1kg)
* 4 rindless bacon slices (260g), sliced thickly
* 160g (5 ounces) mild hungarian salami, sliced thickly
* 800g (1½ pounds) medium potatoes, unpeeled, halved
* 2 tablespoons coarsely chopped fresh flat-leaf parsley

1   Tie juniper berries, seeds, bay leaf and parsley sprigs in muslin.
2   Combine sauerkraut, stock, wine and muslin bag in a 4.5-litre (18-cup) slow cooker. Add hock, bacon and salami, pushing down into sauerkraut; top with potato. Cook, covered, on low, about 8 hours.
3   Season to taste. Discard muslin bag. Serve choucroute sprinkled with chopped parsley.

Not suitable to freeze.

Tip *Choucroute is Alsatian sauerkraut. Traditionally a German and Eastern European dish, sauerkraut was widely adopted by the people of Alsace, the French region situated on the border with Germany and Switzerland.*

Nutritional count per serving *20.5g total fat (7.5g saturated fat); 1593kJ (381 cal); 15.6g carbohydrate; 28.8g protein; 4.8g fibre*

MEXICAN PULL-APART PORK

prep + cook time 8 hours 30 minutes ✳ serves 6

* 2 medium red capsicums (bell peppers) (400g), sliced thinly
* 2 medium brown onions (300g), sliced thinly
* 375g (12 ounces) bottled chunky mild tomato salsa
* 1 cup (280g) barbecue sauce
* 4 cloves garlic, crushed
* 3 teaspoons ground cumin
* 2 teaspoons cayenne pepper
* 1 teaspoon dried oregano
* 1kg (2-pound) boneless pork shoulder
* 12 large flour tortillas
* 1 cup (240g) sour cream
* 1 cup coarsely chopped fresh coriander (cilantro)

1   Combine capsicum, onion, salsa, sauce, garlic, spices and oregano in a 4.5-litre (18-cup) slow cooker; add pork, turn to coat in mixture. Cook, covered, on low, about 8 hours.

2   Carefully remove pork from cooker; shred meat using two forks. Return pork to cooker; stir gently. Season to taste.

3   Divide pork between tortillas. Serve topped with sour cream and coriander.

Suitable to freeze
at the end of step 2.

Serving suggestion
Lime wedges.

Tip *Peel the capsicum with a vegetable peeler if you don't like the skin peeling off when it's cooked.*

Nutritional count per serving *26.3g total fat (13.2g saturated fat); 2842kJ (680 cal); 66.5g carbohydrate; 42.5g protein; 5.4g fibre*

ITALIAN PORK
AND CAPSICUM RAGÙ

prep + cook time 8 hours 30 minutes ✳ serves 8

* 2 tablespoons olive oil
* 1.6kg (3¼-pound) rindless boneless pork belly, chopped coarsely
* 4 Italian-style thin pork sausages (310g)
* 3 medium red capsicums (bell peppers) (600g), sliced thickly
* 2 medium brown onions (300g), sliced thinly
* 1.2kg (2½ pounds) canned white beans, rinsed, drained
* 6 cloves garlic, crushed
* 400g (12½ ounces) canned diced tomatoes
* 1¼ cups (310ml) salt-reduced chicken stock
* 1 tablespoon tomato paste
* 1 teaspoon dried oregano
* ½ teaspoon chilli flakes
* ¼ cup loosely packed fresh oregano leaves

1 Heat oil in a large frying pan; cook pork, in batches, until browned. Transfer to a 4.5-litre (18-cup) slow cooker.
2 Cook sausages in same pan until browned; transfer to cooker with capsicum, onion, beans, garlic, tomatoes, stock, paste, dried oregano and chilli. Cook, covered, on low, about 8 hours.
3 Skim fat from surface. Remove sausages from cooker; chop coarsely, return to cooker. Season to taste.
4 Serve ragù sprinkled with fresh oregano.

Suitable to freeze
at the end of step 3.

Serving suggestion
Ragù is traditionally served with pasta.

Nutritional count per serving *24.8g total fat (8g saturated fat); 2006kJ (480 cal); 10.9g carbohydrate; 51.6g protein; 5g fibre*

CHILLI BEANS
WITH TOMATO SAUCE

prep + cook time 8 hours 30 minutes ✻ serves 6

* 1 tablespoon olive oil
* 6 rindless bacon slices (390g),
chopped finely
* 1 stalk celery (150g), trimmed,
chopped finely
* 1 small brown onion (80g), chopped finely
* 1 small carrot (70g), chopped finely
* 1 fresh long red chilli, chopped finely
* ¼ cup (70g) tomato paste
* 3 cups (700g) bottled tomato pasta sauce
* ¾ cup (180ml) chicken stock
* 2 teaspoons caster (superfine) sugar
* 800g (1½ pounds) canned cannellini
beans, rinsed, drained
* ¼ cup coarsely chopped fresh
flat-leaf parsley

1   Heat oil in a medium frying pan; cook bacon, celery, onion, carrot and chilli, stirring, until onion softens. Add paste; cook, stirring, about 1 minute. Transfer mixture to a 4.5-litre (18-cup) slow cooker. Stir in sauce, stock, sugar and beans. Cook, covered, on low, about 8 hours.
2   Stir in parsley; season to taste.

Suitable to freeze at the end of step 1.

Serving suggestion Toasted sourdough or cornbread.

Tip Instead of cannellini beans, use any canned white beans such as great northern, navy or haricot.

Nutritional count per serving 12.9g total fat (3.9g saturated fat); 1112kJ (266 cal); 17.8g carbohydrate; 17.3g protein; 5.2g fibre

PEPPERED PORK CURRY

prep + cook time 8 hours 30 minutes ✳ serves 4

* 1.2kg (2½ pounds) diced boneless
pork shoulder
* 1 medium red onion (170g), sliced thinly
* 4 cloves garlic, crushed
* 4 teaspoons finely grated fresh ginger
* 2 tablespoons brown sugar
* 2 teaspoons cracked black pepper
* 1 cinnamon stick
* 2 teaspoons ground cumin
* 1 teaspoon ground fenugreek
* ½ teaspoon ground cardamom
* 1 cup (250ml) chicken stock
* 400g (12½ ounces) canned diced tomatoes
* 1 cup (280g) Greek-style yoghurt
* 150g (4½ ounces) baby spinach leaves
* ⅓ cup loosely packed fresh coriander
(cilantro) leaves

1   Combine pork, onion, garlic, ginger, sugar, spices, stock, tomatoes and half the yoghurt in a 5-litre (20-cup) slow cooker. Cook, covered, on low, about 8 hours.
2   Discard cinnamon. Add spinach and remaining yoghurt to cooker; cook, uncovered, on high, for 5 minutes or until spinach wilts. Season to taste. Serve curry sprinkled with coriander; top with extra yoghurt, if you like.

Suitable to freeze
at the end of step 1.

Serving suggestion
*Steamed rice and
warmed roti bread.*

Nutritional count per serving *17.6g total fat (5.2g saturated fat); 2278kJ (545 cal); 21.8g carbohydrate; 72.3g protein; 3.6g fibre*

8
HOURS
AND OVER

POULTRY

BONE-IN CUTS SUCH AS WHOLE CHICKENS AND MARYLANDS
WILL STAND UP BEST TO LONG COOKING TIMES

CHICKEN HOT
AND SOUR SOUP

prep + cook time 9 hours ✳ serves 6

* 1.6kg (3¼-pound) whole chicken
* 2 medium carrots (240g), chopped coarsely
* 2 stalks celery (300g), trimmed, chopped coarsely
* 1 large brown onion (200g), chopped coarsely
* 2.5 litres (10 cups) water
* 6 fresh kaffir lime leaves, crushed
* 2 x 10cm (4-inch) sticks fresh lemon grass (40g), bruised
* 6cm (2½-inch) piece fresh ginger (30g), grated
* 2 fresh long red chillies, sliced thinly
* ½ cup (125ml) lime juice
* ½ cup (125ml) fish sauce
* 3 teaspoons brown sugar
* 425g (13½ ounces) canned straw mushrooms, rinsed, drained
* 2 baby buk choy (300g), trimmed, chopped coarsely
* 200g (6½ ounces) rice vermicelli noodles
* ½ cup firmly packed fresh coriander (cilantro) leaves

1 Remove and discard fat and skin from chicken. Place chicken, carrot, celery, onion and the water in a 4.5-litre (18-cup) slow cooker. Cook, covered, on low, about 8 hours.

2 Carefully remove chicken from cooker; shred meat coarsely using two forks. Discard bones. Strain cooking liquid through a muslin-lined sieve, clean chux or linen tea towel; discard solids.

3 Return strained liquid to cooker with lime leaves, lemon grass, ginger, chilli, juice, sauce, sugar, mushrooms and chicken. Cook, covered, on high about 30 minutes.

4 Stir in buk choy.

5 Meanwhile, place noodles in a medium heatproof bowl, cover with boiling water; stand 10 minutes or until softened, drain. Divide noodles among serving bowls. Ladle hot soup over noodles. Serve sprinkled with coriander, and fresh sliced chilli, if you like.

Suitable to freeze
at the end of step 3.

Nutritional count per serving *16.5g total fat (5g saturated fat); 1482kJ (354 cal); 13.4g carbohydrate; 34.5g protein; 6.2g fibre*

ASIAN NOODLE SOUP

prep + cook time 8 hours 50 minutes ✱ serves 6

* 1kg (2 pounds) chicken necks
* 1 medium brown onion (150g), chopped coarsely
* 1 stalk celery (150g), trimmed, chopped coarsely
* 1 medium carrot (120g), chopped coarsely
* 2 dried bay leaves
* 1 teaspoon black peppercorns
* 2.5 litres (10 cups) water
* 2 tablespoons tamari
* 2.5cm (1-inch) piece fresh ginger (10g), shredded finely
* 250g (8 ounces) dried ramen noodles
* 220g (7 ounces) japanese tofu
* 1 tablespoon vegetable oil
* 90g (3 ounces) fresh shiitake mushrooms, sliced thinly
* 2 baby buk choy (300g), chopped coarsely
* 60g (2 ounces) enoki mushrooms
* 2 green onions (scallions), sliced thinly

1   Combine chicken, brown onion, celery, carrot, bay leaves, peppercorns and the water in a 4.5-litre (18-cup) slow cooker. Cook, covered, on low, about 8 hours.

2   Strain stock through a fine sieve into a large heatproof bowl; discard solids.

3   Return stock to cooker; add tamari and ginger. Cook, uncovered, on high, for 20 minutes or until hot. Season to taste.

4   Meanwhile, cook noodles in a medium saucepan of boiling water until tender; drain. Divide noodles into serving bowls. Chop tofu into cubes.

5   Heat oil in same pan; cook shiitake mushrooms, stirring, until browned all over. Divide shiitake mushrooms, tofu, buk choy, enoki mushrooms, green onion and hot stock between serving bowls.

Suitable to freeze
at the end of step 2.

Nutritional count per serving   *6.2g total fat (0.8g saturated fat); 1012kJ (242 cal); 32.4g carbohydrate; 11.4g protein; 5.1g fibre*

SHREDDED MEXICAN
CHICKEN AND BEANS

prep + cook time 8 hours 45 minutes ✳ serves 4

* 1.6kg (3¼-pound) whole chicken
* 800g (1½ pounds) canned kidney beans, rinsed, drained
* 1 medium brown onion (150g), sliced thinly
* 3 cloves garlic, crushed
* 1 medium red capsicum (bell pepper) (200g), chopped coarsely
* 1 medium green capsicum (bell pepper) (200g), chopped coarsely
* 1 corn cob (250g), trimmed, kernels removed
* 2 tablespoons tomato paste
* 400g (12½ ounces) canned diced tomatoes
* 1 cup (250ml) chicken stock
* 2 teaspoons each ground cumin and dried oregano
* 1 teaspoon each smoked paprika and dried chilli flakes
* ½ cup loosely packed fresh coriander (cilantro)
* 8 flour tortillas (400g)

AVOCADO SALSA
* 1 large avocado (320g), chopped coarsely
* 1 lebanese cucumber (130g), chopped coarsely
* 125g (4 ounces) cherry tomatoes, quartered
* 1 tablespoon lime juice
* 1 green onion (scallion), sliced thinly

1 Rinse chicken under cold water; pat dry, inside and out, with paper towel. Trim excess fat from chicken.
2 Combine beans, onion, garlic, capsicums, corn, paste, tomatoes, stock and spices in a 5-litre (20-cup) slow cooker. Place chicken in cooker, push down into bean mixture. Cook, covered, on low, about 8 hours.
3 Remove chicken from cooker; when cool enough to handle, discard skin and bones. Shred chicken meat coarsely.
4 Return meat to cooker; cook, covered, on low, for 20 minutes or until hot. Season to taste.
5 Meanwhile, make avocado salsa.
6 Sprinkle chicken mixture with coriander; serve with avocado salsa and tortillas. Accompany with sour cream, if you like.

AVOCADO SALSA Combine ingredients in a small bowl; season to taste.

Suitable to freeze
at the end of step 4.

Tip *You can use 250g (8 ounces) of frozen corn kernels or a rinsed and drained 400g (12½-ounce) can of corn kernels instead of the fresh kernels.*

Nutritional count per serving *51.6g total fat (15.5g saturated fat); 4665kJ (1116 cal); 87.2g carbohydrate; 65.2g protein; 18g fibre*

POULE-AU-POT

prep + cook time 8 hours 30 minutes * serves 6

* **12 brown pickling onions (480g)**
* **750g (1½ pounds) kipfler potatoes (fingerlings), unpeeled**
* **1.8kg (3½-pound) whole chicken**
* **3 medium carrots (660g), chopped coarsely**
* **2 medium turnips (460g), halved**
* **1 dried bay leaf**
* **3 sprigs fresh thyme**
* **1 teaspoon black peppercorns**
* **1 litre (4 cups) water**
* **2 teaspoons fresh thyme leaves, extra**

1 Peel onions, leaving the root ends intact. Wash and scrub potatoes well.
2 Place chicken in a 4.5-litre (18-cup) slow cooker; place carrot, turnip and onion around chicken. Add bay leaf, thyme and peppercorns; top with potatoes. Pour the water into cooker. Cook, covered, on low, about 8 hours.
3 Serve chicken and vegetables with a little of the broth; sprinkle with extra thyme.

Not suitable to freeze.

Serving suggestion
Dijon mustard and crusty bread.

Tips *For best results use an old chicken – the meat is generally tougher, making them more suitable for slow cooking; they are available from Asian butchers. Leftover broth can be used as chicken stock in soup or stews.*

Nutritional count per serving *31.7g total fat (9.6g saturated fat); 2747kJ (656 cal); 27.4g carbohydrate; 61g protein; 8.3g fibre*

ITALIAN CHICKEN SOUP

prep + cook time 9 hours ✳ serves 6

* 1.5kg (3-pound) whole chicken
* 3 large tomatoes (650g)
* 1 medium brown onion (150g),
chopped coarsely
* 2 stalks celery (300g), trimmed,
chopped coarsely
* 1 large carrot (180g), chopped coarsely
* 2 dried bay leaves
* 4 cloves garlic, peeled, halved
* 6 black peppercorns
* 2 litres (8 cups) water
* ¾ cup (155g) risoni pasta
* ½ cup coarsely chopped fresh
flat-leaf parsley
* ½ cup coarsely chopped fresh basil
* 2 tablespoons finely chopped fresh oregano
* ¼ cup (60ml) fresh lemon juice

1 Discard as much skin as possible from chicken. Chop 1 tomato coarsely. Chop remaining tomatoes finely; refrigerate, covered, until required.

2 Place chicken, coarsely chopped tomato, onion, celery, carrot, bay leaves, garlic, peppercorns and the water in a 4.5-litre (18-cup) slow cooker. Cook, covered, on low, about 8 hours.

3 Carefully remove chicken from cooker. Strain broth through a fine sieve into a large heatproof bowl; discard solids. Skim and discard any fat from broth. Return broth to cooker; add risoni and finely chopped tomatoes. Cook, covered, on high, for 30 minutes or until risoni is tender.

4 Meanwhile, when cool enough to handle, remove meat from bones; shred coarsely. Discard bones. Add chicken, herbs and juice to soup; cook, covered, on high, about 5 minutes. Season to taste.

Suitable to freeze
at the end of step 2.

Serving suggestion
Crusty bread.

Nutritional count per serving *14.1g total fat (4.4g saturated fat); 1580kJ (378 cal); 23.2g carbohydrate; 37g protein; 4.5g fibre*

CHICKEN MULLIGATAWNY

prep + cook time 8 hours 30 minutes ✳ serves 4

* 2 medium brown onions (300g), chopped coarsely
* 2 cloves garlic, chopped coarsely
* 2 medium carrots (240g), chopped coarsely
* 1 stalk celery (150g), trimmed, chopped coarsely
* 1 fresh long red chilli, chopped coarsely
* 4cm (1½-inch) piece fresh ginger (20g), grated
* 2 chicken marylands (700g)
* 1 tablespoon mild curry powder
* 1 teaspoon ground cumin
* 1 teaspoon garam masala
* 3 cups (750ml) chicken stock
* 1 cup (250ml) coconut milk
* ½ cup loosely packed fresh coriander (cilantro) leaves

1 Place onion, garlic, carrot, celery, chilli, ginger, chicken, curry powder, cumin, garam masala and stock in a 4.5-litre (18-cup) slow cooker. Cook, covered, on low, about 8 hours.

2 Carefully remove chicken from cooker; discard skin and bones. Shred meat coarsely using two forks.

3 Skim fat from surface of vegetable mixture. Blend or process vegetable mixture until smooth. Return chicken to cooker with coconut milk; stir to combine.

4 Ladle soup into serving bowls; sprinkle with coriander, and drizzle with extra coconut milk, if you like.

Suitable to freeze *at the end of step 3.*

Tips *Black pepper and chilli can be added for a hotter version. Garam masala is a blend of spices including cloves, cardamom, cinnamon, coriander, fennel and cumin that are roasted and ground together.*

Nutritional count per serving *20.4g total fat (13.4g saturated fat); 1437kJ (343 cal); 11.1g carbohydrate; 27g protein; 5.3g fibre*

TURKEY WITH BACON,
CELERY AND SAGE SEASONING

prep + cook time 9 hours 30 minutes ✳ serves 6

* ✳ 2 medium brown onions (300g)
* ✳ 2.2kg (5-pound) turkey hindquarter
* ✳ 2 teaspoons vegetable oil
* ✳ 60g (2 ounces) butter
* ✳ 1 garlic clove, chopped finely
* ✳ 4 rindless middle-cut bacon slices (175g), chopped finely
* ✳ 1 stalk celery (150g), trimmed, chopped finely
* ✳ 2 cups (140g) stale breadcrumbs
* ✳ 1 egg
* ✳ 1 tablespoon chopped fresh sage
* ✳ ½ cup (125ml) water
* ✳ 2 tablespoons plain (all-purpose) flour
* ✳ ½ cup (160g) cranberry sauce

1   Cut one onion into wedges; place wedges in a 4.5-litre (18-cup) slow cooker. Finely chop remaining onion; reserve.

2   Cut through thigh joint between turkey drumstick and thigh to separate. Season.

3   Heat oil in a large frying pan over medium heat; cook drumstick and thigh, one piece at a time, until browned. Transfer to cooker; placing thigh on the base and drumstick on top.

4   Melt 20g of the butter in same pan over medium heat. Add chopped onion, garlic, bacon and celery; cook, stirring, until bacon is browned. Transfer to a large bowl; cool slightly. Add breadcrumbs, egg and sage; stir to combine.

5   Grease two 30cm x 40cm (12 inch x 16 inch) pieces of foil. Divide bacon mixture evenly between foil sheets; shape each into a 20cm (8-inch) log. Roll up to enclose. Place foil parcels around turkey.

6   Cook, covered, on low, about 8 hours. Remove foil parcels and turkey from cooker. Cover to keep warm.

7   Strain cooking liquid into a medium heatproof jug; reserve onion. Skim fat from surface. Add enough of the water to make 2½ cups of liquid.

8   Melt remaining butter in a medium saucepan over medium heat; cook reserved onion, stirring, until browned. Add flour; cook, stirring, until mixture thickens and bubbles. Gradually add cooking liquid; stir until mixture boils and thickens.

9   Slice turkey; serve with gravy, seasoning and cranberry sauce.

Not suitable to freeze.

Serving suggestion
Roasted potatoes and pumpkin, or mash, and steamed broccoli or green beans.

Tips *Turkey is often sold frozen in larger supermarkets. Allow at least one day to thaw in the refrigerator before using. If you can't find a turkey hindquarter use two turkey drumsticks (often called turkey shanks) or turkey breast on the bone (called turkey buffe).*

Nutritional count per serving *42.3g total fat (16.6g saturated fat); 3205kJ (766 cal); 31.6g carbohydrate; 64.6g protein; 2.4g fibre*

COUNTRY-STYLE
CHICKEN STEW

prep + cook time 8 hours 45 minutes * serves 4

* 1.4kg (2¾-pound) whole chicken
* 1 medium leek (350g), sliced into 1cm (½-inch) thick rounds
* 2 celery stalks (300g), trimmed, cut into 5cm (2-inch) lengths
* 400g (12½ ounces) baby carrots, trimmed
* 6 shallots (150g), halved
* 4 fresh thyme sprigs
* 2 fresh bay leaves
* 2 fresh flat-leaf parsley stalks
* 1.5 litres (6 cups) salt-reduced chicken stock
* 2 cups (500ml) water
* 50g (1½ ounces) angel hair pasta, broken in half
* 150g (4½ ounces) green beans, halved lengthways
* 1½ tablespoons lemon juice
* ⅓ cup coarsely chopped fresh flat-leaf parsley

1 Place chicken, leek, celery, carrots, shallots, thyme, bay leaves, parsley stalks, stock and the water in a 4.5-litre (18-cup) slow cooker. Cook, covered, on low, about 8 hours. Carefully remove chicken from cooker. Discard bay leaves, thyme and parsley stalks. Skim excess fat from stew.
2 Add pasta and beans to cooker. Cook, covered, on high, for 12 minutes or until pasta and beans are tender. Season to taste.
3 Meanwhile, discard skin from chicken. Break chicken into large pieces (drumstick, thigh, breast etc). Divide chicken into serving bowls.
4 Stir juice and chopped parsley into stew. To serve, spoon vegetables, pasta and broth over chicken.

Not suitable to freeze.

Serving suggestion
Crusty bread.

Nutritional count per serving *29.9g total fat (8.7g saturated fat); 2161kJ (517 cal); 20.2g carbohydrate; 38.5g protein; 8.1g fibre*

CHICKEN AND MUSHROOM SOUP

prep + cook time 10 hours 30 minutes * serves 4

- **1.2kg (2½-pound) whole boiler hen**
- **1 medium brown onion (150g) chopped coarsely**
- **2 cloves garlic, crushed**
- **300g (9½ ounces) swiss brown mushrooms, halved**
- **300g (9½ ounces) button mushrooms, halved**
- **10g (½ ounce) dried porcini mushrooms**
- **1 stalk celery (150g), trimmed, chopped coarsely**
- **2 medium potatoes (400g), chopped coarsely**
- **1 litre (4 cups) water**
- **2 cups (500ml) chicken stock**
- **300ml pouring cream**
- **⅓ cup loosely packed fresh chervil leaves**

1 Rinse chicken under cold water; pat dry, inside and out, with paper towel. Trim excess fat from chicken; place chicken in a 5-litre (20-cup) slow cooker. Add onion, garlic, mushrooms, celery, potato, the water and stock. Cook, covered, on low, about 10 hours.

2 Remove chicken from cooker; when cool enough to handle, discard skin and bones. Shred chicken meat coarsely.

3 Using a stick blender, blend soup in cooker until smooth; stir in cream and shredded chicken. Cook, covered, on high, for 10 minutes or until hot. Season to taste. Serve soup sprinkled with chervil and drizzle with a little extra cream, if you like.

Not suitable to freeze.

Tip *Boiler hens, also known as steamer hens or steamer chickens, are usually 'older' birds used for egg-laying – the meat is generally tougher, making them more suitable for slow cooking; they are available from Asian butchers. You can use a small chicken if you cannot find a boiler; however, you will need to reduce the cooking time from 10 hours to 8 hours on low.*

Nutritional count per serving *51.4g total fat (27.1g saturated fat); 2964kJ (709 cal); 17.5g carbohydrate; 42g protein; 6.9g fibre*

COCK-A-LEEKIE SOUP

prep + cook time 9 hours ✳ serves 6

* 1.2kg (2½-pound) whole chicken
* 2 cloves garlic, sliced thinly
* 4 medium leeks (1.4kg), sliced thinly
* 2 stalks celery (300g), trimmed, sliced thinly
* 4 sprigs fresh thyme
* large pinch cayenne pepper
* 2.5 litres (10 cups) salt-reduced chicken stock
* 1 cup (170g) seeded prunes
* 2 tablespoons coarsely chopped fresh oregano
* 2 tablespoons coarsely chopped fresh flat-leaf parsley

1 Place chicken, garlic, leek, celery, thyme, cayenne pepper and 2 litres of the stock in a 4.5-litre (18-cup) slow cooker. Cook, covered, on low, about 8 hours.

2 Carefully remove chicken from cooker; discard skin and bones. Shred meat coarsely using two forks.

3 Return chicken to cooker with prunes and remaining stock. Cook, covered, on high, for 30 minutes or until prunes soften and stock is hot. Discard thyme; season to taste.

4 Stir oregano and parsley into soup to serve.

Suitable to freeze
at the end of step 3.

Serving suggestion
Damper, mini scones or soda bread.

Nutritional count per serving *14.3g total fat (4.3g saturated fat); 1363kJ (326 cal); 20.6g carbohydrate; 26.4g protein; 7.4g fibre*

CHINESE CHICKEN HOT POT

prep + cook time 8 hours 20 minutes ✳ serves 6

* 1.8kg (3¾-pound) whole chicken
* 1 litre (4 cups) water
* 1 litre (4 cups) chicken stock
* 2 cups (500ml) chinese cooking wine
* ½ cup (125ml) light soy sauce
* ⅓ cup (80ml) oyster sauce
* ⅓ cup (75g) firmly packed light brown sugar
* 4 cloves garlic, bruised
* 6cm (2¼-inch) piece fresh ginger (30g), sliced thinly
* 3 star anise
* 1 teaspoon five-spice powder
* 2 fresh long red chillies, halved lengthways
* 500g (1 pound) baby buk choy, chopped coarsely
* ⅓ cup coarsely chopped fresh coriander (cilantro)
* 1 fresh long red chilli, extra, sliced thinly

1 Rinse chicken under cold water; pat dry, inside and out, with paper towel. Combine the water, stock, cooking wine, sauces, sugar, garlic, ginger, spices and chilli in a 4.5-litre (18-cup) slow cooker. Add chicken; cook, covered, on low, about 8 hours.

2 Remove chicken; strain broth through a fine sieve into a large bowl. Discard solids. Cover chicken to keep warm.

3 Return broth to cooker. Add buk choy to cooker; cook, covered, on high, for 5 minutes or until tender.

4 Cut chicken into 6 pieces; serve with buk choy, drizzle with broth. Sprinkle with coriander and extra chilli.

Suitable to freeze *at the end of step 2.*

Serving suggestion *Steamed fresh rice noodles or rice.*

Tip *Chinese cooking wine is also known as chinese rice wine and shao hsing wine. Dry sherry can be used instead.*

Nutritional count per serving *25.2g total fat (7.9g saturated fat); 2077kJ (487 cal); 20.8g carbohydrate; 34.8g protein; 1.7g fibre*

COQ AU VIN

prep + cook time 8 hours * serves 6

* **20 spring onions (500g)**
* **2 tablespoons olive oil**
* **6 rindless bacon slices (390g), sliced thinly**
* **440g (14 ounces) button mushrooms**
* **2 cloves garlic, crushed**
* **1.8kg (3¾-pound) whole chicken**
* **2 cups (500ml) dry red wine**
* **2 medium carrots (240g), chopped coarsely**
* **3 dried bay leaves**
* **4 sprigs fresh thyme**
* **2 sprigs fresh rosemary**
* **1½ cups (375ml) chicken stock**
* **¼ cup (70g) tomato paste**
* **¼ cup (35g) cornflour (cornstarch)**
* **2 tablespoons water**

1 Trim green ends from onions, leaving about 4cm (1½ inches) of stem attached; trim roots leaving onions intact. Heat half the oil in a large frying pan; cook onions, stirring, until browned all over, remove from pan. Add bacon, mushrooms and garlic to same pan; cook, stirring, until bacon is crisp, remove from pan.

2 Cut chicken into 12 pieces. Heat remaining oil in same pan; cook chicken, in batches, until browned all over; drain on paper towel. Add wine to same pan; bring to the boil, stirring.

3 Place chicken in a 4.5-litre (18-cup) slow cooker with onions, bacon and mushroom mixture, carrot, herbs, stock, wine mixture and paste. Cook, covered, on low, about 7 hours.

4 Stir in blended cornflour and the water; cook, covered, on high, for 20 minutes or until sauce thickens slightly. Season to taste.

Not suitable to freeze.

Serving suggestion
Creamy mashed potato drizzled with some of the sauce; accompany with a green salad.

Tips *Use shallots instead of spring onions. Use chicken pieces if you prefer, such as 6 thigh cutlets and 6 drumsticks or 6 marylands, or ask your butcher to cut the chicken into serving pieces for you.*

Nutritional count per serving *39.6g total fat (11.7g saturated fat); 2750kJ (658 cal); 12.3g carbohydrate; 47.8g protein; 5.1g fibre*

8
HOURS
AND OVER

VEGETABLES

STARTERS AND MAINS – SOME WITH A LITTLE MEAT
BUT ALL BASED ON VEGETABLES

SPLIT PEA
AND CAPSICUM CURRY

prep + cook time 8 hours 30 minutes ✳ serves 4

* 1 medium brown onion (150g), sliced thinly
* 500g (1 pound) baby new potatoes, halved
* 1 large carrot (180g), halved, sliced thickly
* 1 medium red capsicum (bell pepper) (350g), chopped coarsely
* 1 medium yellow capsicum (bell pepper) (350g), chopped coarsely
* ⅓ cup (100g) mild indian curry paste
* ⅓ cup (85g) yellow split peas
* ⅓ cup (85g) green split peas
* 8 fresh curry leaves
* 2 tablespoons tomato paste
* 410g (13 ounces) canned crushed tomatoes
* 2 cups (500ml) vegetable stock
* 2 cups (500ml) water
* 150g (4½ ounces) sugar snap peas
* 1 bunch spinach (500g), chopped coarsely
* ¾ cup (200g) Greek-style yoghurt
* ½ cup loosely packed fresh coriander (cilantro) leaves

1 Place onion, potato, carrot, capsicums, curry paste, split peas, curry leaves, tomato paste, tomatoes, stock and the water in a 4.5-litre (18-cup) slow cooker. Cook, covered, on low, about 8 hours. Season to taste.
2 Stir in sugar snap peas. Cook, uncovered, on low, for 10 minutes or until peas are tender. Stir in spinach. Serve curry topped with yoghurt and sprinkled with coriander.

Not suitable to freeze.

Serving suggestion
Steamed rice and pappadums.

Nutritional count per serving *18g total fat (3.9g saturated fat); 2278kJ (545 cal); 60g carbohydrate; 26g protein; 19g fibre*

SPICED CARROT
AND KUMARA SOUP

prep + cook time 9 hours ✳ serves 4

* 2 medium brown onions (300g),
chopped coarsely
* 5 medium carrots (600g), chopped coarsely
* 3 small kumara (orange sweet potato)
(750g), chopped coarsely
* 1 tablespoon ground coriander
* 2 teaspoons cumin seeds
* ½ teaspoon dried chilli flakes
* 1 litre (4 cups) salt-reduced chicken stock
* 2 cups (500ml) water
* ¾ cup (200g) Greek-style yoghurt
* ½ cup firmly packed fresh coriander
(cilantro) sprigs

1 Place onion, carrot, kumara, ground coriander, cumin, chilli, stock and the water in a 4.5-litre (18-cup) slow cooker. Cook, covered, on low, about 8 hours.
2 Cool soup 10 minutes. Blend or process soup, in batches, until smooth. Return soup to cooker. Cook, covered, on high, for 20 minutes or until hot. Season to taste.
3 To serve, dollop soup with yoghurt and sprinkle with fresh coriander.

Suitable to freeze
at the end of step 2.

Serving suggestion
Warm naan bread.

Tips *If the soup is a little thick add a little more stock or water. Swap chicken stock for vegetable for a vegetarian option.*

Nutritional count per serving *13.5g total fat (3.7g saturated fat); 1396kJ (334 cal); 39.9g carbohydrate; 8.9g protein; 9.6g fibre*

VEGETABLE HARIRA

prep + cook time 8 hours 45 minutes ✳ serves 8

* 2 teaspoons each ground cumin, ground coriander and sweet smoked paprika
* 1 teaspoon each ground ginger, ground cinnamon and dried chilli flakes
* ¼ teaspoon ground nutmeg
* 1 large brown onion (200g), chopped finely
* 2 medium carrots (240g), chopped finely
* 4 stalks celery (600g), trimmed, chopped finely
* 5 medium tomatoes (750g), chopped finely
* 6 cloves garlic, crushed
* 2 tablespoons tomato paste
* 1.5 litres (6 cups) vegetable stock
* 1 litre (4 cups) water
* 1 cup (200g) French-style green lentils
* 400g (12½ ounces) canned chickpeas (garbanzo beans), rinsed, drained
* ⅓ cup each finely chopped fresh flat-leaf parsley and coriander (cilantro)

1 Dry-fry spices in a small frying pan over medium heat for 1 minute or until fragrant.
2 Combine onion, carrot, celery, tomato, garlic, spices, paste, stock, the water and lentils in a 4.5-litre (18-cup) slow cooker. Cook, covered, on low, about 8 hours. Season to taste.
3 Add chickpeas to cooker and stir until heated through.
4 Stir in parsley and coriander to serve.

Suitable to freeze *at the end of step 3.*

Serving suggestion *Lemon wedges and warm flat bread; drizzle over extra virgin olive oil.*

Tip *Harira is a traditional soup that's eaten to break the fast of Ramadan. This is our vegetarian version, but lamb, chicken or beef can be added.*

Nutritional count per serving *2.6g total fat (0.4g saturated fat); 753kJ (180 cal); 23.1g carbohydrate; 12g protein; 9.4g fibre*

ARTICHOKES WITH
GARLIC ANCHOVY CRUMBS

prep + cook time 8 hours 35 minutes ✳ serves 6 [as a starter]

* 6 medium globe artichokes (1.2kg)
* 2 litres (8 cups) water
* 2 cups (500ml) chicken stock
* 2 tablespoons lemon juice
* ¼ cup (60ml) olive oil

GARLIC ANCHOVY CRUMBS
* 1 tablespoon olive oil
* 6 anchovy fillets, drained, chopped finely
* 3 cloves garlic, crushed
* 1½ cups (105g) stale breadcrumbs
* 1 tablespoon finely grated lemon rind
* ⅓ cup finely chopped fresh flat-leaf parsley
* ½ cup (40g) finely grated romano cheese

1 Remove and discard tough outer leaves from artichokes. Trim stems so artichoke bases sit flat. Using a teaspoon, remove and discard hairy chokes from centre of artichokes; rinse artichokes under cold water.

2 Pack artichokes tightly, upside down, into a 4.5-litre (18-cup) slow cooker; pour in the water, stock and juice. Cook, covered, on low, about 8 hours.

3 Make garlic anchovy crumbs before serving.

4 Remove artichokes with a slotted spoon; drain well. Serve artichokes with olive oil and garlic anchovy crumbs for dipping.

GARLIC ANCHOVY CRUMBS Heat oil in a large frying pan; cook anchovy and garlic, stirring, until anchovy softens. Add breadcrumbs and rind; cook, stirring, until crumbs are browned lightly and crisp. Transfer to a medium bowl; cool. Stir in parsley and cheese; season to taste.

Not suitable to freeze.

Serving suggestion
Crusty bread and a green or tomato salad to make a main meal.

Tip *Artichoke leaves are pulled off the whole artichoke, one by one, and eaten by scraping against the teeth to extract the soft flesh at the base of each leaf. Dip the leaves in a full-flavoured olive oil and the flavoured crumbs before eating.*

Nutritional count per serving *6.2g total fat (1.8g saturated fat); 648kJ (155 cal); 13.9g carbohydrate; 9.5g protein; 2.3g fibre*

SILVER BEET DHAL

prep + cook time 10 hours 20 minutes * serves 6

* 500g (1 pound) yellow split peas
* 45g (1½ ounces) ghee
* 2 medium brown onions (300g), chopped finely
* 3 cloves garlic, crushed
* 4cm (1½-inch) piece fresh ginger (20g), grated
* 1 fresh long green chilli, chopped finely
* 2 tablespoons black mustard seeds
* 1 teaspoon cumin seeds
* 1 tablespoon ground coriander
* 2 teaspoons ground turmeric
* 1 teaspoon garam masala
* 800g (1½ pounds) canned diced tomatoes
* 3 cups (750ml) vegetable stock
* 1½ cups (375ml) water
* 1 teaspoon caster (superfine) sugar
* 4 medium silver beet (swiss chard) leaves (320g), stems removed, chopped coarsely

1   Rinse split peas under cold water until water runs clear; drain.

2   Heat ghee in a large frying pan; cook onion, garlic, ginger and chilli, stirring, until onion softens. Add seeds and spices; cook, stirring, until fragrant. Place onion mixture into a 4.5-litre (18-cup) slow cooker; stir in tomatoes, stock, the water, sugar and split peas. Cook, covered, on low, about 10 hours.

3   Stir in silver beet; season to taste.

Suitable to freeze
at the end of step 2.

Serving suggestion
Top with fried or caramelised onions.

Nutritional count per serving *10.1g total fat (5.4g saturated fat); 1689kJ (404 cal); 48.2g carbohydrate; 23.3g protein; 12.5g fibre*

PARMESAN, SPINACH
AND BEAN RAGÙ

prep + cook time 8 hours 45 minutes ✳ serves 6

* 375g (12 ounces) dried four-bean mix
* 50g (1½ ounces) butter, chopped coarsely
* 1 tablespoon olive oil
* 1 large brown onion (200g), chopped finely
* 1 medium carrot (120g), chopped finely
* 2 stalks celery (300g), trimmed, chopped finely
* 3 cloves garlic, crushed
* ½ cup (125ml) dry white wine
* 2 tablespoons tomato paste
* 400g (12½ ounces) canned crushed tomatoes
* 2 cups (500ml) vegetable stock
* 2 teaspoons sea salt flakes
* 2 teaspoons caster (superfine) sugar
* 4 sprigs fresh thyme
* 50g (1½ ounces) baby spinach leaves
* 1 cup (80g) finely grated parmesan

1 Place bean mix in a medium saucepan; cover with 5cm (2 inches) cold water. Bring to the boil over medium-low heat. Boil about 5 minutes; drain. Transfer beans to a 4.5-litre (18-cup) slow cooker.
2 Heat butter and oil in a large frying pan over medium heat; cook onion, carrot, celery and garlic, stirring, for 5 minutes or until softened. Add wine; bring to the boil. Boil until wine has almost evaporated. Add paste, tomatoes, stock, salt, sugar and thyme. Transfer to cooker. Cook, covered, on low, about 8 hours. Season to taste.
3 Discard thyme. Stir in spinach until wilted. Sprinkle ragù with parmesan to serve.

Suitable to freeze *at the end of step 2.*

Serving suggestion *Fresh crusty bread.*

Tip *We used a chardonnay-style wine in this recipe.*

Nutritional count per serving *12.8g total fat (7.4g saturated fat); 1093kJ (261 cal); 19.4g carbohydrate; 12.8g protein; 7g fibre*

VEGETABLE STEW
WITH POLENTA DUMPLINGS

prep + cook time 9 hours ✳ serves 4

* 1 medium red onion (170g), cut into wedges
* 2 medium zucchini (240g), sliced thickly
* 4 yellow patty pan squash (120g), cut into wedges
* 1 medium kumara (orange sweet potato) (400g), chopped coarsely
* 2 medium carrots (240g), chopped coarsely
* 1 trimmed corn cob (250g), cut into 6 rounds
* 1 medium red capsicum (bell pepper) (350g), chopped coarsely
* 2 flat mushrooms (160g) cut into wedges
* 3 cloves garlic, crushed
* 30g (1-ounce) sachet taco seasoning
* 2 teaspoons paprika
* 800g (1½ pounds) canned crushed tomatoes
* 1 cup (250ml) vegetable stock
* 2 tablespoons fresh flat-leaf parsley leaves

POLENTA DUMPLINGS
* 1 cup (150g) self-raising flour
* 2 tablespoons polenta (cornmeal)
* 60g (2 ounces) cold butter, chopped
* 1 egg, beaten lightly
* ¼ cup (20g) finely grated parmesan
* 2 tablespoons milk, approximately

1 Place onion, zucchini, squash, kumara, carrot, corn, capsicum, mushrooms, garlic, seasoning, paprika, tomatoes and stock in a 4.5-litre (18-cup) slow cooker. Cook, covered, on low, about 8 hours.

2 Make polenta dumpling mixture just before required.

3 Drop level tablespoons of dumpling mixture, about 2cm (¾ inch) apart, on top of stew. Cook, covered, on low, for 30 minutes or until dumplings are firm to touch and cooked through. Serve stew with dumplings and sprinkle with parsley.

POLENTA DUMPLINGS Place flour and polenta in a medium bowl; rub in butter. Stir in egg, parmesan and enough milk to make a soft, sticky dough.

Not suitable to freeze.

Tip *Add rinsed, drained canned kidney beans or trimmed green beans for the last 10 minutes of cooking time.*

Nutritional count per serving *22.9g total fat (8g saturated fat); 2483kJ (594 cal); 70g carbohydrate; 19.4g protein; 15.5g fibre*

SMOKY CHICKPEA
AND TOMATO SOUP

prep + cook time 8 hours 30 minutes ✳ serves 6

* 1.5kg (3 pounds) tomatoes, quartered
* 1 large brown onion (200g),
chopped coarsely
* 3 cloves garlic, chopped coarsely
* 1 stalk celery (150g), trimmed,
sliced thickly
* 3 x 400g (12½ ounces) canned chickpeas
(garbanzo beans), rinsed, drained
* 1¾ cups (430ml) chicken stock
* 2 teaspoons smoked paprika
* 1 tablespoon caster (superfine) sugar
* ⅓ cup (80g) sour cream

1   Place tomato, onion, garlic, celery, chickpeas, stock, paprika and sugar in a 4.5-litre (18-cup) slow cooker. Cook, covered, on low, about 8 hours.
2   Using a slotted spoon, transfer 2 cups of the chickpeas to a medium bowl; reserve. Stand remaining soup 10 minutes, then process soup until smooth. Stir in reserved chickpeas. Season to taste.
3   Serve soup topped with sour cream.

Suitable to freeze
at the end of step 2.

Serving suggestion
Char-grilled bread.

Tip *Choose the ripest tomatoes you can find. If you dislike tomato skins, you can either peel the tomatoes before adding to the cooker or strain the pureed soup before returning the chickpeas.*

Nutritional count per serving *8.7g total fat (3.8g saturated fat); 1113kJ (266 cal); 29.9g carbohydrate; 12.3g protein; 10.6g fibre*

CREAM OF CELERIAC SOUP

prep + cook time 8 hours 30 minutes ✳ serves 6

* 2kg (4 pounds) celeriac (celery root), chopped coarsely
* 1 medium brown onion (150g), chopped coarsely
* 3 cloves garlic, quartered
* 1 stalk celery (150g), trimmed, chopped coarsely
* 1.5 litres (6 cups) water
* 1 litre (4 cups) chicken stock
* ½ cup (125ml) pouring cream
* ⅓ cup loosely packed fresh chervil leaves
* 1 tablespoon olive oil

1 Combine celeriac, onion, garlic, celery, the water and stock in a 4.5-litre (18-cup) slow cooker. Cook, covered, on low, about 8 hours.
2 Stand soup 10 minutes, then blend or process, in batches, until smooth. Return soup to cooker; stir in cream. Cook, covered, on high, until hot; season to taste.
3 Serve soup sprinkled with chervil; drizzle with oil.

Suitable to freeze at the end of step 2.

Tip *Be careful when blending or processing hot soup – don't over-fill the container (one-third to half-full as a guide), and make sure that the lid is secure.*

Nutritional count per serving *13.3g total fat (6.7g saturated fat); 995kJ (238 cal); 16.8g carbohydrate; 7.1g protein; 12.6g fibre*

MOROCCAN
CHICKPEA STEW

prep + cook time 9 hours ✳ serves 4

* 3 x 400g (12½ ounces) canned chickpeas (garbanzo beans), rinsed, drained
* 1 large red onion (300g), sliced thinly
* 3 cloves garlic, crushed
* 1 fresh long red chilli, chopped finely
* 1 large carrot (180g), halved, sliced thickly
* ½ medium cauliflower (750g), cut into large florets
* 2 tablespoons moroccan seasoning
* pinch saffron threads
* 1 tablespoon honey
* 400g (12½ ounces) canned diced tomatoes
* 3 cups (750ml) vegetable or chicken stock
* 250g (8 ounces) cavolo nero (tuscan cabbage), trimmed, shredded coarsely
* 250g (8 ounces) yellow patty pan squash, halved
* 1 tablespoon Greek-style yoghurt
* 2 tablespoons finely sliced preserved lemon rind
* ⅓ cup loosely packed fresh flat-leaf parsley leaves

1   Combine chickpeas, onion, garlic, chilli, carrot, cauliflower, seasoning, saffron, honey, tomatoes and stock in a 5-litre (20-cup) slow cooker. Cook, covered, on low, about 8 hours.

2   Add cavolo nero and squash to cooker; cook, covered, on high, for 20 minutes or until squash is tender. Season to taste.

3   Serve stew topped with yoghurt and sprinkled with preserved lemon rind and parsley.

Suitable to freeze
at the end of step 1.

Serving suggestion
Steamed couscous.

Nutritional count per serving   *10.7g total fat (1.7g saturated fat); 1804kJ (431 cal); 50.4g carbohydrate; 23.4g protein; 22.7g fibre*

FOUR THINGS
YOU NEED TO KNOW

1

Browning the meat (and sometimes other ingredients) before adding to a slow cooker is a matter of choice. We think the taste and colour of the final dish is better if the browning is done first. Some slow cookers can be used to brown meat in the cooker itself, but mostly the meat will need to be browned, in batches, in a separate pan.

2

Lean chicken cuts such as fillets (without skin and bones) don't respond well to slow cooking, they dry out and become stringy in texture. Like seafood, though not quite so delicate, they're good to add to a sauce base, then cooked through gently or used in recipes that have a shorter cooking time.

3

Most seafood needs to be cooked quickly, so be careful if you choose to use it as an ingredient in a slow cooker. It's fine to make a sauce or stock then add seafood to it; the trick is to have the liquid as hot as possible so that the seafood will cook quickly without reducing the temperature of the liquid too much.

4

Most of the food cooked in a slow cooker produces a lot of liquid. If it tastes too diluted, boil it quite rapidly in a saucepan on the stovetop until the liquid is reduced and more concentrated. Freeze excess liquid for use as stock in sauces and stews or casseroles.

UNDER 8 HOURS

UNDER
8
HOURS

POULTRY

THE BEST CUTS OF POULTRY TO USE FOR
SLOW COOKING CONTAIN BONES

CHICKEN WITH
LEEKS AND ARTICHOKES

prep + cook time 6 hours 30 minutes ✳ serves 4

* 1.6kg (3¼-pound) whole chicken
* 1 unpeeled lemon, chopped coarsely
* 4 cloves unpeeled garlic
* 4 sprigs fresh tarragon
* 6 sprigs fresh flat-leaf parsley
* 45g (1½ ounces) butter
* ¾ cup (180ml) dry white wine
* 2 medium globe artichokes (400g), quartered
* 8 baby leeks (640g)
* 1 cup (250ml) chicken stock

1 Wash chicken under cold water; pat dry inside and out with paper towel. Place lemon, garlic and herbs in chicken cavity; season with salt and pepper. Tuck wing tips under; tie legs together with kitchen string.

2 Melt butter in a large frying pan; cook chicken until browned all over. Remove chicken. Add wine; bring to the boil.

3 Meanwhile, trim stems from artichokes; remove tough outer leaves. Place artichokes and leeks in a 4.5-litre (18-cup) slow cooker; add wine mixture and stock. Place chicken on vegetables; cook, covered, on low, about 6 hours.

4 Serve chicken with vegetables; drizzle with a little of the juice.

Not suitable to freeze.

Serving suggestion *Creamy mashed potato and a green leafy salad.*

Tip *If you prefer, replace baby leeks with 1 thickly sliced leek.*

Nutritional count per serving *42.2g total fat (16.3g saturated fat); 2571kJ (615 cal); 5.6g carbohydrate; 44.9g protein; 4.2g fibre*

CHICKEN CACCIATORE

prep + cook time 6 hours 25 minutes ✳ serves 6

* 2 tablespoons olive oil
* 12 chicken drumsticks (1.8kg), skin removed
* 1 medium brown onion (150g), sliced thickly
* 3 cloves garlic, crushed
* 3 drained anchovy fillets, crushed
* ½ cup (125ml) dry white wine
* ⅓ cup (80ml) chicken stock
* ⅓ cup (80ml) tomato pasta sauce
* 2 tablespoons tomato paste
* 2 teaspoons finely chopped fresh basil
* 1 teaspoon caster (superfine) sugar
* ⅓ cup (55g) seeded black olives, halved
* 1 tablespoon finely chopped fresh flat-leaf parsley

1 Heat oil in a large frying pan; cook chicken, in batches, until browned all over. Transfer chicken to a 4.5-litre (18-cup) slow cooker.
2 Cook onion, garlic and anchovy in same pan, stirring, until onion softens. Add wine; bring to the boil. Boil, uncovered, until reduced by half; stir into cooker with stock, sauce, paste, basil and sugar. Cook, covered, on low, about 6 hours.
3 Stir in olives and parsley; season to taste.

Suitable to freeze *at the end of step 2.*

Serving suggestion *Creamy mashed potato or crusty bread.*

Tip *Use a plain (unflavoured) tomato-based sauce suitable for serving over pasta. These sauces can be bought in cans and jars and are often labelled 'sugo' or 'passata'.*

Nutritional count per serving *18.5g total fat (4.4g saturated fat); 1501kJ (359 cal); 6.9g carbohydrate; 37.2g protein; 1.3g fibre*

PORTUGUESE TURKEY

prep + cook time 6 hours 30 minutes ✳ serves 6

* **27 cloves garlic, peeled**
* **¼ cup (30g) sea salt flakes**
* **2 teaspoons sweet paprika**
* **2 tablespoons duck fat**
* **3 turkey drumsticks (2.5kg)**
* **2 cups (500ml) tawny port**
* **½ cup (125ml) dry white wine**

1 Blend or process garlic, salt and paprika in a food processor until smooth. Transfer to a small bowl. Stir in duck fat; it will be solid at first, but will soften and combine as it's stirred.

2 Spoon garlic mixture over turkey then, using your hands, rub into the skin.

3 Place turkey legs in a 4.5-litre (18-cup) slow cooker. Add port and wine.

4 Cook, covered, on low, about 6 hours. Using a spoon or small ladle, skim fat from surface of liquid.

5 Serve meat shredded in large chunks with cooking juices spooned over.

Suitable to freeze *at the end of step 4.*

Serving suggestion *Sautéed or roasted potatoes and a bitter greens salad.*

Tips *Depending on the size of your cooker, you may need to ask the butcher to chop the end off each drumstick. We used a chardonnay-style wine in this recipe. This dish is traditionally served at Christmas time.*

Nutritional count per serving *38.8g total fat (12.8g saturated fat); 3028kJ (723 cal); 12g carbohydrate; 62g protein; 2.3g fibre*

GREEN OLIVE
AND LEMON CHICKEN

prep + cook time 6 hours 20 minutes ✳ serves 4

* 15g (½ ounce) butter, softened
* 1 tablespoon olive oil
* 2 teaspoons finely grated lemon rind
* 3 cloves garlic, crushed
* ¼ cup (30g) seeded green olives, chopped finely
* 2 tablespoons finely chopped fresh flat-leaf parsley
* 1.5kg (3-pound) whole chicken
* 2 unpeeled medium lemons (280g), quartered

1 Combine butter, oil, rind, garlic, olives and parsley in a medium bowl; season.
2 Rinse chicken under cold water; pat dry, inside and out, with paper towel. Make a pocket between breasts and skin with your fingers; push half the butter mixture under skin. Rub remaining butter mixture over chicken. Tuck wing tips under; fill cavity with lemon, tie legs together with kitchen string. Trim skin around neck; secure neck flap to underside of chicken with small fine skewers.
3 Place chicken in a 4.5-litre (18-cup) slow cooker. Cook, covered, on low, about 6 hours.
4 Cut chicken into quarters to serve.

Not suitable to freeze.

Serving suggestion
Roasted potatoes and steamed green vegetables, or creamy polenta or mash and a green salad.

Tip *Kitchen string is made of a natural product such as cotton or hemp so that it neither affects the flavour of the food it's tied around nor melts when heated.*

Nutritional count per serving *38.1g total fat (12.1g saturated fat); 2086kJ (499 cal); 2g carbohydrate; 37.7g protein; 0.6g fibre*

CREAMY TURKEY STEW
WITH MUSTARD

prep + cook time 2 hours 30 minutes ✳ serves 8

✱ 4 turkey drumsticks (3kg), skin removed
✱ 2 tablespoons olive oil
✱ 375g (12 ounces) button mushrooms
✱ 2 medium leeks (700g), sliced thickly
✱ 4 rindless bacon slices (260g),
chopped coarsely
✱ 2 cloves garlic, crushed
✱ 2 tablespoons plain (all-purpose) flour
✱ 1 cup (250ml) chicken stock
✱ ½ cup (125ml) dry white wine
✱ 2 tablespoons wholegrain mustard
✱ 6 sprigs fresh lemon thyme
✱ ½ cup (125ml) pouring cream
✱ 2 teaspoons fresh lemon thyme leaves

1   Using a sharp heavy knife, cut turkey meat from bones, chop meat coarsely; discard bones.
2   Heat oil in a large frying pan; cook turkey, in batches, until browned all over. Transfer turkey to a 4.5-litre (18-cup) slow cooker.
3   Add mushrooms, leek, bacon and garlic to same pan; cook, stirring, until leek softens. Add flour; cook, stirring, about 1 minute. Stir in stock, wine, mustard and thyme sprigs; bring to the boil. Boil, uncovered, about 2 minutes. Remove from heat; stir in cream. Transfer mushroom mixture to cooker. Cook, covered, on low, about 2 hours.
4   Season to taste; sprinkle with thyme leaves.

Not suitable to freeze.

Serving suggestion
Mashed potato and steamed green beans.

Tip *Use 3kg turkey marylands if you can't get drumsticks.*

Nutritional count per serving *23.2g total fat (8.8g saturated fat); 1914kJ (458 cal); 5.3g carbohydrate; 53.2g protein; 3.1g fibre*

PORTUGUESE-STYLE
CHICKEN

prep + cook time 6 hours 45 minutes ✳ serves 4

* ¼ cup (60ml) olive oil
* ¼ cup (70g) tomato paste
* 4 cloves garlic, quartered
* 2 tablespoons finely grated lemon rind
* ⅓ cup (80ml) lemon juice
* 4 fresh small red thai (serrano) chillies, chopped coarsely
* 1 tablespoon smoked paprika
* ½ cup firmly packed fresh oregano leaves
* 1.8kg (3¾-pound) whole chicken
* 1 medium unpeeled lemon (140g), quartered
* 3 sprigs fresh lemon thyme

1 Blend or process 2 tablespoons of the oil, paste, garlic, rind, juice, chilli, paprika and oregano until smooth. Season to taste.
2 Rinse chicken under cold water; pat dry inside and out with paper towel. Place lemon and thyme inside cavity of chicken; secure cavity with a fine skewer.
3 Make a pocket under skin of breast, drumsticks and thighs with your fingers. Using disposable gloves, rub ¼ cup of the paste under skin. Tuck wing tips under; tie legs together with kitchen string. Rub ¼ cup of the paste over chicken.
4 Heat remaining oil in a large frying pan; cook chicken until browned all over. Transfer to a 4.5-litre (18-cup) slow cooker. Cook, covered, on low, about 6 hours.
5 Cut chicken into pieces; accompany with remaining paste.

Not suitable to freeze.

Serving suggestion
Potato chips or wedges, a green salad and lemon wedges.

Tip *Fresh chillies can burn your fingers so wear disposable gloves when handling them.*

Nutritional count per serving *50g total fat (13.2g saturated fat); 2688kJ (643 cal); 2.9g carbohydrate; 45.8g protein; 1.5g fibre*

SPICY TOMATO AND
SAFFRON CHICKEN CASSEROLE

prep + cook time 6 hours 25 minutes ✳ serves 6

* ¼ cup (35g) plain (all-purpose) flour
* 2 tablespoons moroccan seasoning
* 6 chicken thigh cutlets (1.2kg)
* 1 tablespoon vegetable oil
* 1 large brown onion (200g), sliced thickly
* 2 cloves garlic, crushed
* 2.5cm (1-inch) piece fresh ginger (15g), grated
* 1 fresh long red chilli, sliced thinly
* 2 cups (500ml) chicken stock
* 400g (12½ ounces) canned diced tomatoes
* ¼ cup (70g) tomato paste
* ¼ teaspoon saffron threads

PRESERVED LEMON GREMOLATA
* ⅓ cup finely chopped fresh flat-leaf parsley
* 1 tablespoon thinly sliced preserved lemon rind
* 1 garlic clove, crushed

1 Combine flour and 1 tablespoon of the seasoning in a small shallow bowl; toss chicken in flour mixture to coat, shake off excess. Heat half the oil in a large frying pan; cook chicken, in batches, until browned. Transfer to a 4.5-litre (18-cup) slow cooker.

2 Heat remaining oil in same pan, add onion, garlic, ginger, chilli and remaining seasoning; cook, stirring, until onion softens. Add ½ cup of the stock; cook, stirring, until mixture boils.

3 Stir onion mixture into cooker with remaining stock, tomatoes, paste and saffron. Cook, covered, on low, about 6 hours. Season to taste.

4 Make preserved lemon gremolata.

5 Sprinkle casserole with gremolata.

PRESERVED LEMON GREMOLATA
Combine ingredients in a small bowl.

Suitable to freeze
at the end of step 3.

Serving suggestion
*Steamed rice
or couscous.*

Tip *Preserved lemons
are available from
delicatessens and some
supermarkets. Remove
and discard the flesh,
wash the rind then use
as the recipe directs.*

Nutritional count per serving *23.8g total fat (7.2g saturated fat); 1522kJ (364 cal); 10.2g carbohydrate; 26.5g protein; 2.5g fibre*

DUCK VINDALOO

prep + cook time 6 hours 45 minutes * serves 6

- **1.8kg (3¾-pound) whole duck**
- **¼ cup (35g) plain (all-purpose) flour**
- **1 tablespoon peanut oil**
- **2 teaspoons each cumin seeds and fenugreek seeds**
- **1 teaspoon each ground coriander and ground turmeric**
- **½ teaspoon ground cardamom**
- **4 fresh small red thai (serrano) chillies, chopped coarsely**
- **3 cloves garlic, quartered**
- **2.5cm (1-inch) piece fresh ginger (15g), sliced thinly**
- **⅓ cup (80ml) white vinegar**
- **½ cup (125ml) chicken stock**
- **1 medium red onion (170g), chopped finely**
- **4 medium potatoes (800g), chopped coarsely**
- **2 tablespoons chicken gravy powder**
- **2 tablespoons water**
- **½ cup loosely packed fresh coriander (cilantro) leaves**

1 Rinse duck under cold water; pat dry. Cut duck into six serving-sized pieces. Toss duck in flour, shake off excess. Heat oil in a large frying pan; cook duck, in batches, until browned. Transfer to a 4.5-litre (18-cup) slow cooker.

2 Meanwhile, dry-fry spices in a small frying pan until fragrant; cool. Blend or process spices, chilli, garlic, ginger and vinegar until smooth.

3 Stir spice mixture into cooker with stock, onion and potato. Cook, covered, on low, about 6 hours. Season to taste.

4 Transfer duck and potato to a serving plate. Skim excess fat from sauce. Stir combined gravy powder and the water into sauce in cooker. Cook, covered, on high, for 10 minutes or until sauce thickens.

5 Drizzle sauce over duck; sprinkle with coriander to serve.

Not suitable to freeze.

Serving suggestion *Steamed rice.*

Tip *This is a mild vindaloo. If you like it hotter, add more fresh chillies when making the paste.*

Nutritional count per serving *66.5g total fat (19.6g saturated fat); 3323kJ (795 cal); 22.7g carbohydrate; 26.7g protein; 3g fibre*

CHICKEN, PORCINI
AND BARLEY SOUP

prep + cook time 6 hours 30 minutes (+ standing) ✻ serves 4

* 20g (¾ ounce) dried porcini mushrooms
* 1 cup (250ml) boiling water
* 2 chicken marylands (700g)
* 1 medium brown onion (150g), chopped finely
* 2 cloves garlic, crushed
* 1 litre (4 cups) chicken stock
* ½ cup (100g) pearl barley
* 1 sprig fresh rosemary
* 1 sprig fresh thyme
* 1 medium parsnip (250g), chopped finely
* 1 small kumara (orange sweet potato) (250g), chopped finely
* 2 stalks celery (300g), trimmed, chopped finely
* 250g (8 ounces) swiss brown mushrooms, quartered
* ½ cup finely chopped fresh flat-leaf parsley

1   Place porcini mushrooms in a small heatproof bowl, cover with the water; stand 15 minutes or until softened. Drain, reserve porcini mushrooms and soaking liquid.

2   Meanwhile, discard as much skin as possible from chicken. Place chicken, onion, garlic, stock, barley, rosemary, thyme, parsnip, kumara, celery, swiss brown mushrooms, porcini mushrooms and strained soaking liquid into a 4.5-litre (18-cup) slow cooker. Cook, covered, on low, about 6 hours.

3   Remove chicken from cooker. When cool enough to handle, remove meat from bone; shred coarsely. Discard bones. Return chicken to cooker; season to taste.

4   Serve soup sprinkled with parsley.

Not suitable to freeze.

Serving suggestion
Crusty bread.

Nutritional count per serving *9.4g total fat (3g saturated fat); 1488kJ (356 cal); 38.9g carbohydrate; 29.2g protein; 8.4g fibre*

POACHED CHICKEN
WITH SOY AND SESAME

prep + cook time 6 hours 30 minutes ✳ serves 4

* 1.6kg (3¼-pound) whole chicken
* 5cm (2-inch) piece fresh ginger (25g), sliced thinly
* 4 cloves garlic, halved
* 2 star anise
* 2 cinnamon sticks
* 1 cup (250ml) light soy sauce
* 1 cup (250ml) chinese cooking wine
* ⅓ cup (75g) white (granulated) sugar
* 1 litre (4 cups) water
* ⅓ cup (80ml) light soy sauce, extra
* 2 teaspoons sesame oil
* 2 cloves garlic, extra, cut into matchsticks
* 2.5cm (1-inch) piece fresh ginger (15g), extra, cut into matchsticks
* 2 fresh long red chillies, sliced thinly
* ⅓ cup (80ml) peanut oil
* 4 green onions (scallions), sliced thinly
* ½ cup loosely packed fresh coriander (cilantro) leaves

1 Trim excess fat from chicken. Place chicken in a 4.5-litre (18-cup) slow cooker. Add ginger, garlic, star anise, cinnamon, sauce, wine, sugar and the water to cooker. Cook, covered, on low, about 6 hours. Remove chicken from cooker; discard poaching liquid.
2 Cut chicken into 12 pieces; place on a heatproof platter. Drizzle extra sauce and sesame oil over chicken; sprinkle with extra garlic and ginger and chilli.
3 Heat peanut oil in a small saucepan, over medium heat, until very hot; carefully drizzle over chicken. Top with onion and coriander.

Suitable to freeze *at the end of step 1.*

Serving suggestion *Steamed noodles or rice.*

Tip *Chinese cooking wine is also known as chinese rice wine and shao hsing wine. Dry sherry can be used instead.*

Nutritional count per serving *52.9g total fat (13.7g saturated fat); 3361kJ (804 cal); 22.7g carbohydrate; 45.5g protein; 1.5g fibre*

CHICKEN, CELERIAC
AND BROAD BEAN CASSEROLE

prep + cook time 4 hours ✻ serves 6

* 1.5kg (3 pounds) chicken thigh fillets
* 2 tablespoons plain (all-purpose) flour
* 2 tablespoons vegetable oil
* 20g (¾ ounce) butter
* 1 large brown onion (200g), chopped coarsely
* 2 medium carrots (240g), sliced thickly
* 2 stalks celery (300g), trimmed, chopped coarsely
* 2 cloves garlic, chopped finely
* 2 cups (500ml) chicken stock
* 2 tablespoons dijon mustard
* 1 medium celeriac (celery root) (750g), chopped coarsely
* 2 cups (300g) frozen broad beans (fava beans)
* ½ cup (50g) walnuts, roasted, chopped coarsely
* ¼ cup coarsely chopped celery leaves

1   Toss chicken in flour to coat, shake off excess. Reserve excess flour. Heat oil in a large frying pan; cook chicken, in batches, until browned. Remove from pan. Wipe pan with paper towel.
2   Heat butter in same pan; cook onion, carrot and celery, stirring, until softened. Add garlic; cook, stirring, until fragrant. Stir in reserved excess flour, then stock and mustard; stir over high heat until mixture boils and thickens.
3   Place celeriac in a 4.5-litre (18-cup) slow cooker. Top with chicken then onion mixture. Cook, covered, on high, about 3 hours.
4   Meanwhile, place beans in a medium heatproof bowl, cover with boiling water; stand 2 minutes, drain. Peel away grey skins.
5   Add beans to cooker; cook, covered, on high, about 30 minutes. Season to taste.
6   Serve sprinkled with nuts and celery leaves.

Suitable to freeze *at the end of step 3.*

Tip *Roast walnuts at 180°C/350°F for 5 minutes or until lightly browned.*

Nutritional count per serving *33.4g total fat (8.6g saturated fat); 2504kJ (599 cal); 16.3g carbohydrate; 54.6g protein; 9.8g fibre*

CHICKEN, LENTIL
AND PUMPKIN CURRY

prep + cook time 7 hours 40 minutes ✱ serves 6

* ⅔ cup (130g) dried brown lentils
* ⅔ cup (130g) dried red lentils
* 1 tablespoon vegetable oil
* 1 large brown onion (200g), chopped finely
* 2 cloves garlic, crushed
* 2.5cm (1-inch) piece fresh ginger (10g), grated
* 2 teaspoons each ground cumin, ground coriander and black mustard seeds
* 1 teaspoon ground turmeric
* 1 fresh long red chilli, chopped finely
* 3 cups (750ml) chicken stock
* 1kg (2 pounds) chicken thigh fillets, chopped coarsely
* 400g (12½ ounces) canned diced tomatoes
* 500g (1 pound) pumpkin, chopped coarsely
* 1¼ cups (270ml) canned coconut milk
* 155g (5 ounces) baby spinach leaves
* ½ cup coarsely chopped fresh coriander (cilantro)

1   Rinse lentils under cold water until water runs clear; drain. Heat oil in a large frying pan; cook onion, garlic and ginger, stirring, until onion softens. Add spices and chilli; cook, stirring, until fragrant. Add stock; bring to the boil.

2   Pour stock mixture into a 4.5-litre (18-cup) slow cooker; stir in chicken, tomatoes, pumpkin and lentils. Cook, covered, on low, about 7 hours.

3   Stir in coconut milk; cook, covered, on high, about 15 minutes, stirring once. Stir in spinach and coriander. Season to taste.

Suitable to freeze
at the end of step 2.

Serving suggestion
Chapatis and plain yoghurt.

Nutritional count per serving *26.3g total fat (12.8g saturated fat); 2312kJ (553 cal); 27.6g carbohydrate; 47g protein; 10g fibre*

SPICED CHICKEN
IN COCONUT SAUCE

prep + cook time 7 hours 45 minutes ✻ serves 6

* 1 tablespoon peanut oil
* 3 chicken thigh fillets (660g), halved
* 6 chicken drumsticks (900g)
* 2 medium brown onions (300g), chopped coarsely
* 1 cup (250ml) chicken stock
* 1⅔ cups (400ml) canned coconut milk
* 3 fresh kaffir lime leaves, shredded thinly
* 315g (10 ounces) green beans, chopped coarsely
* 12 fresh thai eggplants (350g), halved
* ¾ cup loosely packed fresh coriander (cilantro) leaves

SPICE PASTE
* 4 shallots (100g), quartered
* 2 cloves garlic, chopped coarsely
* 5cm (2-inch) piece fresh ginger (25g), chopped coarsely
* 2 teaspoons each ground cumin, ground coriander and ground turmeric
* 3 fresh small red thai (serrano) chillies, chopped coarsely
* 2 tablespoons fish sauce
* 2 tablespoons peanut oil
* 2 tablespoons lime juice
* 1 tablespoon grated palm sugar

1 Make spice paste.

2 Heat half the oil in a large frying pan; cook chicken, in batches, until browned all over, place in a 4.5-litre (18-cup) slow cooker. Heat remaining oil in same pan; cook onion, stirring, until soft. Add spice paste; cook, stirring, until fragrant. Add stock; bring to the boil.

3 Remove from heat; stir in coconut milk and lime leaves, pour over chicken. Cook, covered, on low, about 7 hours.

4 Add beans and eggplant, cook, covered, on high, for 20 minutes or until vegetables are tender. Season to taste; sprinkle with coriander.

SPICE PASTE Blend or process ingredients until mixture is smooth.

Suitable to freeze
at the end of step 3.

Serving suggestion
Steamed rice and lime wedges.

Nutritional count per serving *41.9g total fat (19.4g saturated fat); 2508kJ (600 cal); 11.6g carbohydrate; 42.5g protein; 5.5g fibre*

HONEY MUSTARD CHICKEN

prep + cook time 6 hours 45 minutes ✳ serves 4

* **2 tablespoons cornflour (cornstarch)**
* **2 teaspoons dry mustard powder**
* **½ cup (125ml) dry white wine**
* **1 cup (250ml) chicken stock**
* **¼ cup (70g) wholegrain mustard**
* **2 tablespoons honey**
* **8 chicken thigh cutlets (1.6kg)**
* **1 medium leek (350g), trimmed, sliced thickly**
* **2 stalks celery (300g), trimmed, sliced thickly**
* **400g (12½ ounces) baby carrots, peeled**
* **1 cup (120g) frozen peas**
* **⅓ cup (80ml) pouring cream**
* **¼ cup coarsely chopped fresh flat-leaf parsley**

1   Place cornflour and mustard powder in a 4.5-litre (18-cup) slow cooker. Gradually whisk in wine and stock until smooth. Add mustard and honey; whisk until smooth.
2   Remove and discard fat and skin from chicken. Place chicken, leek, celery and carrots in cooker. Cook, covered, on low, about 6 hours.
3   Add peas to cooker; cook, covered, about 20 minutes. Stir in cream; season to taste.
4   Sprinkle chicken with parsley.

Suitable to freeze
at the end of step 3.

Serving suggestion
Creamy mashed potato, steamed rice or pasta.

Tips *We used a chardonnay-style wine in this recipe. Chicken thigh cutlets usually come with the skin and centre bone intact, although sometimes they can be found skinless. Most major supermarkets sell them.*

Nutritional count per serving *28.9g total fat (10.9g saturated fat); 2636kJ (630 cal); 27.8g carbohydrate; 58.1g protein; 9.1g fibre*

GREEN CHICKEN CURRY

prep + cook time 4 hours 45 minutes ✱ serves 6

* 1kg (2 pounds) chicken thigh fillets, halved
* 2 cloves garlic, crushed
* 2.5cm (1-inch) piece fresh ginger (15g), grated
* 1 fresh long green chilli, chopped finely
* 2 tablespoons green curry paste
* 2 fresh kaffir lime leaves, torn
* 230g (7 ounces) canned sliced bamboo shoots, rinsed, drained
* 400g (12½ ounces) canned baby corn, rinsed, drained, chopped coarsely
* ¾ cup (180ml) chicken stock
* 1⅔ cups (410ml) coconut milk
* 2 tablespoons cornflour (cornstarch)
* 1 tablespoon water
* 1 tablespoon grated palm sugar
* 1 tablespoon lime juice
* 1 tablespoon fish sauce
* ⅔ cup loosely packed fresh thai basil leaves
* ⅓ cup loosely packed fresh coriander (cilantro) leaves

1 Combine chicken, garlic, ginger, chilli, paste, lime leaves, bamboo shoots, corn, stock and coconut milk in a 4.5-litre (18-cup) slow cooker. Cook, covered, on low, about 4 hours.
2 Blend cornflour with the water in a small bowl until smooth. Stir cornflour mixture, sugar, juice, sauce and half the basil into cooker. Cook, uncovered, on high, for 20 minutes or until thickened slightly. Season to taste. Serve sprinkled with coriander and remaining basil.

Suitable to freeze *at the end of step 1.*

Serving suggestion *Steamed jasmine rice and lime wedges.*

Tip *Add curry paste to suit your level of heat tolerance; the strength of the paste will differ between brands.*

Nutritional count per serving *29.2g total fat (16.4g saturated fat); 1981kJ (474 cal); 16.2g carbohydrate; 35.4g protein; 4.7g fibre*

BUTTER CHICKEN

prep + cook time 4 hours 30 minutes (+ refrigeration) ✳ serves 6

✳ 12 chicken thigh cutlets (2.4kg), skin removed

✳ 2 tablespoons lemon juice

✳ 1 teaspoon chilli powder

✳ ¾ cup (200g) Greek-style yoghurt

✳ 5cm (2-inch) piece fresh ginger (25g), grated

✳ 2 teaspoons garam masala

✳ 45g (1½ ounces) butter

✳ 1 tablespoon vegetable oil

✳ 1 medium brown onion (150g), chopped finely

✳ 4 cloves garlic, crushed

✳ 1 teaspoon each ground coriander, ground cumin and sweet paprika

✳ 2 tablespoons tomato paste

✳ 410g (13 ounces) canned tomato puree

✳ ⅔ cup (160ml) chicken stock

✳ 2 tablespoons honey

✳ 1 cinnamon stick

✳ ⅓ cup (80ml) pouring cream

✳ ⅓ cup (80g) ricotta

✳ ½ cup loosely packed fresh coriander (cilantro) leaves

1 Combine chicken, juice and chilli powder in a large bowl. Cover, refrigerate 30 minutes.

2 Stir yoghurt, ginger and half the garam masala into chicken mixture.

3 Heat butter and oil in a large frying pan; cook chicken, in batches, until browned all over. Transfer chicken to a 4.5-litre (18-cup) slow cooker. Add onion and garlic to same pan; cook, stirring, until onion softens. Add remaining garam masala and spices; cook, stirring, until fragrant. Remove from heat; stir in paste, puree, stock, honey and cinnamon. Transfer tomato mixture to cooker. Cook, covered, on low, about 4 hours.

4 Stir in cream; season to taste.

5 Serve topped with ricotta and coriander leaves.

Suitable to freeze
at the end of step 3.

Serving suggestion
Steamed basmati rice and warm naan bread.

Nutritional count per serving *39.3g total fat (17g saturated fat); 2750kJ (658 cal); 17.9g carbohydrate; 57.8g protein; 2.6g fibre*

JERK-SPICED
CHICKEN DRUMSTICKS

prep + cook time 4 hours 30 minutes ✳ serves 4

* ✳ 2 tablespoons olive oil
* ✳ 8 chicken drumsticks (1.2kg)
* ✳ 4 green onions (scallions),
chopped coarsely
* ✳ 5cm (2-inch) piece fresh ginger
(20g), grated
* ✳ 1½ teaspoons ground allspice
* ✳ ½ teaspoon ground cinnamon
* ✳ 2 fresh long green chillies,
chopped coarsely
* ✳ 1 teaspoon cracked black pepper
* ✳ 2 cloves garlic, crushed
* ✳ 3 teaspoons finely chopped fresh thyme
* ✳ 2 tablespoons light brown sugar
* ✳ 1 tablespoon cider vinegar
* ✳ 2 tablespoons orange juice

1 Heat half the oil in a large frying pan; cook chicken, turning, until browned all over. Place chicken in a 4.5-litre (18-cup) slow cooker.
2 Meanwhile, process onion, ginger, spices, chilli, pepper, garlic, thyme and remaining oil until finely chopped. Add sugar, vinegar and juice; process until smooth. Pour paste over chicken. Cook, covered, on low, about 4 hours. Season to taste.
3 Serve chicken with sauce; sprinkle with extra thyme, if you like.

Suitable to freeze
at the end of step 2.

Serving suggestion
Steamed green beans, rice and lime wedges.

Nutritional count per serving *30.1g total fat (7.6g saturated fat); 1831kJ (438 cal); 8.2g carbohydrate; 33.9g protein; 0.9g fibre*

PEKING DUCK

prep + cook time 6 hours 45 minutes ✳ serves 4

✱ 8 green onions (scallions), trimmed, halved crossways
✱ 2 teaspoons five-spice powder
✱ 1 teaspoon ground cinnamon
✱ ½ teaspoon ground nutmeg
✱ 2 teaspoons sea salt flakes
✱ 2 tablespoons honey
✱ 1 tablespoon soy sauce
✱ 2.1kg (4¼-pound) whole duck
✱ 1 medium lemon (140g), sliced thickly
✱ 5cm (2-inch) piece fresh ginger (25g), sliced thickly
✱ 2 star anise

1 Place onion over base of a 4.5-litre (18-cup) slow cooker.
2 Combine five-spice, cinnamon, nutmeg, salt, honey and sauce in a small bowl.
3 Remove excess fat from duck cavity, then cut off the neck and discard with the fat. Rub salt mixture over duck. Fill cavity with lemon, ginger and star anise. Transfer duck to cooker. Cook, covered, on low, about 6 hours.

Not suitable to freeze.

Serving suggestion *Sprinkle with thinly sliced red chillies and green onions.*

Tip *Peking duck is Beijing's most famous dish. Traditionally, it is served with peking duck pancakes and hoisin sauce.*

Nutritional count per serving *21.1g total fat (6.4g saturated fat); 2200kJ (526 cal); 14.8g carbohydrate; 67.7g protein; 1.6g fibre*

SPICED CHICKEN
WITH DATES AND CHICKPEAS

prep + cook time 6 hours 30 minutes ✳ **serves 4**

* 8 skinless chicken thigh cutlets (1.6kg)
* 2 tablespoons plain (all-purpose) flour
* 2 tablespoons olive oil
* 2 medium brown onions (300g),
cut into thin wedges
* 4 cloves garlic, chopped finely
* 1 fresh long red chilli, sliced thinly
* 2 teaspoons each ground cumin and
ground cinnamon
* ¼ teaspoon saffron threads
* 2 tablespoons honey
* 2 cups (500ml) chicken stock
* 400g (12½ ounces) canned chickpeas
(garbanzo beans), rinsed, drained
* 3 small zucchini (270g), sliced thickly
* 6 fresh dates (120g), halved, seeded
* 2 tablespoons lemon juice
* ⅓ cup loosely packed fresh coriander
(cilantro) leaves

1 Toss chicken in flour to coat, shake off excess. Heat half the oil in a large frying pan; cook chicken, in batches, until browned. Remove from pan.
2 Heat remaining oil in same pan; cook onion, stirring, until onion softens. Add garlic, chilli and spices; cook, stirring, for 2 minutes or until fragrant. Stir in honey.
3 Place half the chicken in a 4.5-litre (18-cup) slow cooker; top with half the spice mixture. Top with remaining chicken then remaining spice mixture. Pour stock over chicken. Cook, covered, on low, about 5 hours.
4 Add chickpeas, zucchini and dates around the outside edge of cooker. Cook, covered, about 1 hour. Stir in juice; season to taste. Serve sprinkled with coriander.

Suitable to freeze
at the end of step 3.

Serving suggestion
Couscous or afghani (flat) bread.

Nutritional count per serving *31.3g total fat (7.8g saturated fat); 2926kJ (700 cal); 42.1g carbohydrate; 60.8g protein; 7.4g fibre*

SWEET AND SOUR CHICKEN

prep + cook time 4 hours 30 minutes ✳ serves 4

✳ 1 tablespoon vegetable oil
✳ 4 chicken lovely legs (520g)
✳ 4 skinless chicken thigh cutlets (800g)
✳ 2 medium red onions (340g),
cut into wedges
✳ ½ cup (125ml) japanese soy sauce
✳ ½ cup (130g) bottled passata
✳ ⅓ cup (80ml) pineapple juice
✳ 2 tablespoons firmly packed light
brown sugar
✳ 2 tablespoons white vinegar
✳ 1 fresh long red chilli, chopped finely
✳ 2 cloves garlic, crushed
✳ 1 large red capsicum (bell pepper)
(350g), chopped coarsely
✳ 1 large green capsicum (bell pepper)
(350g), chopped coarsely
✳ 225g (7 ounces) canned pineapple
pieces in juice
✳ 2 tablespoons cornflour (cornstarch)
✳ 2 tablespoons water
✳ 2 green onions (scallions), shredded finely

1 Heat oil in a large frying pan; cook chicken, in batches, until browned. Transfer to a 4.5-litre (18-cup) slow cooker. Add red onion, sauce, passata, juice, sugar, vinegar, chilli, garlic, capsicum and pineapple. Cook, covered, on low, about 4 hours.
2 Blend cornflour with the water in a small bowl until smooth. Add cornflour mixture to cooker. Cook, uncovered, on high, for 5 minutes or until thickened. Season to taste.
3 Serve sprinkled with shredded green onion.

Suitable to freeze
at the end of step 2.

Serving suggestion
*Steamed rice or
rice noodles.*

Tip *Chicken lovely legs
are trimmed, skinless
drumsticks, available
from supermarkets.
Use whatever cuts
of chicken you like but
choose cuts on the bone.*

Nutritional count per serving *16.1g total fat (4.6g saturated fat); 1986kJ (475 cal); 31.7g carbohydrate; 47.8g protein; 4.7g fibre*

APRICOT CHICKEN

prep + cook time 6 hours 30 minutes ✳ serves 6

* 45g (1½-ounce) packet cream of chicken simmer soup mix
* 1⅔ cups (410ml) apricot nectar
* 6 chicken marylands (2.1kg)
* 1 medium leek (350g), trimmed, sliced thickly
* 2 cloves garlic, crushed
* ¾ cup (75g) dried apricot halves
* ¼ cup coarsely chopped fresh flat-leaf parsley

1 Place soup mix in a 4.5-litre (18-cup) slow cooker. Gradually whisk in nectar until smooth. Season to taste.

2 Remove and discard fat and skin from chicken. Place chicken, leek, garlic and apricots in cooker. Cook, covered, on low, about 6 hours.

3 Sprinkle chicken with parsley to serve.

Suitable to freeze *at the end of step 2.*

Serving suggestion *Mashed potato and steamed green beans.*

Tip *Chicken maryland is a traditional crumbed-chicken dish in America, but in Australia it refers to a cut of chicken consisting of the leg (drumstick) and thigh in one piece with the skin and bone intact. It is available from chicken shops and supermarkets.*

Nutritional count per serving *12.1g total fat (3.7g saturated fat); 1400kJ (334 cal); 21.3g carbohydrate; 33.8g protein; 2.7g fibre*

STICKY BALSAMIC
ROAST CHICKEN

prep + cook time 6 hours 30 minutes ✳ serves 4

* 4 cloves garlic, crushed
* ½ cup (125ml) balsamic vinegar
* 2 tablespoons dijon mustard
* 1 tablespoon brown sugar
* 1 tablespoon olive oil
* 2 tablespoons coarsely chopped fresh oregano
* 2 tablespoons coarsely chopped fresh flat-leaf parsley
* 2kg (4-pound) whole chicken

1 Place garlic, vinegar, mustard, sugar, oil and half each of the oregano and parsley in a 4.5-litre (18-cup) slow cooker; stir to combine.

2 Discard excess fat from chicken cavity. Place chicken in cooker; turn to coat in mixture. Cook, covered, on low, about 6 hours.

3 Carefully remove chicken from cooker; cover to keep warm. Transfer cooking liquid to a medium frying pan; skim and discard fat from surface of cooking liquid. Bring liquid to the boil. Boil, uncovered, for 10 minutes or until sauce is reduced to ½ cup. Drizzle chicken with sauce; sprinkle with remaining herbs to serve.

Not suitable to freeze.

Serving suggestion
Rocket, roasted potatoes and truss cherry tomatoes.

Nutritional count per serving *34.7g total fat (9.8g saturated fat); 2408kJ (575 cal); 10.1g carbohydrate; 54g protein; 1.3g fibre*

CHICKEN TIKKA MASALA

prep + cook time 4 hours 15 minutes ✳ serves 6

✳ 1kg (2 pounds) skinless chicken
thigh cutlets
✳ 800g (1½ pounds) canned diced tomatoes
✳ 2 large brown onions (400g), sliced thinly
✳ ⅔ cup (200g) tikka masala paste
✳ ¼ cup (60ml) pouring cream
✳ 1 cup loosely packed fresh coriander
(cilantro) leaves

1   Combine chicken, tomatoes, onion and paste in a 4.5-litre (18-cup) slow cooker; cook, covered, on high, about 4 hours. Season to taste.
2   Drizzle with cream, sprinkle with coriander.

Suitable to freeze
at the end of step 1.

Serving suggestion
Steamed rice, naan bread and raita (minted yoghurt and cucumber).

Nutritional count per serving *22.3g total fat (5.9g saturated fat); 1467kJ (351 cal); 10.8g carbohydrate; 24.2g protein; 6g fibre*

UNDER

8

HOURS

VEGETABLES

A CHAPTER STARRING JUST VEGIES
BUT NOT JUST FOR VEGETARIANS

EGGPLANT, OLIVE
AND PINE NUT PASTA SAUCE

prep + cook time 6 hours 30 minutes ✳ serves 6

* 3 cloves garlic, chopped finely
* 2 medium brown onions (300g), chopped finely
* 1 fresh long red chilli, chopped finely
* 1 large eggplant (500g), chopped coarsely
* 500g (1 pound) ripe tomatoes, chopped coarsely
* 400g (12½ ounces) canned diced tomatoes
* ½ cup lightly packed fresh basil leaves
* 2 tablespoons tomato paste
* ½ cup (75g) seeded black olives
* 2 tablespoons toasted pine nuts
* ⅓ cup finely shredded fresh basil leaves

1   Place garlic, onion, chilli, eggplant, fresh and canned tomatoes, basil leaves (reserve a few of the smallest to serve) and paste in a 4.5-litre (18-cup) slow cooker; stir to combine.
2   Cook, covered, on low, about 6 hours. Season to taste.
3   Add olives, pine nuts and shredded basil to cooker; stir to combine. Sprinkle reserved small basil leaves over sauce before serving.

Suitable to freeze
at the end of step 2.

Serving suggestion
500g (1 pound) cooked short tubular pasta – both casarecce and penne work well.

Nutritional count per serving *6.5g total fat (0.5g saturated fat); 534kJ (128 cal); 9.7g carbohydrate; 4.2g protein; 6.4g fibre*

CHEESE, TOMATO
AND OLIVE BREAD PUDDING

prep + cook time 3 hours 30 minutes ✳ serves 6

* 40g (1½ ounces) butter, softened
* 6 green onions (scallions), trimmed, sliced thinly
* 2 cloves garlic, crushed
* 6 x 1.5cm (¾-inch) thick slices olive bread (360g)
* 200g (6½ ounces) cherry tomatoes
* ½ cup (80g) seeded black olives, halved
* ½ cup (40g) finely grated parmesan
* 100g (3 ounces) drained persian fetta
* 1 tablespoon coarsely chopped fresh basil
* 6 eggs
* 1 cup (250ml) milk
* 300ml (½ pint) reduced-fat thickened (heavy) cream
* ¼ teaspoon sweet paprika

1   Grease a 4.5-litre (18-cup) slow cooker with a little of the butter.
2   Heat 20g (¾ ounce) of the butter in a small frying pan; cook onion and garlic, stirring, for 5 minutes or until softened.
3   Spread bread with remaining butter; cut each slice in half. Place half the bread in the base of cooker. Sprinkle half the onion mixture over bread; layer with half the tomatoes, olives, parmesan, crumbled fetta and basil. Season to taste. Repeat with remaining bread, onion mixture, tomatoes, olives, parmesan, fetta and basil.
4   Whisk eggs, milk and cream together in a large jug; season. Pour egg mixture over bread mixture. Sprinkle with paprika.
5   Cook, covered, on low, for 3 hours or until set. Remove insert from cooker. Stand 5 minutes before serving scattered with baby basil and extra parmesan, if you like.

Not suitable to freeze.

Serving suggestion
Green leafy salad.

Nutritional count per serving   *32.6g total fat (16.5g saturated fat); 2071kJ (495 cal); 29g carbohydrate; 20.3g protein; 3.1g fibre*

STUFFED CAPSICUMS

prep + cook time 3 hours 45 minutes ✳ makes 5

* 2 tablespoons olive oil
* 1 medium brown onion (150g), chopped finely
* 3 cloves garlic, crushed
* 2 tablespoons tomato paste
* 1 cup (280g) bottled passata
* ¾ cup (150g) quinoa
* 1 cup (250ml) chicken stock
* 400g (12½ ounces) canned brown lentils, rinsed, drained
* 180g (5½ ounces) greek fetta, crumbled
* ⅓ cup (50g) seeded black olives, finely chopped
* ¼ cup coarsely chopped fresh flat-leaf parsley
* ¼ cup coarsely chopped fresh basil
* 5 medium capsicums (1kg)

1 Heat oil in a large frying pan over medium heat; cook onion and garlic, stirring, for 5 minutes or until onion softens. Add paste, passata, quinoa and stock; bring to the boil. Remove from heat. Stir in lentils, fetta, olives and herbs. Season to taste.
2 Cut tops from each capsicum; reserve tops. Using a small spoon, scoop out the membranes and seeds. Trim bases level so that the capsicums stand upright. Divide quinoa mixture among capsicums; replace tops.
3 Place capsicums into a 4.5-litre (18-cup) slow cooker. Cook, covered, on high, about 3 hours.

Not suitable to freeze.

Serving suggestion
Greek-style yoghurt.

Tips *Passata is strained tomato puree; it is available from supermarkets. Choose capsicums that are taller rather than wider so that they all fit into the slow cooker.*

Nutritional count per serving *15.4g total fat (7.6g saturated fat); 1638kJ (391 cal); 39g carbohydrate; 20.6g protein; 7.9g fibre*

SPICY LENTIL SOUP

prep + cook time 6 hours 30 minutes ✳ serves 4

* ½ cup (100g) dried red lentils
* 1 litre (4 cups) chicken stock
* 400g (12½ ounces) canned diced tomatoes
* 2 dried bay leaves
* 3 cloves garlic, crushed
* ⅓ cup (100g) mild indian curry paste
* 2 small carrots (240g), chopped coarsely
* 1 stalk celery (150g), trimmed, sliced thinly
* 2 medium potatoes (400g), chopped coarsely
* ½ cup (140g) Greek-style yoghurt
* ½ cup finely chopped fresh coriander (cilantro)

1   Rinse lentils under cold water until water runs clear; drain.
2   Combine lentils, stock, tomatoes, bay leaves, garlic, paste, carrot, celery and potato in a 4.5-litre (18-cup) slow cooker. Cook, covered, on low, about 6 hours. Season to taste.
3   Serve soup topped with yoghurt and coriander.

Suitable to freeze
at the end of step 2.

Serving suggestion
Crusty bread.

Nutritional count per serving *11.8g total fat (2.5g saturated fat); 1376kJ (329 cal); 36.2g carbohydrate; 13.9g protein; 12g fibre*

RATATOUILLE

prep + cook time 4 hours 20 minutes ✳ serves 6

* 2 tablespoons olive oil
* 1 large red onion (300g), chopped coarsely
* 3 cloves garlic, crushed
* ½ cup loosely packed fresh basil leaves
* 2 tablespoons tomato paste
* 3 cups (700g) bottled tomato pasta sauce
* 2 teaspoons caster (superfine) sugar
* 1 large eggplant (500g), chopped coarsely
* 2 medium red capsicums (bell pepper) (400g), chopped coarsely
* 2 large zucchini (300g), chopped coarsely
* 1 medium green capsicum (bell pepper) (200g), chopped coarsely

1 Heat oil in a large frying pan; cook onion, garlic and half the basil, stirring, until onion softens. Add paste; cook, stirring, about 1 minute. Remove from heat, stir in sauce and sugar.

2 Place vegetables and sauce mixture into a 4.5-litre (18-cup) slow cooker. Cook, covered, on low, about 4 hours. Season to taste.

3 Serve ratatouille sprinkled with remaining basil.

Suitable to freeze *at the end of step 2.*

Serving suggestion *Soft creamy polenta or pasta.*

Tip *Although suitable to freeze, this dish is at its best straight after cooking.*

Nutritional count per serving *7.5g total fat (1g saturated fat); 803kJ (192 cal); 22.1g carbohydrate; 5.5g protein; 7g fibre*

INDIAN VEGETABLE CURRY

prep + cook time 5 hours ✴ serves 6

* 1 tablespoon vegetable oil
* 1 medium leek (350g), sliced thickly
* 2 cloves garlic, crushed
* 2 teaspoons each black mustard seeds, ground cumin and garam masala
* 1 teaspoon ground turmeric
* 1½ cups (375ml) vegetable stock
* 400g (12½ ounces) canned diced tomatoes
* 1 large kumara (orange sweet potato) (500g), chopped coarsely
* 1 large carrot (180g), chopped coarsely
* 1⅔ cups (400ml) canned coconut milk
* 375g (12 ounces) brussels sprouts, halved
* 400g (12½ ounces) canned chickpeas (garbanzo beans), rinsed, drained
* 155g (5 ounces) baby spinach leaves
* ½ cup coarsely chopped fresh coriander (cilantro)

1 Heat oil in a large frying pan; cook leek and garlic, stirring, until leek softens. Add spices; cook, stirring, until fragrant. Add stock; bring to the boil.

2 Pour stock mixture into a 4.5-litre (18-cup) slow cooker; stir in tomatoes, kumara, carrot and coconut milk. Cook, covered, on low, about 4 hours.

3 Add sprouts and chickpeas to curry. Cook, covered, on high, for 40 minutes or until sprouts are just tender.

4 Stir in spinach and coriander. Season to taste.

Suitable to freeze
at the end of step 3.

Serving suggestion
Naan bread and lemon wedges.

Nutritional count per serving *18.7g total fat (12.8g saturated fat); 1388kJ (332 cal); 25.4g carbohydrate; 10.7g protein; 10.6g fibre*

MOROCCAN-STYLE
VEGETABLE STEW WITH HARISSA

prep + cook time 6 hours 45 minutes ✳ serves 4

* 1 medium red onion (170g), chopped coarsely
* 4 cloves garlic, quartered
* 2 teaspoons each ground cumin, ground coriander and sweet paprika
* 1 fresh long red chilli, chopped finely
* ½ cup loosely packed fresh flat-leaf parsley leaves and stalks, chopped coarsely
* 1 cup loosely packed fresh coriander (cilantro) leaves and stalks, chopped coarsely
* 2 cups (500ml) vegetable stock
* 4 baby eggplants (240g), chopped coarsely
* 4 small zucchini (360g), chopped coarsely
* 2 small parsnips (240g), chopped coarsely
* 2 medium carrots (240g), halved lengthways, then halved crossways
* ¼ medium butternut pumpkin (500g), skin on, cut into 8 pieces
* 2 medium potatoes (400g), quartered
* 2 tablespoons honey
* 1 cup (280g) Greek-style yoghurt
* 2 tablespoons mild harissa sauce
* ⅓ cup loosely packed fresh coriander (cilantro) leaves, extra

1 Blend or process onion, garlic and spices until a smooth paste. Combine paste with chilli, herbs and stock in a large jug.
2 Combine vegetables and stock mixture in a 4.5-litre (18-cup) slow cooker. Cook, covered, on low, about 6 hours. Stir in honey; season to taste.
3 Serve stew topped with yoghurt, harissa and extra coriander.

Not suitable to freeze.

Serving suggestion
Buttered couscous.

Nutritional count per serving *12.2g total fat (5.3g saturated fat); 1659kJ (397 cal); 52.1g carbohydrate; 13.4g protein; 11.9g fibre*

CREAMY POTATO BAKE

prep + cook time 6 hours 25 minutes ✳ serves 8 [as a side]

* 1 tablespoon olive oil
* 2 medium leeks (700g), sliced thinly
* 4 rindless bacon slices (260g), chopped finely
* 2 tablespoons coarsely chopped fresh flat-leaf parsley
* 1.5kg (3 pounds) potatoes, sliced thinly
* 2 cups (500ml) pouring cream
* ¼ cup (60ml) milk
* 1 tablespoon dijon mustard
* 50g packet dried chicken noodle soup mix
* ½ cup (60g) coarsely grated cheddar
* ½ cup (40g) finely grated parmesan

1   Heat oil in a large frying pan; cook leek and bacon, stirring, until leek softens. Remove from heat; stir in parsley.

2   Layer one third of the potato in a 4.5-litre (18-cup) slow cooker; top with half the leek mixture. Repeat layering with remaining potato and leek, finishing with potato layer.

3   Combine cream, milk, mustard and soup mix in a large jug, pour over potato; sprinkle with combined cheddar and parmesan. Cook, covered, on low, about 6 hours.

Not suitable to freeze.

Serving suggestion
A green leafy salad for a light meal, or serve as an accompaniment to a main course.

Tip *It's important to slice the potatoes thinly; a mandoline or V-slicer makes the job quick and easy.*

Nutritional count per serving *38.7g total fat (22.7g saturated fat); 2257kJ (540 cal); 29.5g carbohydrate; 17.3g protein; 4.3g fibre*

PUMPKIN, SAGE
AND ZUCCHINI LASAGNE

prep + cook time 4 hours 45 minutes ✻ serves 6

* 1kg (2 pounds) pumpkin, chopped coarsely
* 60g (2 ounces) butter, chopped
* 5 cloves garlic, crushed
* 1½ tablespoons finely chopped fresh sage
* 3 cups (720g) firm ricotta
* 1 egg
* ¼ teaspoon ground nutmeg
* 1 cup (80g) finely grated parmesan
* 3 medium zucchini (360g)
* cooking-oil spray
* ⅓ cup (80ml) pouring cream
* 8 dried instant lasagne sheets (120g)
* 1 cup (100g) coarsely grated mozzarella

1 Boil, steam or microwave pumpkin until tender; drain.

2 Melt butter in a large frying pan over medium heat; cook garlic and sage for 1 minute or until fragrant. Stir in pumpkin; remove from heat. Season.

3 Combine ricotta, egg, nutmeg and half the parmesan in a large bowl; season.

4 Thinly slice zucchini lengthways using a vegetable peeler.

5 Lightly spray a 4.5-litre (18-cup) slow cooker with cooking oil. Drizzle 2 tablespoons of the cream over base; top with 2 lasagne sheets, breaking to fit.

6 Spread one-third of the pumpkin mixture over pasta; top with one-third of the zucchini slices, then one-quarter of the ricotta mixture. Top with 2 more lasagne sheets. Repeat layering, finishing with pasta. Pour over remaining cream, then spread with remaining ricotta mixture. Sprinkle with mozzarella and remaining parmesan. Cook, covered, on low, for 4 hours or until pasta is tender.

Suitable to freeze
at the end of step 6.

Serving suggestion
Green leafy salad.

Nutritional count per serving *37.1g total fat (22.6g saturated fat); 2377kJ (568 cal); 27.9g carbohydrate; 28.9g protein; 4.7g fibre*

SPINACH AND
THREE CHEESE CANNELLONI

prep + cook time 5 hours ✳ serves 6

* **750g (1½ pounds) frozen spinach, thawed**
* **3½ cups (840g) firm ricotta**
* **2 eggs**
* **1 egg yolk**
* **¾ cup (60g) finely grated parmesan**
* **225g (7 ounces) jar char-grilled eggplant in olive oil, drained, chopped finely**
* **3 cloves garlic, crushed**
* **1 litre (4 cups) bottled passata**
* **¾ cup (180ml) pouring cream**
* **¾ cup coarsely chopped fresh basil**
* **400g (12½ ounces) dried instant cannelloni tubes**
* **1½ cups (180g) pizza cheese**

1 Squeeze excess moisture from spinach. Place spinach, ricotta, eggs, egg yolk, parmesan, eggplant and garlic in a large bowl; stir to combine. Season.
2 Combine passata, cream and basil in a large jug; season.
3 Lightly oil a 4.5-litre (18-cup) slow cooker. Pour half the passata mixture over base of cooker.
4 Spoon or pipe spinach mixture into cannelloni tubes; arrange cannelloni vertically in cooker. Top with remaining passata mixture; sprinkle with pizza cheese. Cook, covered, on low, about 4 hours. Stand 10 minutes before serving.

Not suitable to freeze.

Serving suggestion
Extra basil leaves and grated parmesan.

Tips *Firm ricotta is available from cheese shops and supermarket delicatessens. It is not the same as the soft ricotta found in tubs in the dairy section. Cannelloni are large pasta tubes usually stuffed with a meat or cheese filling and baked. The name is also used for the finished dish.*

Nutritional count per serving *41.8g total fat (24.7g saturated fat); 3493kJ (834 cal); 66.6g carbohydrate; 45.3g protein; 3.4g fibre*

MUSHROOM RISOTTO

prep + cook time 2 hours 45 minutes ✳ serves 4

* 30g (1 ounce) butter
* 1 large brown onion (200g), chopped finely
* ½ cup (125ml) dry white wine
* 1 litre (4 cups) vegetable stock
* 2 cups (500ml) water
* 10g (½ ounce) dried porcini mushroom slices, torn
* 2 cups (400g) arborio rice
* 60g (2 ounces) butter, extra
* 300g (9½ ounces) button mushrooms, sliced thinly
* 200g (6½ ounces) swiss brown mushrooms, sliced thinly
* 2 cloves garlic, crushed
* 2 teaspoons finely chopped fresh thyme
* 1 cup (80g) finely grated parmesan

1 Heat butter in a large frying pan; cook onion, stirring, until softened. Add wine; bring to the boil. Boil, uncovered, until liquid is almost evaporated. Add stock, the water and porcini mushrooms; bring to the boil.

2 Place rice in a 4.5-litre (18-cup) slow cooker; stir in onion mixture. Cook, covered, on high, about 1½ hours. Stir well.

3 Meanwhile, heat 20g (¾ ounce) of the extra butter in same pan; cook button mushrooms, stirring occasionally, until browned. Remove from pan. Heat another 20g (¾ ounce) butter in same pan; cook swiss brown mushrooms, stirring occasionally, until browned. Add garlic and thyme; cook, stirring, until fragrant.

4 Stir button mushrooms and swiss brown mushroom mixture into cooker. Cook, uncovered, on high, for 20 minutes or until rice is tender.

5 Stir in parmesan and remaining butter; season to taste. Serve immediately, sprinkled with extra thyme and parmesan, if you like.

Not suitable to freeze.

Tip *This risotto has the texture of an oven-baked version rather than the creaminess of a traditional stirred risotto; it must be served immediately.*

Nutritional count per serving *26.6g total fat (16.6g saturated fat); 2947kJ (705 cal); 88.7g carbohydrate; 20g protein; 4.7g fibre*

PUMPKIN SOUP

prep + cook time 6 hours 30 minutes * serves 6

- **30g (1 ounce) butter**
- **1 tablespoon olive oil**
- **1 large leek (500g), sliced thinly**
- **1.8kg (3¾ pounds) pumpkin, chopped coarsely**
- **1 large potato (300g), chopped coarsely**
- **3 cups (750ml) chicken stock**
- **3 cups (750ml) water**
- **½ cup (125ml) pouring cream**
- **1 tablespoon finely chopped fresh chives**

1 Heat butter and oil in a large frying pan; cook leek, stirring, until soft.

2 Combine leek mixture, pumpkin, potato, stock and the water in a 4.5-litre (18-cup) slow cooker. Cook, covered, on low, about 6 hours.

3 Cool soup 10 minutes. Blend or process soup, in batches, until smooth. Return soup to cooker. Cook, covered, on high, for 20 minutes or until hot. Stir in ⅓ cup of the cream. Season to taste.

4 Serve soup topped with remaining cream and chives.

Suitable to freeze *at the end of step 2.*

Serving suggestion *Toasted sourdough or rye bread.*

Nutritional count per serving *17.9g total fat (10.1g saturated fat); 1275kJ (305 cal); 24.8g carbohydrate; 9g protein; 5.1g fibre*

SPICY RED LENTIL
AND CHICKPEA SOUP

prep + cook time 6 hours 20 minutes ✳ serves 6

* 2 teaspoons vegetable oil
* 1 medium brown onion (150g), chopped finely
* 2 cloves garlic, crushed
* 2.5cm (1-inch) piece fresh ginger (15g), grated
* 2 teaspoons smoked paprika
* 1 teaspoon ground cumin
* ½ teaspoon dried chilli flakes
* 375g (12 ounces) pumpkin, chopped coarsely
* 1 stalk celery (150g), trimmed, sliced thickly
* ¾ cup (150g) red lentils
* 400g (12½ ounces) canned chickpeas (garbanzo beans), rinsed, drained
* 400g (12½ ounces) canned diced tomatoes
* 3 cups (750ml) water
* 3 cups (750ml) vegetable stock
* ⅓ cup (80ml) finely chopped fresh flat-leaf parsley

1 Heat oil in a small frying pan; cook onion, garlic and ginger, stirring, until onion softens. Add spices and chilli; cook, stirring, until fragrant.

2 Place onion mixture into a 4.5-litre (18-cup) slow cooker; stir in pumpkin, celery, lentils, chickpeas, tomatoes, the water and stock. Cook, covered, on low, about 6 hours. Season to taste.

3 Serve soup sprinkled with parsley.

Suitable to freeze
at the end of step 2.

Serving suggestion
Crusty bread.

Nutritional count per serving *3.9g total fat (0.8g saturated fat); 815kJ (195 cal); 23.5g carbohydrate; 12.4g protein; 7.9g fibre*

SPINACH AND
RICOTTA LASAGNE

prep + cook time 4 hours 30 minutes ✳ serves 6

* 500g (1 pound) frozen spinach, thawed
* 3 cups (720g) ricotta
* 2 eggs
* 1 cup (80g) finely grated parmesan
* cooking-oil spray
* 750g (1½ pounds) bottled passata
* ⅓ cup (90g) basil pesto
* 6 dried instant lasagne sheets
* 1 cup (100g) coarsely grated mozzarella

1 Squeeze excess moisture from spinach; place spinach in a large bowl. Add ricotta, eggs and half the parmesan; season, mix well.

2 Spray a 4.5-litre (18-cup) slow cooker lightly with cooking oil. Combine passata and pesto in a medium bowl, season; spread ½ cup of the sauce mixture over base of cooker.

3 Place 2 lasagne sheets in cooker, breaking to fit. Spread one-third of the spinach mixture over pasta; top with one-third of the sauce, then 2 more lasagne sheets. Repeat layering twice, finishing with sauce. Sprinkle with mozzarella and remaining parmesan. Cook, covered, on low, for 4 hours or until pasta is tender.

Suitable to freeze
at the end of step 3.

Serving suggestion
*Rocket salad and
thick crusty bread.*

Nutritional count per serving *31.9g total fat (15.8g saturated fat); 2211kJ (529 cal); 25.1g carbohydrate; 32.7g protein; 8.3g fibre*

CREAMY VEGETABLE
AND ALMOND KORMA

prep + cook time 6 hours 45 minutes ✳ serves 6

* ½ cup (150g) korma paste
* ½ cup (60g) ground almonds
* 1 large brown onion (200g), sliced thinly
* 2 cloves garlic, crushed
* ½ cup (125ml) vegetable stock
* ½ cup (125ml) water
* 300ml pouring cream
* 375g (12 ounces) baby carrots
* 125g (4 ounces) baby corn
* 500g (1 pound) baby potatoes, halved
* 375g (12 ounces) pumpkin, chopped coarsely
* 315g (10 ounces) cauliflower, cut into florets
* 6 medium yellow patty-pan squash (180g), halved
* ½ cup (60g) frozen peas
* ½ cup (70g) roasted slivered almonds
* 2 teaspoons black sesame seeds

1   Combine paste, ground almonds, onion, garlic, stock, the water, cream, carrots, corn, potato, pumpkin and cauliflower in a 4.5-litre (18-cup) slow cooker. Cook, covered, on low, about 6 hours.
2   Add squash and peas; cook, covered, on high, about 20 minutes. Season to taste.
3   Sprinkle curry with nuts and seeds.

Suitable to freeze *at the end of step 2.*

Serving suggestion *Steamed rice, naan bread and yoghurt.*

Tip *This is a mild curry. For more heat, serve sprinkled with sliced fresh red chilli.*

Nutritional count per serving *42.8g total fat (16.2g saturated fat); 2429kJ (581 cal); 29.6g carbohydrate; 14.4g protein; 12.4g fibre*

EGGPLANT, CHILLI
AND TOMATO STEW WITH RICOTTA

prep + cook time 2 hours 45 minutes ✱ serves 4

* 2 celery stalks (300g), trimmed
* 4 cloves garlic, sliced thinly
* 1 fresh long red chilli, sliced thinly
* 2 x 400g (12½ ounces) canned cherry tomatoes
* 2 medium red onions (340g), unpeeled
* ¼ cup (60ml) olive oil
* 2 medium eggplants (600g)
* 400g (12½ ounces) fresh firm ricotta
* ½ teaspoon dried chilli flakes
* 2 teaspoons olive oil, extra
* ¼ cup lightly packed fresh basil leaves

1   Cut celery into 7.5cm (3-inch) lengths. Place garlic, sliced chilli, celery and tomatoes in a 4.5-litre (18-cup) slow cooker. Season.

2   Peel onions leaving root end intact. Cut each onion into eight wedges.

3   Heat 1 tablespoon of the oil in a medium frying pan over medium-high heat; cook onion, turning, until browned. Transfer to cooker.

4   Meanwhile, chop eggplant into 5cm (2-inch) pieces. Heat remaining oil in same pan over medium heat; cook eggplant, turning occasionally, until browned. Transfer to cooker.

5   Cook, covered, on high, about 2 hours. Season to taste.

6   Cut ricotta into 4 wedges; place on serving platter. Sprinkle with chilli flakes; drizzle with extra oil.

7   To serve, sprinkle stew with basil; accompany with ricotta wedges.

Not suitable to freeze.

Serving suggestion
Soft polenta and grilled crusty bread.

Tip *Canned cherry tomatoes are available from supermarkets. You can use canned chopped or diced tomatoes instead.*

Nutritional count per serving *29.3g total fat (10g saturated fat); 1603kJ (383 cal); 12.5g carbohydrate; 14.4g protein; 7.7g fibre*

CAULIFLOWER SOUP

prep + cook time 7 hours 30 minutes ✳ serves 8

* 40g (1½ ounces) butter
* 2 large brown onions (400g), chopped coarsely
* 3 cloves garlic, crushed
* 1 litre (4 cups) vegetable stock
* 1.2kg (2½ pounds) cauliflower, cut into florets
* 2 medium potatoes (400g), chopped coarsely
* 2 cups (500ml) water
* 300ml pouring cream
* 2 tablespoons finely chopped fresh flat-leaf parsley

1 Heat butter in a large frying pan; cook onion, stirring, until softened. Add garlic; cook, stirring, until fragrant. Add stock; bring to the boil.
2 Transfer onion mixture to a 4.5-litre (18-cup) slow cooker with cauliflower, potato and the water. Cook, covered, on low, about 6½ hours.
3 Blend or process soup, in batches, until smooth. Return to cooker; stir in cream. Cook, covered, on high, for 30 minutes or until soup is hot. Season to taste.
4 Sprinkle with parsley.

Suitable to freeze *at the end of step 3.*

Serving suggestion *Hot buttery toast or muffins.*

Tip *You will need 2 small cauliflowers.*

Nutritional count per serving *19.3g total fat (12.3g saturated fat); 1105kJ (264 cal); 114.9g carbohydrate; 6g protein; 4.1g fibre*

CHANA MASALA

prep + cook time 3 hours * serves 6

* 2 large brown onions (400g), chopped coarsely
* 8 cloves garlic, quartered
* 6cm (2¼-inch) piece fresh ginger (60g), grated
* 2 tablespoons tomato paste
* 125g (4 ounces) ghee
* 2 teaspoons each ground coriander and garam masala
* 1 teaspoon ground turmeric
* ½ teaspoon ground chilli
* 2 x 400g (12½ ounces) canned chickpeas (garbanzo beans), rinsed, drained
* 1½ cups (375ml) water
* ½ cup loosely packed fresh coriander (cilantro) leaves

1 Blend onion, garlic, ginger and paste until smooth.

2 Heat ghee in a large saucepan; cook onion mixture, stirring, about 5 minutes. Add spices; cook, stirring, about 2 minutes. Transfer to a 4.5-litre (18-cup) slow cooker with chickpeas and the water. Cook, covered, on high, about 2½ hours. Season to taste.

3 Serve sprinkled with coriander.

Suitable to freeze *at the end of step 2.*

Serving suggestion *Steamed rice, yoghurt and naan bread.*

Tip *Chana masala is a spicy vegetarian curry popular in Pakistan and India. It has a slightly sour flavour.*

Nutritional count per serving *22.1g total fat (13.4g saturated fat); 1283kJ (307 cal); 17.9g carbohydrate; 7.2g protein; 6.3g fibre*

CAULIFLOWER CHEESE

prep + cook time 3 hours 30 minutes * serves 6

* 50g (1½ ounces) butter, chopped coarsely
* 2 tablespoons plain (all-purpose) flour
* 2 cups (500ml) milk
* 1¼ cups (150g) grated swiss cheese
* 1 medium cauliflower (1.5kg), cut into florets
* 1 medium brown onion (150g), chopped finely
* ½ cup (40g) finely grated parmesan
* ⅓ cup (25g) flaked almonds
* ¼ cup coarsely chopped fresh flat-leaf parsley

1   Melt butter in a medium saucepan over medium heat, add flour; cook, stirring, for 2 minutes or until mixture thickens and bubbles. Gradually stir in milk; cook, stirring, until sauce boils and thickens. Remove from heat; stir in swiss cheese until melted.

2   Place cauliflower and onion into a 4.5-litre (18-cup) slow cooker; toss to combine. Season to taste. Pour over cheese sauce; toss to coat. Sprinkle with parmesan.

3   Cook, covered, on low, about 3 hours. Sprinkle with nuts and parsley to serve.

Not suitable to freeze.

Serving suggestion
Pan-fried steaks, chicken breasts or grilled lamb cutlets.

Nutritional count per serving *22.5g total fat (12.8g saturated fat); 1421kJ (339 cal); 12.3g carbohydrate; 18.9g protein; 7.2g fibre*

EGGPLANT PARMIGIANA

prep + cook time 6 hours 45 minutes ✳ serves 4

* ⅔ cup (160ml) olive oil
* 1 medium brown onion (150g),
chopped finely
* 2 cloves garlic, crushed
* 400g (12½ ounces) canned diced tomatoes
* 1 cup (260g) bottled passata
* ¼ teaspoon dried chilli flakes
* 2 medium eggplants (600g), sliced thickly
* ¼ cup (35g) plain (all-purpose) flour
* ⅓ cup loosely packed fresh basil leaves
* 200g (6½ ounces) bocconcini, sliced thinly
* ⅔ cup (50g) finely grated parmesan
* ½ teaspoon sweet paprika

1   Heat 1 tablespoon of the oil in a large frying pan; cook onion, stirring, until onion softens. Add garlic; cook, stirring, until fragrant. Stir in tomatoes, passata and chilli. Transfer to a medium jug.
2   Toss eggplant in flour to coat, dust off excess. Heat remaining oil in same pan; cook eggplant, in batches, until browned. Drain on paper towel.
3   Layer half the eggplant in a 4.5-litre (18-cup) slow cooker; season. Top with half the tomato mixture, basil and bocconcini. Repeat layering, finishing with parmesan. Sprinkle with paprika. Cook, covered, on low, about 6 hours.

Not suitable to freeze.

Serving suggestion
Crusty bread and rocket salad.

Nutritional count per serving *49.9g total fat (12.8g saturated fat); 2562kJ (613 cal); 20.6g carbohydrate; 18.5g protein; 7.2g fibre*

OKRA CURRY

prep + cook time 3 hours ✳ serves 4

* ¼ cup (60ml) peanut oil
* 2 large brown onions (400g), sliced thinly
* 2 fresh long green chillies, quartered lengthways
* 4cm (1½-inch) piece fresh ginger (20g), grated
* 5 cloves garlic, crushed
* 2 teaspoons ground coriander
* 1 teaspoon garam masala
* ½ teaspoon each ground turmeric and chilli powder
* 2 medium tomatoes (300g), chopped coarsely
* 1kg (2 pounds) okra, trimmed
* 2½ cups (625ml) coconut milk

1   Heat oil in a large saucepan; cook onion, stirring, until soft and browned lightly. Add chilli, ginger and garlic; cook, stirring, until fragrant. Stir in spices; cook, stirring, about 1 minute. Add tomato; cook, stirring, about 2 minutes.
2   Transfer tomato mixture to a 4.5-litre (18-cup) slow cooker with okra and coconut milk; season. Cook, covered, on high, about 2½ hours.

Not suitable to freeze.

Serving suggestion
Steamed rice and lime wedges.

Tip *Okra, also known as lady fingers, is a green, ridged, oblong pod with a furry skin. While native to Africa, it is used in Indian, Middle-Eastern and southern US cooking. It often serves as a thickener in stews.*

Nutritional count per serving *46.8g total fat (30.9g saturated fat); 2395kJ (573 cal); 17.4g carbohydrate; 14g protein; 16.9g fibre*

UNDER
8
HOURS

PORK

BUDGET-SMART PORK PRODUCTS
MAKE HEARTY MEALS FOR THE FAMILY

THE AUSTRALIAN WOMEN'S WEEKLY
TRIPLE TESTED
TEST KITCHEN

SMOKY STICKY PORK RIBS
WITH COLESLAW

prep + cook time 4 hours 45 minutes ✳ serves 4

* 2kg (4 pounds) American-style pork ribs
* 3 cloves garlic, crushed
* 1 cup (280g) barbecue sauce
* ¼ cup (60ml) lemon juice
* ¼ cup (55g) brown sugar
* 2 teaspoons sweet smoked paprika
* 1 teaspoon Tabasco sauce

CHEESY COLESLAW
* ¼ small green cabbage (300g), shredded finely
* ¼ small red cabbage (300g), shredded finely
* 1 large carrot (180g), grated coarsely
* ½ small red onion (50g), sliced thinly
* 1 cup (120g) coarsely grated vintage cheddar
* 2 tablespoons coarsely chopped fresh chives
* ¾ cup (225g) mayonnaise
* ¼ cup (60ml) cider vinegar

1 Cut pork into pieces that will fit into a 4.5-litre (18-cup) slow cooker.
2 Combine remaining ingredients in a large shallow dish; add pork, turn to coat in marinade. Transfer pork and marinade to cooker. Cook, covered, on high, about 4 hours. Turn ribs twice during cooking time for even cooking.
3 Make cheesy coleslaw.
4 Carefully remove ribs from cooker; cover to keep warm. Transfer sauce to a medium frying pan; bring to the boil. Reduce heat; simmer, uncovered, skimming fat from surface, for 10 minutes or until sauce has reduced to 1 cup.
5 Drizzle pork with sauce. Serve with coleslaw.

CHEESY COLESLAW Combine ingredients in a large bowl; toss gently to combine. Season to taste.

Not suitable to freeze.

Tip *Ask the butcher to cut the ribs into pieces that will fit into your slow cooker.*

Nutritional count per serving *57.1g total fat (19.7g saturated fat); 4592kJ (1097 cal); 64g carbohydrate; 80g protein; 6.9g fibre*

SLOW-ROASTED CHILLI
AND FENNEL PORK

prep + cook time 7 hours 30 minutes ✻ serves 6

* 1kg (2-pound) piece pork shoulder bone in, rind on
* 1 medium lemon (140g)
* 1½ tablespoons fennel seeds
* 2 teaspoons dried chilli flakes
* 2 teaspoons sea salt
* ½ teaspoon cracked black pepper
* 3 cloves garlic, chopped coarsely
* ⅓ cup (80ml) olive oil
* 1 large brown onion (200g), chopped coarsely
* ½ cup (125ml) chicken stock

1 Using a sharp knife, score pork rind in a criss-cross pattern. Coarsely grate rind from lemon; chop lemon coarsely.
2 Cook fennel seeds in a dry large frying pan until fragrant. Using mortar and pestle, crush seeds. Add chilli, salt, pepper, garlic, lemon rind and 2 tablespoons of the oil; pound until ground finely.
3 Heat remaining oil in same pan; cook pork, skin-side down, until browned and crisp. Turn pork; cook until browned all over. Spread fennel mixture over pork. Place onion, stock and chopped lemon in a 4.5-litre (18-cup) slow cooker; top with pork, skin-side up. Cook, covered, on low, about 7 hours.
4 Remove pork from cooker; stand, covered, 10 minutes before slicing thinly.

Not suitable to freeze.

Serving suggestion
Your favourite chutney or relish in crusty bread rolls or baguettes with a green salad.

Tip *Ask the butcher to score the rind on the pork for you.*

Nutritional count per serving *24.3g total fat (6.4g saturated fat); 1384kJ (331 cal); 2.1g carbohydrate; 26.1g protein; 0.7g fibre*

RED PORK CURRY

prep + cook time 4 hours 30 minutes (+ refrigeration) ✳ serves 4

* 1⅔ cups (400ml) coconut cream
* 1 cup (250ml) salt-reduced chicken stock
* ¼ cup (75g) red curry paste
* 2 tablespoons fish sauce
* 3 fresh kaffir lime leaves, shredded finely
* 1.5kg (3 pounds) rindless boneless pork belly, chopped coarsely
* 2 large kumara (orange sweet potato) (1kg), chopped coarsely
* 500g (1 pound) snake beans, chopped coarsely
* 1 cup loosely packed fresh thai basil leaves
* 2 fresh long red chillies, sliced thinly
* 1 fresh kaffir lime leaf, extra, shredded finely

1 Combine coconut cream, stock, paste, sauce and lime leaves in a 4.5-litre (18-cup) slow cooker; add pork and kumara. Cook, covered, on high, about 4 hours.

2 Skim fat from surface. Stir in beans; cook, covered, on high, about 30 minutes. Season to taste.

3 Serve sprinkled with basil, chilli and extra lime leaf.

Suitable to freeze *at the end of step 2.*

Serving suggestion *Steamed rice.*

Tip *Ask the butcher to chop the pork belly for you so that it will fit into your slow cooker.*

Nutritional count per serving *21.9g total fat (12.1g saturated fat); 1831kJ (438 cal); 18.9g carbohydrate; 39.2g protein; 5.1g fibre*

BARBECUED
AMERICAN-STYLE PORK RIBS

prep + cook time 4 hours 30 minutes (+ refrigeration) ✳ serves 4

* 2kg (4 pounds) American-style pork ribs
* ½ cup (140g) barbecue sauce
* ½ cup (140g) tomato sauce (ketchup)
* ½ cup (125ml) cider vinegar
* ¼ cup (85g) orange marmalade
* 3 cloves garlic, crushed
* ½ teaspoon chilli flakes

1   Cut pork into pieces that will fit into a 4.5-litre (18-cup) slow cooker. Combine remaining ingredients in a large shallow dish; add pork, turn to coat in marinade. Cover; refrigerate mixture overnight.
2   Transfer pork and marinade to cooker; cook, covered, on high, about 4 hours. Turn ribs twice during cooking time for even cooking.
3   Carefully remove ribs from cooker; cover to keep warm. Transfer sauce to a large frying pan; bring to the boil. Reduce heat; simmer, uncovered, skimming fat from surface, for 10 minutes or until sauce has reduced to 1¾ cups. Serve pork drizzled with sauce.

Not suitable to freeze.

Serving suggestion
Steamed rice and lime wedges.

Nutritional count per serving *10.6g total fat (3.8g saturated fat); 1860kJ (445 cal); 38.2g carbohydrate; 48.6g protein; 1.7g fibre*

PORK NECK
WITH CIDER AND PEAR

prep + cook time 6 hours 30 minutes ✳ serves 4

* 1kg (2-pound) piece pork neck
* 185g (6 ounces) italian pork sausages
* 1 egg yolk
* ½ cup (70g) coarsely chopped pistachios
* 2 tablespoons coarsely chopped fresh sage
* 1 tablespoon olive oil
* 1 medium brown onion (150g), quartered
* 4 cloves garlic, halved
* 2 medium unpeeled pears (460g), quartered
* ⅔ cup (160ml) apple cider
* 6 fresh sage leaves

1 Place pork on a board; slice through thickest part of pork horizontally, without cutting all the way through. Open pork out to form one large piece; trim pork.

2 Squeeze filling from sausages into a small bowl, mix in egg yolk, nuts and chopped sage; season. Press sausage mixture along one long side of pork; roll pork to enclose filling. Tie pork with kitchen string at 2.5cm (1-inch) intervals.

3 Heat oil in a large frying pan; cook pork until browned all over. Remove from pan. Add onion and garlic to same pan; cook, stirring, until onion softens.

4 Place onion mixture and pear in a 4.5-litre (18-cup) slow cooker; top with pork then add cider and sage leaves. Cook, covered, on low, about 6 hours.

5 Serve sliced pork with onion mixture and pear. Sprinkle with extra sage leaves, if you like.

Not suitable to freeze.

Serving suggestion
Creamy mashed potato and a radicchio or witlof salad.

Tip *Italian sausages are coarse pork sausages generally sold in plump links. They are usually flavoured with garlic and fennel seed or anise seed, and come in two styles – hot (flavoured with thai red chilli) and sweet (without the added heat).*

Nutritional count per serving *45.3g total fat (13g saturated fat); 3164kJ (757 cal); 19g carbohydrate; 63g protein; 5.6g fibre*

FIVE-SPICE
CARAMEL PORK BELLY

prep + cook time 7 hours ✳ serves 6

* **2kg (4-pound) boneless pork belly, rind removed, cut into 4cm (1½-inch) pieces**
* **2 litres (8 cups) water**
* **1 cup (250ml) coconut water**
* **1 cup (250ml) water, extra**
* **¾ cup (180ml) fish sauce**
* **½ cup (110g) firmly packed brown sugar**
* **2 teaspoons five-spice powder**
* **16 garlic cloves, unpeeled**
* **6 eggs**
* **6 fresh small thai red (serrano) chillies**
* **¼ cup fresh coriander (cilantro) sprigs**

CARAMEL
* **1 cup (220g) caster (superfine) sugar**
* **½ cup (125ml) water**

1 Place pork and the water in a large saucepan, bring to the boil over medium heat. Boil about 5 minutes, skimming impurities from surface; drain.
2 Meanwhile, make caramel.
3 Place pork in a 4.5-litre (18-cup) slow cooker with caramel, coconut water, the extra water, sauce, sugar, five spice and garlic. Cook, covered, on low, about 6 hours.

4 Meanwhile, place eggs in a medium saucepan; cover with cold water. Bring to the boil; boil for 6 minutes or until hard-boiled. Transfer to a bowl of cold water and cool slightly before peeling.
5 Add eggs and chillies to cooker. Cook, uncovered, on high, about 30 minutes; skim fat from surface. Sprinkle with coriander to serve.

CARAMEL Combine sugar and the water in a small saucepan; stir over high heat, without boiling, until sugar dissolves. Bring to the boil. Boil, uncovered, without stirring, until a deep golden caramel.

Suitable to freeze *at the end of step 3.*
Serving suggestion *Steamed jasmine rice.*

Tips *Coconut water is the liquid from the centre of an immature coconut. It is available in tetra packs and cans from supermarkets. Ensure that it's labelled 100 per cent coconut water, and that it is not sweetened. Have eggs at room temperature.*

Nutritional count per serving *33.8g total fat (12.7g saturated fat); 3550kJ (848 cal); 59.4g carbohydrate; 78.3g protein; 2g fibre*

LEMON GRASS PORK CURRY

prep + cook time 6 hours 30 minutes ✳ serves 6

* 2 x 10cm (4-inch) sticks fresh lemon grass (40g), chopped coarsely
* 3 cloves garlic, quartered
* 4cm (1½-inch) piece fresh galangal (20g), sliced thinly
* 1 fresh small red thai (serrano) chilli, chopped coarsely
* 1 teaspoon ground turmeric
* ½ teaspoon ground cumin
* ¼ teaspoon ground cardamom
* 3 fresh kaffir lime leaves, shredded thinly
* 1 medium red onion (170g), chopped coarsely
* ½ cup (125ml) water
* 1 tablespoon peanut oil
* 1.2kg (2½ pounds) pork neck, chopped coarsely
* 3⅓ cups (800ml) canned coconut milk
* 3 baby eggplants (180g), sliced thickly
* 375g (12 ounces) baby carrots, halved lengthways
* 1 tablespoon fish sauce
* 2 tablespoons lime juice
* ½ cup loosely packed fresh coriander (cilantro) leaves

1 Blend or process lemon grass, garlic, galangal, chilli, spices, lime leaves, onion and the water until mixture is smooth.
2 Heat oil in a medium frying pan; cook lemon grass mixture, stirring, for 5 minutes or until fragrant.
3 Transfer lemon grass mixture to a 4.5-litre (18-cup) slow cooker; stir in pork, coconut milk and eggplant. Cook, covered, on low, about 4 hours.
4 Add carrots; cook, covered, on low, about 2 hours. Stir in sauce and juice; season to taste. Sprinkle curry with coriander.

Not suitable to freeze.

Serving suggestion
Steamed rice.

Nutritional count per serving *46.9g total fat (30.2g saturated fat); 2759kJ (660 cal); 10.9g carbohydrate; 46.6g protein; 5.8g fibre*

CHAR SIU PORK RIBS

prep + cook time 7 hours 25 minutes ✳ serves 6

* 2.5kg (5¼ pounds) American-style pork ribs
* 2 tablespoons peanut oil
* ½ cup (125ml) char siu sauce
* 2 tablespoons light soy sauce
* ¼ cup (60ml) orange juice
* 5cm (2-inch) piece fresh ginger (25g), grated
* 2 cloves garlic, crushed
* 1 fresh long red chilli, chopped finely
* 2 teaspoons sesame oil

1   Cut pork into pieces that will fit into a 4.5-litre (18-cup) slow cooker. Heat peanut oil in a large frying pan; cook ribs, in batches, until browned all over.

2   Meanwhile, combine sauces, juice, ginger, garlic, chilli and sesame oil in a jug; brush over ribs. Place ribs in cooker; pour over remaining sauce. Cook, covered, on low, about 7 hours.

3   Remove ribs from sauce; cover to keep warm. Place sauce in a medium saucepan; bring to the boil. Boil, uncovered, for 5 minutes or until sauce is thickened slightly.

4   Serve ribs drizzled with sauce.

Not suitable to freeze.

Serving suggestion
Steamed rice and stir-fried asian greens.

Nutritional count per serving *23.9g total fat (6.6g saturated fat); 1760kJ (421 cal); 9.6g carbohydrate; 40.7g protein; 2.7g fibre*

TAMARIND AND COCONUT
PORK CURRY

prep + cook time 6 hours 40 minutes ✱ serves 6

* 1 tablespoon peanut oil
* 1.2kg (2½ pounds) boneless pork shoulder, chopped coarsely
* 1 medium brown onion (150g), chopped finely
* 2 cloves garlic, crushed
* 1 fresh long red chilli, sliced thinly
* 4cm (1½-inch) piece fresh ginger (20g), grated
* 2 teaspoons fenugreek seeds
* 1 teaspoon each ground cumin and ground ginger
* ½ teaspoon each ground cinnamon and ground cardamom
* 8 fresh curry leaves
* 1 tablespoon tamarind concentrate
* 1¼ cups (270ml) canned coconut cream
* 1 cup (250ml) chicken stock
* 185g (6 ounces) green beans, halved
* 1 cup (75g) toasted shredded coconut

1 Heat oil in a large frying pan; cook pork, in batches, until browned. Remove from pan.
2 Cook onion, garlic, chilli and ginger in same heated pan, stirring, until onion softens. Add spices and curry leaves; cook, stirring, until fragrant.
3 Transfer onion mixture to a 4.5-litre (18-cup) slow cooker; stir in pork, tamarind, coconut cream and stock. Cook, covered, on low, about 6 hours.
4 Add beans and half the coconut; cook, covered, on high, for 20 minutes or until beans are tender. Season to taste; sprinkle curry with remaining coconut.

Not suitable to freeze.

Serving suggestion
Steamed rice.

Nutritional count per serving *36.8g total fat (21.4g saturated fat); 2253kJ (539 cal); 5.2g carbohydrate; 45.6g protein; 4.1g fibre*

PORK AND VEAL MEATBALLS

prep + cook time 4 hours (+ refrigeration) ✳ serves 6

* 500g (1 pound) minced (ground) pork
* 500g (1 pound) minced (ground) veal
* 1 cup (70g) stale breadcrumbs
* 1 cup (120g) finely grated cheddar
* 2 eggs
* 1 cup finely chopped fresh flat-leaf parsley
* 4 cloves garlic, crushed
* 3½ cups (900g) bottled passata
* 1 medium fennel bulb (300g), trimmed, sliced thinly
* 2 medium brown onions (300g), chopped finely
* 1 cup (80g) finely grated parmesan

1 Combine pork, veal, breadcrumbs, cheddar, eggs, parsley and half the garlic in a large bowl, season. Roll rounded tablespoons of mixture into balls. Place on a tray, cover; refrigerate 20 minutes.
2 Combine passata, fennel, onion and remaining garlic in a 4.5-litre (18-cup) slow cooker; add meatballs. Cook, covered, on high, about 3½ hours. Season to taste.
3 Serve sprinkled with parmesan and crusty bread, if you like.

Suitable to freeze *at the end of step 2.*

Serving suggestion *Spaghetti, soft polenta or couscous.*

Tip *Some butchers sell a pork and veal mince mixture.*

Nutritional count per serving *25.2g total fat (12.2g saturated fat); 2220kJ (531 cal); 20.3g carbohydrate; 52.4g protein; 6.1g fibre*

CHORIZO, CHILLI
AND BEAN STEW

prep + cook time 3 hours 20 minutes ✳ serves 6

* 1 tablespoon olive oil
* 1 large red onion (300g), chopped coarsely
* 3 raw chorizo sausages (500g),
chopped coarsely
* 4 cloves garlic, crushed
* 1 teaspoon dried chilli flakes
* 1 medium red capsicum (bell pepper)
(200g), chopped coarsely
* 150g baby green beans, halved
* 800g (1½ pounds) canned cannellini beans,
rinsed, drained
* 800g (1½ pounds) canned diced tomatoes
* ⅓ cup (80ml) chicken stock
* 2 dried bay leaves
* ⅓ cup coarsely chopped fresh
flat-leaf parsley

1 Heat oil in a large frying pan; cook onion and chorizo, stirring, until browned lightly. Add garlic and chilli flakes; cook, stirring, until fragrant.
2 Combine capsicum, beans, tomatoes, stock, bay leaves and chorizo mixture in a 4.5-litre (18-cup) slow cooker. Cook, covered, on low, about 3 hours.
3 Discard bay leaves. Season to taste.
4 Sprinkle stew with parsley.

Suitable to freeze
at the end of step 3.

Serving suggestion
*Green salad and
crusty bread.*

Nutritional count per serving *28.7g total fat (9.6g saturated fat); 1689kJ (404 cal); 13.1g carbohydrate; 21.3g protein; 5.8g fibre*

PORK AND FENNEL SOUP

prep + cook time 6 hours 40 minutes ✳ serves 6

* 500g (1-pound) piece pork neck
* 4 small potatoes (500g), chopped coarsely
* 2 large fennel bulbs (1kg), chopped coarsely, fronds reserved
* 1 medium brown onion (150g), chopped coarsely
* 2 cloves garlic, quartered
* 1 dried bay leaf
* 6 black peppercorns
* 1.5 litres (6 cups) water
* 2 cups (500ml) chicken stock
* ½ cup (125ml) pouring cream

1 Tie pork at 2.5cm (1-inch) intervals with kitchen string. Combine pork, potato, fennel, onion, garlic, bay leaf, peppercorns, the water and stock in a 4.5-litre (18-cup) slow cooker. Cook, covered, on low, about 6 hours.
2 Discard bay leaf. Transfer pork to a medium bowl; remove string. Using two forks, shred pork coarsely.
3 Stand soup 10 minutes, then blend or process, in batches, until smooth. Return soup to cooker; stir in cream. Cook, covered, on high, until hot. Season to taste.
4 Serve soup topped with pork and reserved fennel fronds.

Suitable to freeze
at the end of step 1.

Serving suggestion
Crusty bread.

Nutritional count per serving *16.2g total fat (8.4g saturated fat); 1258kJ (301 cal); 14.9g carbohydrate; 22g protein; 4.3g fibre*

UNDER 8 HOURS

LAMB

IT'S EASY TO MAKE A CURRY OR A STEW USING THE CHEAPEST CHOPS

THE AUSTRALIAN WOMEN'S WEEKLY
TRIPLE TESTED
TEST KITCHEN

BALTI LAMB
AND RICE MEATBALLS

prep + cook time 4 hours 30 minutes (+ refrigeration) * serves 6

* 750g (1½ pounds) minced (ground) lamb
* ¾ cup (150g) jasmine rice
* 1 cup (70g) stale breadcrumbs
* 1 egg
* 2 tablespoons finely chopped fresh coriander (cilantro)
* ½ cup (150g) balti curry paste
* 2½ cups (625ml) water
* 400g (12½ ounces) canned diced tomatoes
* 2 medium brown onions (300g), chopped finely
* 650g (1¼ pounds) baby eggplant, halved lengthways, chopped coarsely
* ½ cup loosely packed fresh coriander (cilantro) leaves, extra

1 Combine lamb, rice, breadcrumbs, egg and coriander in a large bowl, season; roll level tablespoons of mixture into balls. Place on a tray, cover; refrigerate 20 minutes.
2 Combine paste and the water in a large jug; pour into a 4.5-litre (18-cup) slow cooker. Stir in tomatoes and onion; add meatballs and eggplant. Cook, covered, on high, about 4 hours. Season to taste.
3 Serve sprinkled with extra coriander.

Suitable to freeze
at the end of step 2.

Tip *Meatballs must be completely submerged in the liquid during cooking time.*

Nutritional count per serving *19g total fat (5.4g saturated fat); 1969kJ (471 cal); 37.5g carbohydrate; 33.7g protein; 7.3g fibre*

LAMB TAGINE
WITH HARISSA AND GREEN OLIVES

prep + cook time 4 hours 35 minutes ✳ serves 6

* 1.2kg (2½ pounds) boneless lamb shoulder, chopped coarsely
* 1 large red onion (300g), grated coarsely
* 2 cloves garlic, crushed
* 2 tablespoons finely chopped coriander (cilantro) root and stem mixture
* 1 cinnamon stick, halved
* 1 teaspoon each ground cumin, ground ginger and sweet paprika
* ⅓ cup (80ml) olive oil
* 1 tablespoon harissa
* 800g (1½ pounds) canned diced tomatoes
* ¼ cup (70g) tomato paste
* ½ cup (125ml) beef stock
* 400g (12½ ounces) canned chickpeas (garbanzo beans), rinsed, drained
* 2 tablespoons honey
* ½ cup (90g) seeded small green olives
* 2 teaspoons finely chopped preserved lemon rind
* ½ cup loosely packed fresh mint leaves

1   Combine lamb, onion, garlic, coriander, spices and half the oil in a large bowl.
2   Heat remaining oil in a large frying pan; cook lamb, in batches, until browned all over. Transfer lamb to a 4.5-litre (18-cup) slow cooker.
3   Stir harissa, tomatoes, paste, stock, chickpeas and honey into cooker. Cook, covered, on low, about 4 hours.
4   Remove cinnamon; stir in olives and preserved lemon rind. Season to taste; sprinkle with mint.

Suitable to freeze *at the end of step 3.*

Serving suggestion *Couscous flavoured with preserved lemon rind and fresh mint.*

Tip *Lamb mixture can be marinated overnight at the end of step 1.*

Nutritional count per serving *32g total fat (10.2g saturated fat); 2424kJ (580 cal); 26.3g carbohydrate; 44.1g protein; 5.7g fibre*

GREEK LAMB STIFADO

prep + cook time 6 hours 45 minutes ✳ serves 4

* 1kg (2 pounds) boneless lamb shoulder, cut into 5cm (2-inch) pieces
* 2 tablespoons plain (all-purpose) flour
* 800g (1½ pounds) brown pickling onions
* 4 cloves garlic, chopped finely
* 2 fresh bay leaves
* 1 sprig fresh rosemary
* 1 sprig rigani (greek dried oregano)
* 1 cinnamon stick
* 1 teaspoon ground cumin
* 2 whole cloves
* 2 tablespoons red wine vinegar
* 2 tablespoons tomato paste
* ½ cup (125ml) dry red wine
* 2 cups (500ml) chicken stock
* 100g (3 ounces) fetta, crumbled

1   Toss lamb in flour to coat, shake off excess; place in a 4.5-litre (18-cup) slow cooker. Sprinkle lamb evenly with excess flour.

2   Peel onions, leaving root ends intact. Add onions, garlic, herbs and spices to cooker. Pour over combined vinegar, paste, wine and stock. Cook, covered, on low, about 6 hours. Discard bay leaves, rosemary, rigani, cinnamon and cloves. Season to taste.

3   Serve sprinkled with fetta and extra rigani, if you like.

Suitable to freeze *at the end of step 2.*

Serving suggestion *Mashed potato.*

Tips *Stifado is a meat stew, usually lamb or beef, full of sweet baby onions in a rich red wine sauce. To peel pickling onions, place them in a heatproof bowl, cover with boiling water; stand 2 minutes, drain. The skins will slip off easily.*

Nutritional count per serving *20.6g total fat (10.7g saturated fat); 2207kJ (528 cal); 18.2g carbohydrate; 59.8g protein; 3.8g fibre*

LAMB STEW
WITH ARTICHOKES AND PEAS

prep + cook time 7 hours ✱ serves 6

* 1.5kg (3 pounds) lamb shoulder chops
* 2 tablespoons plain (all-purpose) flour
* 2 tablespoons olive oil
* 12 fresh sage leaves
* 1 large brown onion (200g), chopped coarsely
* 2 stalks celery (300g), trimmed, chopped coarsely
* 1 large carrot (180g), chopped coarsely
* 4 cloves garlic, chopped finely
* ½ cup (125ml) dry white wine
* 1½ cups (375ml) chicken stock
* 1 tablespoon coarsely chopped fresh sage
* ½ cup (60g) frozen peas
* 360g (11½ ounces) small fresh artichokes, trimmed, halved, centre chokes removed

1   Trim excess fat from lamb. Toss lamb in flour to coat, shake off excess. Reserve excess flour. Heat half the oil in a large frying pan, cook sage leaves until browned lightly and crisp; drain on paper towel.

2   Cook lamb in same pan, in batches, until browned. Transfer to a 4.5-litre (18-cup) slow cooker. Sprinkle reserved excess flour over lamb.

3   Heat remaining oil in same pan; cook onion, celery and carrot, stirring, until softened. Add garlic; cook, stirring, until fragrant. Add wine; bring to the boil. Boil, uncovered, until liquid is almost evaporated. Stir onion mixture, stock and chopped sage into cooker. Cook, covered, on low, about 6 hours.

4   Add peas and artichoke to cooker; cook, covered, about 30 minutes. Season to taste. Serve sprinkled with crisp sage leaves.

Suitable to freeze *at the end of step 3.*

Serving suggestion *Creamy mashed potato or polenta.*

Tip *Lamb forequarter and chump chops are also suitable.*

Nutritional count per serving *14g total fat (4.5g saturated fat); 1271kJ (304 cal); 8.9g carbohydrate; 30.1g protein; 4g fibre*

MOROCCAN LAMB
WITH KUMARA AND RAISINS

prep + cook time 6 hours 25 minutes ✳ serves 6

* 2 tablespoons olive oil
* 1.2kg (2½ pounds) boneless lamb shoulder, chopped coarsely
* 1 large brown onion (200g), sliced thickly
* 4 cloves garlic, crushed
* 2 tablespoons ras el hanout
* 2 cups (500ml) chicken stock
* ½ cup (125ml) water
* 1 tablespoon honey
* 2 medium kumara (orange sweet potato) (800g), chopped coarsely
* 400g (12½ ounces) canned chickpeas (garbanzo beans), rinsed, drained
* 1 cinnamon stick
* 3 cardamom pods, bruised
* ⅓ cup (50g) raisins, halved
* ½ cup loosely packed fresh coriander (cilantro) leaves
* ⅓ cup (55g) coarsely chopped blanched almonds, roasted

1 Heat half the oil in a large frying pan; cook lamb, in batches, until browned all over. Remove from pan. Heat remaining oil in same pan; cook onion and garlic, stirring, until onion is soft. Add ras el hanout; cook, stirring, until fragrant. Remove from heat; stir in stock, the water and honey.

2 Place kumara in a 4.5-litre (18-cup) slow cooker; stir in chickpeas, cinnamon, cardamom, lamb and onion mixture. Cook, covered, on low, about 6 hours. Season to taste.

3 Stir in raisins and coriander; sprinkle with nuts to serve.

Suitable to freeze *at the end of step 2.*

Serving suggestion *Buttered couscous and steamed baby green beans.*

Tip *Ras el hanout is a blend of Moroccan spices available in delis and specialist food stores. If you can't find it, use a moroccan seasoning available in supermarkets.*

Nutritional count per serving *30.5g total fat (9.7g saturated fat); 2567kJ (614 cal); 34.9g carbohydrate; 47.2g protein; 6.3g fibre*

HONEY SOY LAMB CHOPS

prep + cook time 6 hours ✳ serves 6

* ¼ cup (60ml) salt-reduced soy sauce
* ¼ cup (90g) honey
* 3 cloves garlic, crushed
* 1 teaspoon sesame oil
* 2 large red onions (600g),
cut into thick wedges
* 6 lamb forequarter chops (1.2kg)
* 6 sprigs fresh rosemary
* 15g (½ ounce) butter, melted
* 1 tablespoon plain (all-purpose) flour

1   Combine sauce, honey, garlic and oil in a small jug.
2   Place onion in a 4.5-litre (18-cup) slow cooker; top with lamb, soy sauce mixture and rosemary. Cook, covered, on low, about 5 hours. Discard rosemary.
3   Remove lamb from cooker; cover to keep warm.
4   Combine butter and flour in a small bowl; stir into cooker. Cook, covered, on high, for 25 minutes or until sauce thickens; season to taste. Strain sauce through a fine sieve into a medium heatproof jug; discard onion.
5   Serve lamb drizzled with sauce.

Suitable to freeze
at the end of step 2.

Serving suggestion
Steamed kipfler potatoes, baby peas and carrots.

Nutritional count per serving *16.9g total fat (8.2g saturated fat); 1588kJ (380cal); 19.5g carbohydrate; 36.2g protein; 1.6g fibre*

FRENCH ONION
LAMB CHOPS

prep + cook time 6 hours 30 minutes ✳ serves 6

* 12 lamb forequarter chops (2kg)
* 2 tablespoons plain (all-purpose) flour
* 2 tablespoons olive oil
* 80g (2½ ounces) packaged french onion soup mix
* 2 medium leeks (700g), sliced thinly
* 3 stalks celery (450g), trimmed, chopped coarsely
* 2 cups (500ml) salt-reduced chicken stock
* ¼ cup coarsely chopped fresh flat-leaf parsley

1 Trim excess fat from lamb. Toss lamb in flour to coat, shake off excess. Heat oil in a large frying pan; cook lamb, in batches, until browned.

2 Place 4 lamb chops into a 4.5-litre (18-cup) slow cooker. Sprinkle one-third of the soup mix then one-third of the leek and celery over chops. Repeat layering twice with remaining lamb, soup mix, leek and celery. Pour stock into cooker. Cook, covered, on low, about 6 hours.

3 Remove lamb from cooker; cover to keep warm. Skim fat from surface of sauce; season to taste.

4 Serve lamb and sauce sprinkled with parsley.

Suitable to freeze
at the end of step 3.

Serving suggestion
Mashed potato and steamed green beans.

Tip *Lamb shoulder chops and chump chops are also suitable.*

Nutritional count per serving *16.9g total fat (5.9g saturated fat); 1532kJ (366 cal); 11.6g carbohydrate; 39.8g protein; 4.4g fibre*

LAMB AND POTATO STEW
WITH SPINACH

prep + cook time 6 hours 20 minutes * serves 6

* 3 medium potatoes (600g), unpeeled,
cut into thick wedges
* 2 large brown onions (400g), sliced thickly
* 2 large carrots (360g), sliced thickly
* 4 cloves garlic, sliced thinly
* 1.2kg (2½ pounds) boneless lamb leg,
chopped coarsely
* 1½ cups (375ml) chicken stock
* 410g (13 ounces) canned tomato puree
* 4 sprigs fresh thyme
* 60g (2 ounces) baby spinach leaves

1 Place potato, onion, carrot, garlic and lamb in a 4.5-litre (18-cup) slow cooker; stir in stock, puree and thyme. Cook, covered, on low, about 6 hours.
2 Discard thyme. Stir in spinach; season to taste.

Not suitable to freeze.

Serving suggestion
Crusty bread and steamed green vegetables.

Nutritional count per serving *11.4g total fat (4.9g saturated fat); 1676kJ (401 cal); 21.6g carbohydrate; 49.6g protein; 5.9g fibre*

SHREDDED LAMB
AND PUMPKIN SOUP

prep + cook time 6 hours 30 minutes ✳ serves 4

* ½ cup (100g) dried brown lentils
* 3 french-trimmed lamb shanks (750g)
* 2 tablespoons moroccan seasoning
* 500g (1 pound) pumpkin, chopped coarsely
* 1 litre (4 cups) chicken stock
* 400g (12½ ounces) canned diced tomatoes
* 400g (12½ ounces) canned chickpeas (garbanzo beans), rinsed, drained
* ½ cup finely chopped fresh flat-leaf parsley

1 Rinse lentils under cold water until water runs clear; drain.
2 Combine lamb, seasoning, pumpkin, stock, tomatoes, chickpeas and lentils in a 4.5-litre (18-cup) slow cooker. Cook, covered, on low, about 6 hours.
3 Remove lamb from cooker. When cool enough to handle, remove meat from bones; shred coarsely. Discard bones. Return meat to cooker; season to taste.
4 Serve sprinkled with parsley.

Suitable to freeze
at the end of step 3.

Serving suggestion
A dollop of thick yoghurt.

Nutritional count per serving *13g total fat (5.4g saturated fat); 1797kJ (430 cal); 34.7g carbohydrate; 39.7g protein; 10.3g fibre*

PANANG LAMB CURRY

prep + cook time 4 hours 30 minutes ✳ serves 8

✳ 1 tablespoon peanut oil
✳ 1.5kg (3 pounds) boneless lamb shoulder, cut into 5cm (2-inch) pieces
✳ ½ cup (150g) panang curry paste
✳ 2½ cups (625ml) coconut cream
✳ 2 tablespoons fish sauce
✳ ¼ cup (65g) grated palm sugar
✳ 2 tablespoons peanut butter
✳ 4 fresh kaffir lime leaves
✳ 225g (7 ounces) canned sliced bamboo shoots, rinsed, drained
✳ 1 small red capsicum (bell pepper) (150g), sliced thinly
✳ 200g (6½ ounces) green beans, trimmed, halved
✳ ½ cup loosely packed fresh coriander (cilantro) leaves

1 Heat oil in a large frying pan; cook lamb, in batches, until browned. Transfer to a 4.5-litre (18-cup) slow cooker.
2 Add paste to same pan; cook, stirring, for 1 minute or until fragrant. Add coconut cream, sauce, sugar, peanut butter and lime leaves; bring to the boil. Transfer to cooker.
3 Cook, covered, on low, about 3½ hours. Add bamboo shoots, capsicum and beans to cooker; cook, covered, on low, for 30 minutes or until vegetables are tender. Season to taste.
4 Serve curry sprinkled with coriander.

Not suitable to freeze.

Tip *Panang curry has a distinct peanut flavour; the addition of peanut butter helps to bring out the flavour when using a bought paste.*

Nutritional count per serving *37.1g total fat (20.2g saturated fat); 2347kJ (501 cal); 13.5g carbohydrate; 42.3g protein; 3.7g fibre*

LAMB KORMA

prep + cook time 6 hours 30 minutes ✻ serves 6

* 1.5kg (3 pounds) boneless lamb shoulder, chopped coarsely
* 2 medium brown onions (300g) sliced thinly
* 5cm (2-inch) piece fresh ginger (25g), grated
* 3 cloves garlic, crushed
* ⅔ cup (200g) korma paste
* 3 medium tomatoes (450g), chopped coarsely
* ½ cup (125ml) chicken stock
* 300ml pouring cream
* 1 cinnamon stick
* 2 teaspoons poppy seeds
* ½ cup loosely packed fresh coriander (cilantro) leaves
* 1 fresh long red chilli, sliced thinly
* ⅓ cup (25g) roasted flaked almonds

1 Combine lamb, onion, ginger, garlic, paste, tomato, stock, cream, cinnamon and seeds in a 4.5-litre (18-cup) slow cooker. Cook, covered, on low, about 6 hours. Discard cinnamon stick. Season to taste.

2 Serve korma sprinkled with coriander, chilli and nuts.

Suitable to freeze
at the end of step 1.

Serving suggestion
Steamed basmati rice, grilled naan bread and yoghurt.

Nutritional count per serving *49.9g total fat (22.8g saturated fat); 3005kJ (719 cal); 9.3g carbohydrate; 55.7g protein; 6.2g fibre*

LAMB, HARISSA
AND CHICKPEA CASSEROLE

prep + cook time 7 hours 35 minutes ✳ serves 6

* 1.2kg (2½ pounds) boneless lamb shoulder, chopped coarsely
* ¼ cup (35g) plain (all-purpose) flour
* 1 tablespoon olive oil
* 1 medium red onion (170g), sliced thinly
* 2 cloves garlic, crushed
* 2cm (¾-inch) piece fresh ginger (10g), grated
* 1 teaspoon ground allspice
* 1½ cups (375ml) beef stock
* 2 tablespoons harissa paste
* 2 x 5cm (2-inch) strips orange rind
* 2 x 400g (12½ ounces) canned chickpeas (garbanzo beans), rinsed, drained
* ⅓ cup coarsely chopped fresh mint

1 Toss lamb in flour to coat; shake off excess. Heat half the oil in a large frying pan; cook lamb, in batches, until browned. Transfer to a 4.5-litre (18-cup) slow cooker.
2 Heat remaining oil in same pan; cook onion, garlic and ginger, stirring, until onion softens. Add allspice; cook, stirring, until fragrant. Add ½ cup of the stock; cook, stirring, until mixture boils.
3 Stir onion mixture into cooker with remaining stock, harissa, rind and chickpeas. Cook, covered, on low, about 7 hours. Season to taste.
4 Sprinkle casserole with mint.

Suitable to freeze
at the end of step 3.

Serving suggestion
Rice pilaf, steamed rice or couscous.

Nutritional count per serving *23.1g total fat (9g saturated fat); 2019kJ (483 cal); 19.9g carbohydrate; 46.2g protein; 5.5g fibre*

UNDER 8 HOURS

BEEF

BEEF IS THE EASIEST MEAT TO SLOW COOK
FREEZE ANY LEFTOVERS FOR LATER

BEEF POT AU FEU

prep + cook time 6 hours 30 minutes ✳ serves 6

* 9 brown pickling onions (360g)
* 2 teaspoons cracked black pepper
* 1.5kg (3-pound) piece beef sirloin or beef blade steak
* 150g (4½-ounce) piece smoked speck
* 400g (12½ ounces) baby carrots, trimmed
* 9 baby new potatoes (360g), halved
* 3 stalks celery (450g), trimmed, chopped coarsely
* 1 litre (4 cups) chicken stock
* 6 cloves garlic, peeled
* 1 sprig fresh rosemary
* 1 sprig fresh thyme
* 2 fresh bay leaves
* 1 tablespoon coarsely chopped fresh flat-leaf parsley

1 Peel onions, leaving the root ends intact.
2 Rub pepper over beef. Place in a 4.5-litre (18-cup) slow cooker with onions. Add speck, carrots, potato, celery, stock, garlic, rosemary, thyme and bay leaves. Cook, covered, on low, about 6 hours. Season to taste.
3 Remove beef from cooker; shred into large pieces. Discard speck, herbs and bay leaves. Skim fat from surface of broth.
4 Serve meat with vegetables and broth. Sprinkle with parsley before serving.

Not suitable to freeze.

Tip *French for 'pot on the fire', pot au feu is the traditional, classic beef stew.*

Nutritional count per serving *16.4g total fat (6.8g saturated fat); 2094kJ (501 cal); 16.4g carbohydrate; 69g protein; 4.6g fibre*

PHO BO

prep + cook time 6 hours ✳ serves 4

* 1kg (2 pounds) chopped beef bones
* 1 large brown onion (200g),
chopped coarsely
* 5cm (2-inch) piece fresh ginger (25g),
chopped coarsely
* 2.5 litres (10-cups) boiling water
* 6 star anise
* 2 cinnamon sticks
* 10 cloves
* 2 tablespoons coriander seeds
* ¼ cup (60ml) fish sauce
* ¼ cup (60ml) lime juice
* 2 tablespoons brown sugar
* 200g (6½ ounces) rice stick noodles
* 250g (8 ounces) beef eye fillet, sliced thinly
* 2 cups (160g) bean sprouts
* ½ cup firmly packed fresh mint
* ½ cup firmly packed fresh
coriander (cilantro)
* ½ cup firmly packed fresh vietnamese
mint leaves
* 2 fresh long red chillies, sliced thinly

1 Place bones, onion and ginger in a 4.5-litre (18-cup) slow cooker. Cook, covered, on high, about 2 hours.

2 Add the water, star anise, cinnamon, cloves and coriander seeds. Cook, covered, on high, about 3 hours. Add sauce, juice and sugar. Strain cooking liquid through a muslin-lined sieve, clean chux or linen tea towel; discard solids.

3 Place noodles in a medium heatproof bowl, cover with boiling water; stand 15 minutes or until softened; drain.

4 Divide noodles and beef among serving bowls. Ladle hot soup over (the heat will gently cook the beef); scatter over sprouts, mint, fresh coriander, vietnamese mint and chilli to serve.

Suitable to freeze *at the end of step 2.*

Tip *Freeze the beef to make it easier to slice thinly.*

Nutritional count per serving *3.7g total fat (1.3g saturated fat); 695kJ (166 cal); 14.6g carbohydrate; 17.1g protein; 3.1g fibre*

VEAL WITH
BALSAMIC SAGE SAUCE

prep + cook time 6 hours 30 minutes ✳ serves 6

* 6 pieces veal osso buco (1.2kg)
* 2 tablespoons plain (all-purpose) flour
* 1 tablespoon olive oil
* 20g (¾ ounce) butter
* 2 cloves garlic, sliced thinly
* 2 tablespoons coarsely chopped fresh sage
* ½ cup (125ml) balsamic vinegar
* 1 cup (250ml) chicken stock

1 Trim excess fat from veal; toss in flour to coat, shake off excess. Heat oil and butter in a large frying pan; cook veal, in batches, until browned. Transfer to a 4.5-litre (18-cup) slow cooker.
2 Add garlic and sage to same pan; cook, stirring, until fragrant. Add vinegar; boil, uncovered, for 2 minutes or until reduced by half. Stir in stock. Transfer to cooker.
3 Cook, covered, on low, about 6 hours. Season to taste.
4 Serve sprinkled with extra sage, if you like.

Suitable to freeze *at the end of step 3.*

Serving suggestion *Cheese risotto, soft polenta or mashed potato and steamed green vegetables.*

Tips *Veal forequarter chops are also suitable. Use regular balsamic vinegar, not an aged vinegar or glaze.*

Nutritional count per serving *9.8g total fat (3.7g saturated fat); 945kJ (226 cal); 3.4g carbohydrate; 30.1g protein; 0.3g fibre*

MEATBALLS
IN TOMATO SAUCE

prep + cook time 6 hours 45 minutes ✳ serves 6

* 2 slices white bread (90g), crusts removed
* ½ cup (125ml) milk
* 1kg (2 pounds) minced (ground) beef
* 1 large brown onion (200g), chopped finely
* 1 medium carrot (120g), grated finely
* 3 cloves garlic, crushed
* 1 egg
* 2 tablespoons tomato paste
* ½ teaspoon dried oregano leaves
* 2 tablespoons finely chopped fresh basil
* 1 tablespoon olive oil
* 1 medium brown onion (150g), extra, chopped finely
* 2 cloves garlic, extra, crushed
* 400g (12½ ounces) canned diced tomatoes
* 400g (12½ ounces) canned cherry tomatoes
* 2 tablespoons tomato paste, extra
* 1 cup (250ml) beef stock
* ¼ cup loosely packed fresh basil leaves

1 Combine bread and milk in a large bowl; stand 10 minutes. Add beef, onion, carrot, garlic, egg, paste, oregano and chopped basil; season, mix well. Shape level tablespoons of mixture into balls. Transfer to a 4.5-litre (18-cup) slow cooker.
2 Heat oil in a large frying pan; cook extra onion and garlic, stirring, until onion softens. Stir in tomatoes, extra paste and stock; transfer to cooker. Cook, covered, on low, about 6 hours. Season to taste.
3 Serve sprinkled with basil leaves.

Suitable to freeze
at the end of step 2.

Serving suggestion
Spaghetti or mashed potato, sprinkle with parmesan.

Nutritional count per serving *18.1g total fat (7.5g saturated fat); 1689kJ (404 cal); 18.4g carbohydrate; 39.7g protein; 4.4g fibre*

MOROCCAN
BEEF MEATBALLS

prep + cook time 6 hours 45 minutes ✷ serves 6

* 2 slices white bread (90g)
* ½ cup (125ml) milk
* 1kg (2 pounds) minced (ground) beef
* 1 egg
* 2 tablespoons finely chopped fresh coriander (cilantro) root and stem mixture
* 1 tablespoon each ground cumin, ground coriander and sweet paprika
* 2 teaspoons ground ginger
* 1 teaspoon ground cinnamon
* 1 large brown onion (200g), chopped finely
* 4 cloves garlic, chopped finely
* 1 tablespoon olive oil
* 2 tablespoons tomato paste
* 700g (1½ pounds) bottled passata
* ½ cup (125ml) beef stock
* 2 tablespoons honey
* ½ cup firmly packed fresh coriander (cilantro) leaves

1   Remove and discard crusts from bread. Combine bread and milk in a small bowl; stand 10 minutes.

2   Combine bread mixture, beef, egg, coriander root and stem mixture, spices and half the onion and garlic in a large bowl; roll level tablespoons of mixture into balls, place in a 4.5-litre (18-cup) slow cooker.

3   Heat oil in a large frying pan over medium heat. Cook remaining onion and garlic, stirring, for 5 minutes or until onion softens. Stir in paste, passata, stock and honey; transfer to cooker. Cook, covered, on low, about 6 hours. Season to taste.

4   Sprinkle with fresh coriander to serve.

Suitable to freeze
at the end of step 3.

Serving suggestion
Couscous and Greek-style yoghurt.

Nutritional count per serving *18.6g total fat (7.5g saturated fat); 1570kJ (375 cal); 12.7g carbohydrate; 38.4g protein; 2g fibre*

TUSCAN BEEF STEW

prep + cook time 6 hours 30 minutes ✳ serves 6

* 6 pieces beef osso buco (1.2kg)
* 1 tablespoon olive oil
* 1 large brown onion (200g),
chopped coarsely
* 3 cloves garlic, crushed
* 6 anchovy fillets, drained, chopped finely
* 2 tablespoons plain (all-purpose) flour
* ¼ cup (60ml) balsamic vinegar
* 2 tablespoons tomato paste
* 400g (12½ ounces) canned
crushed tomatoes
* 1 cup (250ml) beef stock
* ¼ cup (60ml) water
* 4 sprigs fresh rosemary
* 1 cup (120g) seeded green olives

1   Trim excess fat from beef. Heat oil in a large frying pan over medium-high heat. Cook beef, in batches, until browned. Transfer to a 4.5-litre (18-cup) slow cooker.

2   Add onion, garlic and anchovy to same pan; cook, stirring, for 1 minute or until fragrant. Add flour; cook, stirring, about 1 minute. Stir in vinegar and paste, then tomatoes, stock, the water and rosemary. Transfer mixture to cooker.

3   Cook, covered, on low, about 6 hours. Season to taste.

4   Just before serving, stir in olives.

Suitable to freeze
at the end of step 3.

Serving suggestion
Soft polenta and baby rocket leaves.

Tip *In Italian, osso buco literally means 'bone with a hole'. It is cut from the shin of the hind leg (shank) and is also known as knuckle. The hole is filled with rich bone marrow, also known as 'jelly'; stand the bones upright to cook, so you don't lose the delicious jelly inside.*

Nutritional count per serving *8.2g total fat (1.9g saturated fat); 1437kJ (343 cal); 9g carbohydrate; 55.7g protein; 2.5g fibre*

VEAL STROGANOFF

prep + cook time 6 hours 30 minutes ✳ serves 6

* 1.5kg (3 pounds) stewing veal,
cut into 2.5cm (1-inch) pieces
* ¼ cup (35g) plain (all-purpose) flour
* 1 tablespoon sweet paprika
* 2 medium brown onions (300g),
chopped coarsely
* 3 cloves garlic, crushed
* 400g (12½ ounces) button mushrooms
* 1½ cups (375ml) beef stock
* 2 tablespoons tomato paste
* ½ cup (120g) sour cream
* ¼ cup coarsely chopped fresh
flat-leaf parsley

1   Toss veal in combined flour and paprika to coat, shake off excess; place in a 4.5-litre (18-cup) slow cooker. Sprinkle veal evenly with excess flour mixture.
2   Add onion, garlic and mushrooms to cooker; pour over combined stock and paste. Cook, covered, on low, about 6 hours. Stir in sour cream; season to taste.
3   Serve stroganoff sprinkled with parsley.

Suitable to freeze
at the end of step 2.

Serving suggestion
*Buttered fettuccine,
mashed potato or
steamed rice.*

Nutritional count per serving *14.4g total fat (7g saturated fat); 1743kJ (416 cal); 10.2g carbohydrate; 59.5g protein; 3.2g fibre*

TOMATO TRIPE STEW
WITH PANCETTA

prep + cook time 6 hours 30 minutes * serves 6

*** 1.5kg (3 pounds) honeycomb tripe**
*** 1 tablespoon olive oil**
*** 1 medium brown onion (150g), chopped coarsely**
*** 2 cloves garlic, crushed**
*** 6 slices pancetta (90g), chopped coarsely**
*** ⅓ cup (80ml) dry white wine**
*** 1 large carrot (180g), chopped coarsely**
*** 1 stalk celery (150g), trimmed, chopped coarsely**
*** 3 cups (700g) bottled tomato pasta sauce**
*** 2 dried bay leaves**
*** ½ cup coarsely chopped fresh flat-leaf parsley**

1 Cover tripe with cold water in a large saucepan; bring to the boil. Boil, covered, about 10 minutes. Drain. Cut tripe into 4cm (1½-inch) pieces, transfer to a 4.5-litre (18-cup) slow cooker.

2 Meanwhile, heat oil in a small frying pan; cook onion, garlic and pancetta, stirring, until onion softens and pancetta is browned and crisp.

3 Transfer onion mixture to cooker; stir in wine, carrot, celery, sauce and bay leaves. Cook, covered, on low, about 6 hours.

4 Discard bay leaves. Season to taste. Sprinkle stew with parsley.

Not suitable to freeze.

Serving suggestion *Crusty bread.*

Tip *Check with the butcher to make sure the tripe has been cleaned and blanched. We suggest you blanch it again – see step 1 – before cutting it into pieces. You might have to order tripe in advance.*

Nutritional count per serving *11.3g total fat (3.6g saturated fat); 1371kJ (328 cal); 14g carbohydrate; 38.3g protein; 3.9g fibre*

VEAL WITH
MARSALA AND MUSHROOMS

prep + cook time 6 hours 30 minutes ✳ serves 6

✳ 300g (9½ ounces) button mushrooms
✳ ¼ cup (35g) plain (all-purpose) flour
✳ 6 pieces veal osso buco (1.5kg)
✳ 1 tablespoon olive oil
✳ 20g (¾ ounce) butter
✳ 6 shallots (150g), chopped finely
✳ 2 cloves garlic, chopped finely
✳ ½ cup (125ml) marsala
✳ 2 cups (500ml) salt-reduced beef stock
✳ ½ cup (125ml) pouring cream
✳ 1 tablespoon wholegrain mustard
✳ ¼ cup coarsely chopped fresh
flat-leaf parsley

1 Place mushrooms over base of a 4.5-litre (18-cup) slow cooker.
2 Reserve 1 tablespoon of the flour. Toss veal in remaining flour to coat, shake off excess. Heat oil and butter in a large frying pan over medium-high heat. Cook veal, in batches, until browned. Transfer to cooker.
3 Cook shallots and garlic in same pan, stirring, for 5 minutes or until shallots are softened. Add reserved flour; cook, stirring, about 1 minute. Stir in marsala and stock; bring to the boil. Transfer to cooker.
4 Cook, covered, on low, about 6 hours. Carefully remove veal from cooker; cover to keep warm.
5 Add cream and mustard to cooker; stir to combine. Cook, covered, on high, for 10 minutes or until heated through. Season to taste.
6 Serve veal with mushrooms and sauce sprinkled with parsley.

Not suitable to freeze.

Serving suggestion
Mashed potato, soft polenta, buttered pasta or risotto and steamed green vegetables.

Nutritional count per serving *14.2g total fat (7.2g saturated fat); 874kJ (201 cal); 10.2g carbohydrate; 4.8g protein; 2.2g fibre*

VEAL WITH
PARSLEY AND CAPERS

prep + cook time 6 hours 30 minutes ✳ serves 6

* 1.2kg (2½ pounds) boneless veal shoulder, chopped coarsely
* ⅓ cup (50g) plain (all-purpose) flour
* ¼ cup (60ml) olive oil
* 8 shallots (200g)
* 375g (12 ounces) button mushrooms
* 1 cup (250ml) dry white wine
* 4 bacon bones (320g)
* 1 cup (250ml) chicken stock
* 4 dried bay leaves
* 1 cup (120g) frozen peas, thawed
* 1 cup coarsely chopped fresh flat-leaf parsley
* 1 tablespoon rinsed, drained baby capers
* 2 teaspoons finely grated lemon rind
* 2 cloves garlic, chopped finely

1 Coat veal in flour; shake off excess. Heat 2 tablespoons of the oil in a large frying pan; cook veal, in batches, until browned all over. Transfer veal to a 4.5-litre (18-cup) slow cooker.

2 Meanwhile, peel shallots, leave roots intact. Heat remaining oil in same pan; cook shallots and mushrooms, stirring, until browned. Add wine, bring to the boil; boil, uncovered, until reduced by half.

3 Add bacon bones, stock, bay leaves and shallot mixture to cooker. Cook, covered, on low, about 6 hours.

4 Discard bacon bones and bay leaves. Stir in peas, parsley, capers, rind and garlic; season to taste.

Not suitable to freeze.

Serving suggestion
Creamy mashed potato and a green leafy salad.

Tip *If the butcher has some good stewing veal available, it's fine to use in this recipe.*

Nutritional count per serving *16.5g total fat (3.4g saturated fat); 1814kJ (434 cal); 9.1g carbohydrate; 53.4g protein; 4g fibre*

SHREDDED BEEF TACOS

prep + cook time 6 hours 30 minutes ✳ makes 6

* 1kg (2-pound) piece beef chuck steak
* ¼ teaspoon chilli powder
* 1 teaspoon each ground cumin, ground coriander and smoked paprika
* 1 cup (250ml) beef stock
* 2 tablespoons tomato paste
* 1 fresh long red chilli, sliced thinly
* 2 cloves garlic, crushed
* 6 large flour tortillas, warmed

1 Rub beef with combined spices; place in a 4.5-litre (18-cup) slow cooker. Pour over combined stock, paste, chilli and garlic. Cook, covered, on low, about 6 hours.
2 Remove beef from cooker. When cool enough to handle, shred meat coarsely using two forks. Discard half the liquid from cooker. Return meat to cooker; season to taste.
3 Serve shredded beef in tortillas.

Suitable to freeze
at the end of step 2.

Serving suggestion
Guacamole, tomato salsa, grated cheese, sour cream, shredded lettuce and fresh coriander (cilantro).

Nutritional count per serving *8.2g total fat (2.5g saturated fat); 1354kJ (324 cal); 18.9g carbohydrate; 42.4g protein; 1.6g fibre*

UNDER

8

HOURS

SEAFOOD

ONLY SOME RECIPES BASED ON SEAFOOD
WILL WORK IN A SLOW COOKER

THE AUSTRALIAN WOMEN'S WEEKLY · TEST KITCHEN · TRIPLE TESTED

PORTUGUESE CALDEIRADA

prep + cook time 4 hours 30 minutes ✳ serves 6

* 2 tablespoons olive oil
* 2 large brown onions (400g), sliced thickly
* 3 medium red capsicums (bell peppers) (600g), sliced thickly
* 1kg (2 pounds) potatoes, sliced thickly
* 1 cup (250ml) dry white wine
* ½ cup (125ml) water
* 800g (1½ pounds) firm white fish fillets, chopped coarsely
* 2 tablespoons olive oil, extra

1 Pour oil into a 4.5-litre (18-cup) slow cooker; layer onion, capsicum and potato in cooker, seasoning between each layer. Add wine and the water. Cook vegetable mixture, covered, on high, about 3½ hours.
2 Add fish to cooker, season; spoon vegetable mixture over fish. Cook, covered, on high, about 30 minutes.
3 Serve drizzled with extra oil.

Not suitable to freeze.

Serving suggestion
Crusty bread.

Tips Caldeirada is a Portuguese fish stew. It varies from region to region but usually contains a variety of fish, and occasionally shellfish, with potato, onion and tomato, or capsicum, as we use here. It is similar to the French seafood stew, bouillabaisse. Use any firm white fish you like; choose large pieces. We used a mixture of angel and monk fish.

Nutritional count per serving 15.4g total fat (2.6g saturated fat); 1689kJ (404 cal); 24.6g carbohydrate; 32.7g protein; 3.9g fibre

SEAFOOD
IN ROMESCO SAUCE

prep + cook time 4 hours 45 minutes * serves 6

* **1kg (2 pounds) cleaned whole baby octopus**
* **800g (1½ pounds) canned crushed tomatoes**
* **4 cloves garlic, crushed**
* **1 teaspoon dried chilli flakes**
* **2 teaspoons smoked paprika**
* **2 medium red capsicums (bell peppers) (400g), sliced thinly**
* **2 tablespoons red wine vinegar**
* **500g (1 pound) uncooked medium king prawns (shrimp)**
* **500g (1 pound) cleaned mussels**
* **½ cup (60g) ground almonds**
* **½ cup coarsely chopped fresh flat-leaf parsley**
* **⅓ cup coarsely chopped fresh oregano**

1 Combine octopus, tomatoes, garlic, chilli, paprika, capsicum and vinegar in a 4.5-litre (18-cup) slow cooker; cook, covered, on low, about 4 hours.

2 Meanwhile, shell and devein prawns, leaving tails intact. Add prawns, mussels and ground almonds to cooker; cook, covered, stirring occasionally, on high, for 20 minutes or until prawns change colour and mussels open.

3 Serve sprinkled with herbs.

Not suitable to freeze.

Serving suggestion *Steamed rice or crusty bread.*

Tip *Ground almonds are also sold as almond meal. They are available from health-food stores and supermarkets.*

Nutritional count per serving *9.5g total fat (1.2g saturated fat); 1509kJ (361 cal); 9.5g carbohydrate; 57.1g protein; 3.7g fibre*

OCTOPUS
WITH CHILLI RICE

prep + cook time 4 hours 30 minutes ✳ serves 8

* 800g (1½ pounds) canned diced tomatoes
* 2 large brown onions (400g), chopped finely
* 6 cloves garlic, sliced thinly
* 1 dried bay leaf
* 1 litre (4 cups) water
* 1.5kg (3 pounds) large octopus, cleaned
* 1½ cups (300g) jasmine rice
* 1 cup coarsely chopped fresh coriander (cilantro)
* 2 fresh long red chillies, chopped finely

1 Combine tomatoes, onion, garlic, bay leaf and the water in a 4.5-litre (18-cup) slow cooker; add octopus, season. Cook, covered, on high, about 3½ hours.
2 Carefully remove octopus from cooker to a board. Stir rice into cooker; cook, covered, on high, about 30 minutes.
3 When octopus is cool enough to handle, discard black skin; cut octopus into large chunks. Return octopus to cooker for remaining cooking time of rice.
4 Serve octopus and rice sprinkled with coriander and chilli.

Not suitable to freeze.

Tip *Ask the fishmonger to clean the octopus.*

Nutritional count per serving *3.9g total fat (0.8g saturated fat); 1685kJ (403 cal); 37.8g carbohydrate; 51.8g protein; 2.7g fibre*

SIDE DISHES

45 SUGGESTIONS FOR SIDES THAT ARE
ALSO JUST RIGHT FOR A LIGHT MEAL

WHICH SIDE DISHES GO BEST WITH YOUR SLOW COOKER MEAL

1

Potatoes are one of our favourite vegetables as they're versatile, forgiving to cook and take on flavours from other ingredients in a delicious way. There are many varieties available and some are more suited to certain cooking methods than others. Experiment with different types until you find the flavours and textures you prefer.

2

Root vegetables are mostly boiled or steamed in a pan covered with a tight-fitting lid. If you forget whether to cover them or not, think where the vegetable grows; if it's under the ground, then almost always, the vegie is cooked 'in the dark' – under a lid.

3

Pulses include lentils, dried beans and peas. They are a great source of carbohydrates, protein, vitamins and minerals. Some pulses need to be soaked overnight before cooking. All kidney-shaped beans need to be cooked separately before adding to a slow cooker.

4

Leafy green vegetables are a valuable source of vitamins and minerals essential for good health. You can eat a lot of them in one sitting as they are high in water and low in kilojoules. Wash and drain them well before cooking – steam, stir-fry, boil, microwave, pan-fry - all methods work well. Salad leaves need to be dried well before use.

ASPARAGUS HOLLANDAISE

prep + cook time 35 minutes ⁂ serves 4

Combine 2 tablespoons water, 2 tablespoons white wine vinegar and ¼ teaspoon cracked black pepper in a small saucepan; bring to the boil. Reduce heat; simmer, uncovered, until liquid is reduced to 1 tablespoon. Strain mixture through a fine sieve into a medium heatproof bowl; cool 10 minutes. Whisk 2 egg yolks into vinegar mixture. Set bowl over a medium saucepan of simmering water (don't let water touch base of bowl). Whisk mixture over heat until thickened. Remove bowl from heat; gradually whisk in 200g (6½ ounces) melted butter in a thin, steady stream, whisking constantly until sauce is thick and creamy. Boil, steam or microwave 1kg (2 pounds) trimmed asparagus until tender. Serve asparagus on a large platter drizzled with hollandaise sauce; season to taste with cracked black pepper.

Nutritional count per serving *44g total fat (26.9g saturated fat); 1797kJ (430 cal); 2.8g carbohydrate; 6.1g protein; 2.6g fibre*

403

SIDE DISHES

CAPRESE SALAD

prep time 15 minutes ✳ **serves 4**

Overlap 3 thinly sliced large roma (egg) tomatoes and 310g (10 ounces) thinly sliced bocconcini on a serving platter. Drizzle with 2 tablespoons olive oil; sprinkle with ¼ cup firmly packed torn fresh basil leaves.

Nutritional count per serving *20.6g total fat (8.8g saturated fat); 1028kJ (246 cal); 1.6g carbohydrate; 13.6g protein; 1.1g fibre*

cheesy pesto polenta

green onion couscous

soft polenta

lemon pistachio couscous

See recipes page 406

CHEESY PESTO POLENTA

prep + cook time 35 minutes ✳ serves 4

Blend or process 2 tablespoons each finely grated parmesan, pine nuts and olive oil, 1 crushed garlic clove and 1 cup firmly packed basil leaves until mixture forms a paste. Combine 2⅓ cups water and 2⅓ cups milk in a large saucepan; bring to the boil. Gradually sprinkle 1 cup polenta over milk mixture; cook, stirring, until polenta thickens slightly. Reduce heat; simmer, uncovered, for 20 minutes or until polenta is thickened, stirring constantly. Stir in ½ cup finely grated parmesan, 30g butter (1 ounce) and pesto. Season to taste.

Tip *If you don't want to make your own pesto, use 95g (3 ounces) of the store-bought variety.*

Nutritional count per serving *31.2g total fat (12.3g saturated fat); 1594kJ (381 cal); 39.2g carbohydrate; 15.5g protein; 2.2g fibre*

GREEN ONION COUSCOUS

prep + cook time 10 minutes ✳ serves 4

Bring 1½ cups chicken stock to the boil in a large saucepan. Remove from heat; add 1½ cups couscous and 25g (¾ ounce) butter; stir to combine. Cover; stand 5 minutes or until liquid is absorbed, fluffing with a fork occasionally. Stir in 3 thinly sliced green onions (scallions).

Nutritional count per serving *6g total fat (3.6g saturated fat); 1404kJ (336 cal); 58.5g carbohydrate; 10.8g protein; 0.8g fibre*

SOFT POLENTA

prep + cook time 20 minutes ✳ serves 6

Combine 3 cups milk and 2 cups chicken stock in a large saucepan; bring to the boil. Gradually add 2 cups polenta to liquid, stirring constantly. Reduce heat; simmer, stirring, for 10 minutes or until polenta thickens. Add 1 cup milk and ¼ cup finely grated parmesan; stir until cheese melts.

Nutritional count per serving *12.1g total fat (7.5g saturated fat); 621kJ (148 cal); 23.9g carbohydrate; 9.4g protein; 0.7g fibre*

LEMON PISTACHIO COUSCOUS

prep + cook time 15 minutes ✳ serves 4

Combine 1 cup couscous, ¾ cup boiling water, 2 teaspoons finely grated lemon rind and ¼ cup lemon juice in a medium heatproof bowl. Cover; stand 5 minutes or until liquid is absorbed, fluffing with a fork occasionally. Meanwhile, dry-fry ½ cup pistachios in a heated small frying pan until fragrant; remove nuts from pan, chop coarsely. Heat 2 teaspoons olive oil in same pan, add 1 crushed garlic clove and 1 finely chopped small red onion; cook, stirring, until onion softens. Fluff couscous then stir nuts, onion mixture and ½ cup shredded fresh mint through couscous.

Nutritional count per serving *10.6g total fat (1.3g saturated fat); 1321kJ (316 cal); 42.8g carbohydrate; 10.2g protein; 2.8g fibre*

Pictured on page 405

PRESERVED LEMON AND OLIVE COUSCOUS

prep time 15 minutes ✳ serves 6

Combine 1¼ cups couscous with 1¼ cups boiling water and 1 tablespoon oil in a large heatproof bowl, cover; stand 5 minutes or until water is absorbed, fluffing with a fork occasionally. Stir 400g (12½ ounces) rinsed, drained canned chickpeas (garbanzo beans), ½ cup coarsely chopped seeded green olives, 2 tablespoons lemon juice, 3 thinly sliced green onions (scallions), 2 tablespoons finely chopped fresh flat-leaf parsley and 1 tablespoon thinly sliced preserved lemon rind into couscous. Season to taste.

Nutritional count per serving *5.4g total fat (0.8g saturated fat); 1113kJ (266 cal); 41.8g carbohydrate; 9.8g protein; 6.1g fibre*

PINE NUT AND DRIED FIG COUSCOUS

prep + cook time 15 minutes ✳ serves 4

Bring 1 cup chicken stock to the boil in a medium saucepan. Remove from heat, add 1 cup couscous, cover; stand 5 minutes or until liquid is absorbed, fluffing with a fork occasionally. Stir ⅔ cup coarsely chopped dried figs, ½ cup toasted pine nuts, 2 teaspoons finely grated lemon rind, ¼ cup lemon juice and ¼ cup finely chopped fresh flat-leaf parsley into couscous; season to taste.

Tips *Add your favourite dried fruit or nuts to the couscous. Serve warm or cold.*

Nutritional count per serving *9.9g total fat (0.7g saturated fat); 1179kJ (282 cal); 38.5g carbohydrate; 7.4g protein; 4.2g fibre*

SPICY RED COUSCOUS

prep + cook time 15 minutes ✳ serves 6

Heat 1 tablespoon olive oil in a medium saucepan, add 2 teaspoons harissa paste, 2 teaspoons sweet paprika and 2 thinly sliced green onions (scallions); cook, stirring, for 2 minutes or until fragrant. Add 1 cup chicken stock and ½ cup water; bring to the boil. Remove from heat, add 1½ cups couscous; cover, stand 5 minutes or until liquid is absorbed, fluffing with a fork occasionally. Stir 1 tablespoon lemon juice into couscous; season to taste. Serve sprinkled with 2 thinly sliced green onions (scallions).

Tip *Harissa is a hot paste; there are many different brands available on the market and the strengths vary enormously.*

Nutritional count per serving *3.7g total fat (0.6g saturated fat); 900kJ (215 cal); 37.4g carbohydrate; 6.2g protein; 2.6g fibre*

PILAF

prep + cook time 30 minutes ✳ serves 4

Melt 20g (¾ ounce) butter in a medium saucepan; cook 1 crushed garlic clove, stirring, until fragrant. Add 1 cup basmati rice; cook, stirring, about 1 minute. Add 1 cup chicken stock and 1 cup water; bring to the boil. Reduce heat; simmer, covered, for 20 minutes or until rice is just tender. Remove from heat; fluff rice with a fork. Stir in ¼ cup coarsely chopped fresh flat-leaf parsley and ¼ cup toasted flaked almonds.

Nutritional count per serving *8.1g total fat (3g saturated fat); 1092kJ (261 cal); 41.2g carbohydrate; 5g protein; 1.5g fibre*

Pictured on page 408

preserved lemon and olive couscous

pine nut and dried fig couscous

spicy red couscous

pilaf

See recipes page 407

COUSCOUS SALAD WITH MIXED PEAS AND BEANS

prep + cook time 25 minutes (+ cooling) ✳ serves 8

Combine 1 cup couscous, 2 tablespoons lemon juice and 1 cup boiling water in a medium heatproof bowl; stand 5 minutes or until liquid is absorbed, fluffing with a fork occasionally, cool. Boil, steam or microwave 150g (4½ ounces) trimmed, halved baby beans and 150g (4½ ounces) trimmed sugar snap peas, separately, until just tender; drain. Rinse under cold water; drain. Combine 1½ tablespoons wholegrain mustard and ¼ cup olive oil in a large bowl; add couscous, beans, peas and ¼ cup finely chopped fresh chives, toss gently to combine.

Nutritional count per serving *7.2g total fat (1g saturated fat); 748kJ (179 cal); 22g carbohydrate; 5.2g protein; 2.2g fibre*

YELLOW COCONUT RICE

prep + cook time 30 minutes (+ standing) ✳ serves 4

Stand 1¾ cups white long grain rice in a large bowl of cold water 30 minutes. Rinse rice under cold water until water runs clear; drain. Place 1¼ cups water, 1⅔ cups coconut cream, 1 teaspoon each white sugar and salt, ½ teaspoon ground turmeric, a pinch saffron threads and rice in a large heavy-based saucepan; cover, bring to the boil, stirring occasionally. Reduce heat; simmer, covered, without stirring, for 15 minutes or until rice is tender. Remove from heat; stand, covered, 5 minutes. Season to taste.

Nutritional count per serving *20.2g total fat (17.8g saturated fat); 1999kJ (477 cal); 66.9g carbohydrate; 6.5g protein; 1.4g fibre*

rice and peas

steamed ginger rice

pea mash

celeriac mash

See recipes page 412

RICE AND PEAS

prep + cook time 30 minutes ✳ serves 6

Combine 1½ cups water, 1½ cups chicken stock and ¼ cup olive oil in a medium saucepan; bring to the boil. Stir in 2 cups white medium-grain rice; cook, uncovered, without stirring, for 10 minutes or until liquid has almost evaporated. Reduce heat; simmer, covered, about 5 minutes. Meanwhile, thinly slice 4 green onions (scallions). Gently stir in onion and 1 cup frozen peas; simmer, covered, for 5 minutes or until rice and peas are tender. Season to taste.

Nutritional count per serving *9.8g total fat (1.6g saturated fat); 1437kJ (343 cal); 56.1g carbohydrate; 6.1g protein; 2.5g fibre*

STEAMED GINGER RICE

prep + cook time 20 minutes ✳ serves 4

Heat 1 tablespoon olive oil in a medium saucepan; cook 6 thinly sliced green onions (scallions), stirring, until softened. Add 2½ teaspoons finely grated fresh ginger and 1½ cups basmati rice; stir to coat in oil. Add 2 cups chicken stock; bring to the boil. Reduce heat; simmer, covered, over low heat, about 10 minutes. Remove from heat; stand, covered, 5 minutes, then fluff with a fork; stir in 2 tablespoons each finely chopped fresh coriander (cilantro) and mint, season to taste.

Nutritional count per serving *5.5g total fat (0.9g saturated fat); 1342kJ (321 cal); 61g carbohydrate; 5.7g protein; 1.1g fibre*

PEA MASH

prep + cook time 30 minutes ✳ serves 4

Place 1kg (2 pounds) coarsely chopped peeled pontiac potatoes in a medium saucepan with enough cold water to barely cover potato. Boil, uncovered, over medium heat, for 15 minutes or until potato is almost tender. Add 1½ cups frozen peas to potato; boil, uncovered, 3 minutes or until tender; drain. Mash vegetables with 50g (1½ ounces) butter and ¾ cup hot milk.

Tip *Any all-round or mashing potato is fine to use here. Desiree or sebago are good choices.*

Nutritional count per serving *12.4g total fat (7.9g saturated fat); 1183kJ (283 cal); 31.1g carbohydrate; 9g protein; 5.8g fibre*

CELERIAC MASH

prep + cook time 30 minutes ✳ serves 6

Place 800g (1½ pounds) coarsely chopped peeled potatoes in a medium saucepan with enough cold water to barely cover potato. Boil, uncovered, over medium heat for 15 minutes or until potato is tender. Drain. Meanwhile, boil, steam or microwave 1kg (2 pounds) coarsely chopped peeled celeriac (celery root) until tender; drain. Mash potato and celeriac together; stir in 60g (2 ounces) butter and ½ cup hot pouring cream. Drizzle with 2 teaspoons olive oil and sprinkle with cracked black pepper to taste.

Nutritional count per serving *17.6g total fat (8.6g saturated fat); 1226kJ (293 cal); 23.5g carbohydrate; 5.7g protein; 9g fibre*

Pictured on page 411

WASABI MASH

prep + cook time 30 minutes ✳ **serves 4**

Boil, steam or microwave 1kg (2 pounds) coarsely chopped peeled desiree potatoes until tender; drain. Mash potato; stir in ⅔ cup warm pouring cream and 1½ teaspoons wasabi paste. Season to taste.

Tip *Any all-round or mashing potato is fine to use here. Pontiac or sebago are good choices.*

Nutritional count per serving *14.7g total fat (9.2g saturated fat); 1255kJ (300 cal); 32.5g carbohydrate; 6.7g protein; 4.2g fibre*

POTATO PUREE

prep + cook time 30 minutes ✳ **serves 4**

Place 1kg (2 pounds) coarsely chopped peeled potatoes in a medium saucepan with enough cold water to barely cover the potato. Boil, uncovered, over medium heat, for 15 minutes or until potato is tender; drain. Using the back of a wooden spoon, push potato through a fine sieve into a large bowl. Stir 40g (1½ ounces) butter and ¾ cup hot milk into potato, folding gently until mash is smooth and fluffy.

Tip *We used lasoda potatoes, but use any general purpose or mashing variety – desiree, sebago, coliban and king edward are all fine to use.*

Nutritional count per serving *10.2g total fat (6.6g saturated fat); 991kJ (237 cal); 28.4g carbohydrate; 6.4g protein; 3.2g fibre*

PARSNIP MASH

prep + cook time 30 minutes ✳ **serves 4**

Boil, steam or microwave 1kg (2 pounds) coarsely chopped peeled parsnips until tender; drain. Mash parsnip with 40g (1½ ounces) butter, 1 crushed garlic clove and ¾ cup hot pouring cream. To serve, sprinkle with 1 tablespoon torn parsley leaves and cracked black pepper to taste.

Nutritional count per serving *10.5g total fat (6.6g saturated fat); 955kJ (228 cal); 24.9g carbohydrate; 5.7g protein; 5.9g fibre*

FETTA AND OLIVE MASH

prep + cook time 30 minutes ✳ **serves 4**

Boil, steam or microwave 1kg (2 pounds) coarsely chopped peeled potatoes until tender; drain. Mash potato with 1 tablespoon olive oil until smooth. Stir in ⅔ cup warmed buttermilk, 200g (6½ ounces) finely chopped fetta and ½ cup thinly sliced black olives. Season with pepper. To serve, drizzle with another tablespoon of olive oil.

Nutritional count per serving *25.5g total fat (10g saturated fat); 1865kJ (446 cal); 33.7g carbohydrate; 16.6g protein; 4.8g fibre*

Pictured on page 414

wasabi mash

potato puree

parsnip mash

fetta and olive mash

See recipes page 413

FENNEL MASH

prep + cook time 30 minutes ✳ **serves 4**

Thinly slice 1 large fennel bulb; reserve 1 tablespoon fennel fronds. Melt 60g (2 ounces) butter in a large frying pan; cook fennel, covered, over low heat, for 10 minutes or until fennel is very soft. Blend or process fennel until smooth. Meanwhile, boil, steam or microwave 1kg (2 pounds) coarsely chopped peeled potatoes until tender; drain. Mash potato; stir in fennel mixture and ½ cup hot pouring cream. Season to taste; sprinkle with fennel fronds.

Nutritional count per serving *13.8g total fat (8.9g saturated fat); 1296kJ (310 cal); 36g carbohydrate; 7.3g protein; 6.1g fibre*

ROASTED CAPSICUM MASH

prep + cook time 30 minutes ✳ serves 4

Quarter 2 medium red capsicums (bell peppers); discard seeds and membranes. Roast under hot grill (broiler), skin-side up, until skin blisters and blackens. Cover capsicum with plastic or paper about 5 minutes, then peel away skin. Blend capsicum until smooth. Meanwhile, boil, steam or microwave 1kg (2 pounds) coarsely chopped peeled potatoes until tender, drain. Mash potato; stir in ½ cup hot pouring cream and 20g (¾ ounce) softened butter. Add capsicum; stir until combined. Season to taste.

Nutritional count per serving *18g total fat (11.6g saturated fat); 1446kJ (346 cal); 36.2g carbohydrate; 7.7g protein; 4.7g fibre*

kumara mash

pumpkin mash

spinach mash

white bean puree

See recipes page 418

KUMARA MASH

prep + cook time 30 minutes ✳ serves 4

Boil, steam or microwave 500g (1 pound) coarsely chopped peeled kumara (orange sweet potato) and 500g (1 pound) coarsely chopped peeled potatoes together until tender; drain. Mash potato and kumara. Combine ¼ cup chicken stock and 40g (1½ ounces) butter in a small saucepan over medium high heat until butter is melted. Stir into kumara mixture until combined. Season to taste.

Nutritional count per serving *8.5g total fat (5.4g saturated fat); 1024kJ (245 cal); 34.2g carbohydrate; 5.6g protein; 4.3g fibre*

PUMPKIN MASH

prep + cook time 30 minutes ✳ serves 4

Boil, steam or microwave 500g (1 pound) coarsely chopped peeled pontiac potatoes and 500g (1 pound) coarsely chopped peeled pumpkin together until tender; drain. Mash potato and pumpkin; stir in 30g (1 ounce) butter. Season to taste.

Tip *Any all-round or mashing potato is fine to use here. Desiree or sebago are good choices.*

Nutritional count per serving *6.5g total fat (2.6g saturated fat); 800kJ (191 cal); 25.6g carbohydrate; 4.7g protein; 5.3g fibre*

SPINACH MASH

prep + cook time 30 minutes ✳ serves 4

Place 1kg (2 pounds) coarsely chopped peeled pontiac potatoes in a medium saucepan with enough cold water to barely cover potato. Boil, uncovered, over medium heat for 15 minutes or until potato is tender; drain. Meanwhile, boil, steam or microwave 200g (6½ ounces) baby spinach leaves until wilted; drain. Squeeze out excess liquid. Blend or process spinach with 40g (1½ ounces) butter until almost smooth. Mash potato; stir in ¼ teaspoon nutmeg, ½ cup hot pouring cream and spinach mixture. Season to taste.

Tip *Any all-round or mashing potato is fine to use here. Desiree or sebago are good choices*

Nutritional count per serving *22.1g total fat (14.3g saturated fat); 1430kJ (342 cal); 27.5g carbohydrate; 6.7g protein; 4.6g fibre*

WHITE BEAN PUREE

prep + cook time 25 minutes ✳ serves 4

Melt 20g (¾ ounce) butter in a medium frying pan; cook 1 finely chopped small brown onion and 1 crushed garlic clove, stirring, until onion softens. Add ¼ cup dry white wine; cook, stirring, until liquid is reduced by half. Add ¾ cup chicken stock and 800g (1½ pounds) rinsed, drained canned white beans; bring to the boil. Reduce heat; simmer, uncovered, for 10 minutes or until liquid is almost evaporated. Blend or process bean mixture and 2 tablespoons pouring cream until smooth. Season to taste. Top with thinly sliced green onions (scallions) to serve.

Nutritional count per serving *7.1g total fat (3g saturated fat); 825kJ (197 cal); 18.6g carbohydrate; 10.6g protein; 9.8g fibre*

Pictured on page 417

SPICED LENTILS

prep + cook time 20 minutes ✳ serves 4

Cook 1½ cups red lentils, uncovered, in a large saucepan of boiling water until just tender; drain. Meanwhile, melt 25g (¾ ounce) butter in a large frying pan; cook 1 finely chopped small brown onion, 1 crushed garlic clove, ½ teaspoon each ground coriander and cumin, and ¼ teaspoon each ground turmeric and cayenne pepper, stirring, until onion softens. Add lentils, ½ cup chicken stock and an extra 25g (¾ ounce) butter; cook, stirring, until hot. Remove pan from heat, stir in 2 tablespoons coarsely chopped fresh flat-leaf parsley.

Nutritional count per serving *11.9g total fat (7g saturated fat); 1354kJ (324 cal); 29.9g carbohydrate; 18.9g protein; 10.8g fibre*

PEAS WITH MINT BUTTER

prep + cook time 10 minutes ✳ serves 4

Boil, steam or microwave 2¼ cups fresh shelled peas until tender; drain. Meanwhile, combine 40g (1½ ounces) butter, 1 tablespoon finely chopped fresh mint and 1 tablespoon thinly sliced lemon rind in a small bowl. Serve peas topped with butter mixture.

Tip *You will need approximately 1kg (2 pounds) fresh pea pods to get the amount of shelled peas needed for this recipe.*

Nutritional count per serving *8.6g total fat (5.4g saturated fat); 589kJ (141 cal); 8.6g carbohydrate; 5.2g protein; 5g fibre*

CAULIFLOWER GRATIN

prep + cook time 30 minutes ✳ serves 6

Preheat oven to 220°C/400°F. Boil, steam or microwave 6 trimmed baby cauliflowers until tender; drain. Place in a medium shallow ovenproof dish. Meanwhile, melt 50g (1½ ounces) butter in a medium saucepan, add ¼ cup plain (all-purpose) flour; cook, stirring, until mixture bubbles and thickens. Gradually stir in 1¾ cups hot milk until smooth; cook, stirring, until mixture boils and thickens. Remove from heat; stir in ½ cup coarsely grated cheddar and ¼ cup finely grated parmesan. Pour cheese sauce over cauliflower in dish; sprinkle with 1 tablespoon japanese (panko) breadcrumbs. Bake for 15 minutes or until browned lightly.

Nutritional count per serving *18g total fat (10.1g saturated fat); 1121kJ (268 cal); 12.4g carbohydrate; 12.7g protein; 3.7g fibre*

BRUSSELS SPROUTS WITH CREAM AND ALMONDS

prep + cook time 10 minutes ✳ serves 4

Melt 10g (½ ounce) butter in a large frying pan; cook ⅓ cup flaked almonds, stirring, until browned lightly; remove from pan. Melt 40g (1½ ounce) extra butter in same pan; cook 1kg (2 pounds) halved brussels sprouts and 2 crushed garlic cloves, stirring, until sprouts are browned lightly. Add 300ml pouring cream; bring to the boil. Reduce heat; simmer, uncovered, until sprouts are tender and sauce thickens slightly. Serve sprout mixture sprinkled with nuts.

Nutritional count per serving *46.7g total fat (28.4g saturated fat); 2061kJ (493 cal); 6.6g carbohydrate; 9.5g protein; 7.3g fibre*

Pictured on page 420

spiced lentils

peas with mint butter

cauliflower gratin

brussels sprouts with cream and almonds

See recipes page 419

FRIED CAULIFLOWER

prep + cook time 15 minutes ✳ serves 4

Whisk 2 eggs, ½ cup self-raising flour and ½ cup water in a medium shallow bowl until smooth. Stir in 2 tablespoons finely chopped fresh coriander (cilantro); season to taste. Heat enough vegetable oil to come half way up a wok. Dip 900g (1¾ pounds) cauliflower florets in batter; drain off excess. Deep-fry cauliflower, in batches, until browned lightly and tender. Drain on paper towel. Combine 2 tablespoons very finely chopped coriander (cilantro) and 1 cup Greek-style yoghurt in a small bowl; season to taste. Serve cauliflower with coriander yoghurt.

Nutritional count per serving *9g total fat (2.8g saturated fat); 1083kJ (259 cal); 27.4g carbohydrate; 14.2g protein; 5.2g fibre*

LIME AND COCONUT SNAKE BEAN SALAD

prep + cook time 20 minutes ✳ serves 4

Boil, steam or microwave 350g (11 ounces) coarsely chopped snake beans until tender; drain. Meanwhile, combine ¼ cup coconut cream, 1 tablespoon lime juice, 2 teaspoons fish sauce and 1 thinly sliced long red chilli in a screw-top jar; shake well. Combine beans, coconut mixture, ½ cup coarsely shredded fresh coconut and ¾ cup loosely packed fresh coriander (cilantro) leaves in a medium bowl.

Tip *To open a fresh coconut, pierce one of the eyes then roast coconut briefly in a very hot oven only until cracks appear in the shell. Cool the coconut, then break it apart and grate the flesh.*

Nutritional count per serving *11.5g total fat (9.9g saturated fat); 598kJ (143 cal); 3.2g carbohydrate; 4.5g protein; 4.9g fibre.*

steamed gai lan in oyster sauce

potato salad with herbed cream

grilled asian vegetables

lyonnaise potatoes

See recipes page 424

STEAMED GAI LAN IN OYSTER SAUCE

prep + cook time 10 minutes ✳ serves 8

Boil, steam or microwave 1kg (2 pounds) halved gai lan until tender; drain. Heat 1 tablespoon peanut oil in a wok; stir-fry gai lan, 2 tablespoons oyster sauce and 1 tablespoon light soy sauce for 2 minutes or until mixture is heated through.

Nutritional count per serving *2.6g total fat (0.4g saturated fat); 205kJ (49 cal); 2.7g carbohydrate; 2.3g protein; 2.4g fibre*

POTATO SALAD WITH HERBED CREAM

prep + cook time 25 minutes ✳ serves 8

Combine ½ cup each mayonnaise and sour cream, ¼ cup warm water, 3 teaspoons dijon mustard, ¼ cup finely chopped fresh chives and ½ cup coarsely chopped fresh flat-leaf parsley in a screw-top jar; shake well. Boil, steam or microwave 1.5kg (3 pounds) scrubbed, unpeeled medium kipfler (fingerling) potatoes until tender; drain. Cool, then slice potatoes crossways into 2cm (¾-inch) thick rounds. Drizzle potato with herbed cream.

Nutritional count per serving *12.2g total fat (4.6g saturated fat); 1074kJ (257 cal); 29g carbohydrate; 5.2g protein; 4.1g fibre*

GRILLED ASIAN VEGETABLES

prep + cook time 25 minutes ✳ serves 4

Boil, steam or microwave 400g (12½ ounces) trimmed, halved baby pak choy until wilted; drain. Brush with 1 tablespoon peanut oil; cook on a heated oiled flat plate until tender. Cut 200g (6½ ounces) baby corn in half lengthways; combine in a large bowl with 175g (5½ ounces) halved broccolini, 100g (3 ounces) trimmed snow peas and an extra 1 tablespoon peanut oil; mix well. Cook vegetables on a flat plate until tender. Meanwhile, combine 2 tablespoons mirin, 1 tablespoon each oyster sauce and light soy sauce, 1 clove crushed garlic, 1 teaspoon white sugar and ½ teaspoon sesame oil in same bowl; mix in vegetables.

Nutritional count per serving *11.2g total fat (1.9g saturated fat); 948kJ (226 cal); 16.7g carbohydrate; 8.7g protein; 8.6g fibre*

LYONNAISE POTATOES

prep + cook time 30 minutes ✳ serves 4

Boil, steam or microwave 900g (1¾ pounds) coarsely chopped peeled desiree potatoes until just tender; drain. Meanwhile, heat 2 teaspoons olive oil in a large frying pan; cook 2 thinly sliced medium red onions and 3 cloves crushed garlic, stirring, until onion softens. Remove from pan. Cook 6 coarsely chopped rindless bacon slices in same pan, stirring, until crisp; drain on paper towel. Heat an extra 2 teaspoons olive oil in same pan; cook potato, stirring, for 5 minutes or until browned lightly. Return onion mixture and bacon to pan; stir gently to combine with potato. Remove from heat; stir in ¼ cup coarsely chopped fresh mint.

Tip *You can also use sebago or ruby lou potatoes.*

Nutritional count per serving *18.8g total fat (6g saturated fat); 1754kJ (419 cal); 32g carbohydrate; 26.9g protein; 5.9g fibre*

Pictured on page 423

CREAMED SPINACH

prep + cook time 15 minutes ✻ serves 4

Melt 20g (¾ ounce) butter in a large frying pan; cook 600g (1¼ pounds) trimmed spinach, stirring, until wilted. Add ½ cup pouring cream; bring to the boil. Reduce heat; simmer, uncovered, until liquid reduces by half.

Nutritional count per serving *38.7g total fat (25.4g saturated fat); 1555kJ (372 cal); 2.8g carbohydrate; 3.5g protein; 2.1g fibre*

MAPLE-GLAZED BABY CARROTS

prep + cook time 25 minutes ✻ serves 4

Melt 30g (1 ounce) butter in a large frying pan over medium heat; cook 750g (1½ pounds) trimmed baby carrots, turning occasionally, for 8 minutes or until almost tender. Add 2 teaspoons finely grated orange rind, ¼ cup orange juice, 2 tablespoons dry white wine and 2 tablespoons maple syrup to pan; bring to the boil. Reduce heat; simmer, uncovered, until liquid has almost evaporated and carrots are tender and caramelised. Serve carrots sprinkled with ½ cup coarsely chopped roasted hazelnuts.

Nutritional count per serving *17.2g total fat (4.5g saturated fat); 1145kJ (274 cal); 20.8g carbohydrate; 4.1g protein; 7.7g fibre*

PROSCIUTTO-WRAPPED BEAN BUNDLES

prep + cook time 30 minutes ✻ serves 8

Cook 200g (6½ ounces) each trimmed green and yellow beans in a medium saucepan of boiling water until just tender; drain. Rinse under cold water; drain. Divide beans into eight equal bundles. Place 8 prosciutto slices on a board; top each with one bean bundle. Wrap beans with prosciutto, rolling to enclose tightly. Cook bundles in a heated oiled large frying pan, over high heat, turning, until prosciutto is crisp. Remove from pan; cover to keep warm. Melt 60g (2 ounces) butter in same pan; cook 1 tablespoon rinsed, drained baby capers, stirring, about 1 minute. Stir in 1 tablespoon lemon juice. Serve bundles drizzled with caper mixture; sprinkle with ⅓ cup coarsely chopped fresh flat-leaf parsley.

Nutritional count per serving *6.9g total fat (4.3g saturated fat); 347kJ (83 cal); 1.5g carbohydrate; 3.3g protein; 1.5g fibre*

GARLICKY BEANS WITH PINE NUTS

prep + cook time 20 minutes ✻ serves 4

Boil, steam or microwave 400g (12½ ounces) trimmed baby beans until just tender; drain. Rinse under cold water; drain. Transfer to a large bowl. Heat ¼ cup olive oil and 1 thinly sliced garlic clove in a small frying pan over low heat until garlic just changes colour. Add 2 tablespoons roasted pine nuts; stir until heated through. Drizzle mixture over beans.

Nutritional count per serving *18.9g total fat (2.2g saturated fat); 828kJ (198 cal); 2.8g carbohydrate; 3.2g protein; 3.2g fibre*

Pictured on page 426

creamed spinach

maple-glazed baby carrots

prosciutto-wrapped bean bundles

garlicky beans with pine nuts

See recipes page 425

MIXED BEAN SALAD WITH HAZELNUT BUTTER

prep + cook time 15 minutes ✻ serves 4

Boil, steam or microwave 250g (8 ounces) each trimmed green beans and yellow beans until tender; drain. Combine warm beans with 60g (2 ounces) chopped butter, ⅓ cup finely chopped roasted hazelnuts, ½ cup torn fresh flat-leaf parsley and 2 teaspoons finely grated lemon rind in a medium bowl.

Nutritional count per serving *19.5g total fat (8.4g saturated fat); 907kJ (217 cal); 3.8g carbohydrate; 4.7g protein; 5g fibre*

tomato and herb salad

baby spinach and parmesan salad

coleslaw

bean and tomato salad with hazelnut dressing

See recipes page 429

TOMATO AND HERB SALAD

prep time 10 minutes ✳ serves 4

Place 5 coarsely chopped medium tomatoes, 2 tablespoons coarsely chopped fresh mint, ¼ cup coarsely chopped fresh flat-leaf parsley and 2 tablespoons finely chopped fresh dill in a medium bowl. Place 2 crushed garlic cloves, 2 tablespoons lemon juice, 1 tablespoon olive oil and 2 teaspoons white vinegar in a screw-top jar; shake well. Drizzle dressing over salad; toss gently to combine.

Nutritional count per serving *4.9g total fat (0.7g saturated fat); 362kJ (87 cal); 5.7g carbohydrate; 2.6g protein; 3.5g fibre*

BABY SPINACH AND PARMESAN SALAD

prep time 10 minutes ✳ serves 4

Place 100g (3 ounces) baby spinach leaves, 50g (1½ ounces) shaved parmesan and 1 tablespoon toasted pine nuts in a large bowl. Combine 2 tablespoons balsamic vinegar and 1 tablespoon olive oil in a screw-top jar; shake well, season to taste. Drizzle dressing over salad; toss gently to combine.

Nutritional count per serving *13.4g total fat (1.3g saturated fat); 561kJ (134 cal); 0.7g carbohydrate; 2.3g protein; 1.1g fibre*

COLESLAW

prep time 15 minutes ✳ serves 4

Place 2 tablespoons mayonnaise and 1 tablespoon white wine vinegar in a screw-top jar; shake well. Place dressing in a large bowl with 2 cups finely shredded white cabbage, 1 cup finely shredded red cabbage, 1 coarsely grated medium carrot and 3 thinly sliced green onions (scallions); toss gently to combine.

Nutritional count per serving *3.1g total fat (0.4g saturated fat); 251kJ (60 cal); 4.9g carbohydrate; 1.6g protein; 3.3g fibre*

BEAN AND TOMATO SALAD WITH HAZELNUT DRESSING

prep + cook time 20 minutes ✳ serves 4

Combine ½ cup roasted, skinned, coarsely chopped hazelnuts, 2 tablespoons each hazelnut oil and apple cider vinegar and 1 teaspoon wholegrain mustard in a screw-top jar; shake well. Boil, steam or microwave 200g (6½ ounces) trimmed green beans until tender; drain. Rinse under cold water; drain. Combine beans, 250g (8 ounces) quartered cherry tomatoes and hazelnut mixture in a medium bowl; toss gently to combine.

Nutritional count per serving *20.2g total fat (1.8g saturated fat); 920kJ (220 cal); 3.6g carbohydrate; 4.2g protein; 4.3g fibre*

Pictured on page 428

PUDDINGS

AN AMAZING SELECTION OF DELICIOUS
EASY-TO-MAKE DESSERTS FOR ALL SEASONS

THE AUSTRALIAN WOMEN'S WEEKLY
TRIPLE TESTED
★ TEST KITCHEN ★

SAGO PLUM PUDDINGS

prep + cook time 4 hours (+ cooling & refrigeration) ✷ makes 4

You need to soak the sago overnight, so start the recipe the day before.

* **1 cup (250ml) milk**
* **⅓ cup (65g) sago (seed tapioca)**
* **1½ teaspoons bicarbonate of soda**
* **40g (1½ ounces) butter, chopped**
* **1 teaspoon finely grated orange rind**
* **1 egg**
* **½ cup (110g) caster (superfine) sugar**
* **⅔ cup (110g) sultanas**
* **1 cup (70g) stale breadcrumbs**

1 Place milk in a medium saucepan; bring to the boil then remove from heat. Stir in sago and soda (mixture will foam). Transfer to a large bowl; cool to room temperature. Cover sago, refrigerate overnight.

2 Grease four ¾-cup (180ml) straight sided or fluted dariole moulds; line bases with baking paper.

3 Melt butter. Add butter, rind, egg, sugar, sultanas and breadcrumbs to sago mixture; stir to combine.

4 Spoon sago mixture into moulds. Cut out rounds of baking paper 2cm (¾-inch) larger than top of moulds. Make a vertical pleat down the centre of the paper; place paper over moulds and secure with kitchen string.

5 Place moulds in a 4.5-litre (18-cup) slow cooker. Pour in enough boiling water to come halfway up side of moulds. Cook, covered, on high, for 3½ hours or until mixture is firm to touch.

6 Remove puddings from cooker; stand 5 minutes before turning onto serving plates.

Suitable to freeze.

Serving suggestion
Ice-cream or custard.

Tips *Sago and tapioca, while similar, are not the same and can't be substituted for each other. Sago may be found labelled as 'seed tapioca' on some packets. It is available from most health-food stores and supermarkets. Ensure the four moulds fit into your slow cooker before you start to cook.*

Nutritional count per serving *7.1g total fat (4.2g saturated fat); 1045kJ (250 cal); 43.2g carbohydrate; 3.8g protein; 1.2g fibre*

MIXED BERRY PUDDING

prep + cook time 3 hours ✳ serves 6

* 90g (3 ounces) butter
* ¾ cup (180ml) milk
* 1 teaspoon vanilla extract
* ½ cup (110g) caster (superfine) sugar
* 1⅔ cups (250g) self-raising flour
* 1 egg, beaten lightly
* 500g (1 pound) frozen mixed berries
* ½ cup (160g) raspberry jam
* 2 cups (500ml) boiling water

1 Grease a 4.5-litre (18-cup) slow cooker.
2 Heat butter and milk in a medium saucepan over low heat until butter is melted. Remove from heat; cool 5 minutes. Stir in extract and sugar, then sifted flour and egg.
3 Sprinkle berries over base of cooker; drop tablespoons of jam over berries. Spread pudding mixture over berry mixture. Gently pour the water over pudding mixture. Cook, covered, on high, for 2½ hours or until centre of pudding feels firm.
4 Remove insert from cooker. Stand pudding 10 minutes before serving warm.

Not suitable to freeze.

Serving suggestion
Dust with a little sifted icing (confectioners') sugar and accompany with custard.

Nutritional count per serving *15.2g total fat (9.2g saturated fat); 1935kJ (463 cal); 71.8g carbohydrate; 7.4g protein; 6.4g fibre*

SPANISH CARAMEL
RICE PUDDING

prep + cook time 2 hours 45 minutes ✳ serves 8

* 30g (1 ounce) butter
* 1¾ cups (350g) arborio rice
* 2 litres (8 cups) milk
* 2 cups (500ml) water
* 2 cinnamon sticks
* 1 vanilla bean, split, seeds scraped
* 2 x 380g (12 ounces) canned caramel filling
* ½ cup (80g) sultanas
* 1 cup (250ml) sweet sherry
* 1 teaspoon finely grated orange rind
* ¾ cup (100g) flaked almonds, toasted

1   Melt butter in a large saucepan over medium heat. Add rice; stir 2 minutes to coat well. Stir in milk, the water, cinnamon, vanilla bean and seeds; bring mixture to the boil.

2   Meanwhile, spoon caramel into a 4.5-litre (18-cup) slow cooker; whisk until smooth. Add rice mixture to caramel; whisk well to combine. Cover surface of pudding with baking paper. Cook, covered, on high, for 2¼ hours, stirring twice during cooking, or until rice is tender and liquid thickened.

3   Meanwhile, combine sultanas and sherry in a small saucepan; bring to the boil. Reduce heat to medium; cook mixture for 5 minutes or until liquid is reduced by half. Stir in rind and set aside until needed.

4   Discard cinnamon stick and vanilla bean. Serve warm or chilled topped with sherry sultanas and nuts.

Not suitable to freeze.

Serving suggestion
Pouring cream or yoghurt.

Tips *Italian arborio rice will hold its shape better than locally grown arborio. Canned caramel filling is found in the baking aisle in supermarkets. Any sweet sherry is fine, however one of the best is Pedro Ximénez, a sweet dark sherry with a rich raisin flavour. Leftover rice pudding will keep refrigerated for up to 1 week.*

Nutritional count per serving   *26.3g total fat (7.3g saturated fat); 2839kJ (678 cal); 92.7g carbohydrate; 11.9g protein; 1.6g fibre*

STEAMED
CHRISTMAS PUDDING

prep + cook time 5 hours 30 minutes ✳ serves 12

* 2½ cups (375g) chopped mixed dried fruit
* ¾ cup (120g) finely chopped dried seedless dates
* ½ cup (65g) finely chopped dried cranberries
* ¾ cup (180ml) water
* 1 cup (220g) firmly packed dark brown sugar
* 90g (3 ounces) butter, chopped coarsely
* 1 teaspoon bicarbonate of soda (baking soda)
* 2 eggs, beaten lightly
* ¾ cup (110g) plain (all-purpose) flour
* ¾ cup (110g) self-raising flour
* 1 teaspoon mixed spice
* ½ teaspoon ground cinnamon
* ¼ cup (60ml) dark rum

1 Combine dried fruit, the water, sugar and butter in a medium saucepan. Stir over heat until butter melts and sugar dissolves; bring to the boil. Reduce heat; simmer, uncovered, about 5 minutes. Transfer mixture to a large heatproof bowl, stir in soda; cool 10 minutes.

2 Stir eggs, sifted dry ingredients and rum into fruit mixture.

3 Grease a 2-litre (8-cup) pudding steamer; spoon mixture into steamer. Top with pleated baking paper and foil; secure with kitchen string or lid.

4 Place pudding in a 4.5-litre (18-cup) slow cooker with enough boiling water to come halfway up side of steamer. Cook, covered, on high, about 5 hours, replenishing with boiling water as necessary to maintain level.

5 Remove pudding from cooker, stand 10 minutes before turning onto a plate.

Suitable to freeze.

Serving suggestion *Cream or custard.*

Tips *The pleat in the baking paper and foil allow the pudding mixture to rise. Pudding can be frozen whole or in serving-sized wedges.*

Nutritional count per serving *7.6g total fat (4.5g saturated fat); 1463kJ (350 cal); 61.5g carbohydrate; 4.1g protein; 3.7g fibre*

POACHED PEARS
IN CHAMPAGNE AND ROSEWATER

prep + cook time 5 hours (+ cooling) ✳ serves 6

* 6 medium firm pears (1.4kg)
* 3 cups (750ml) sparkling wine
* 1 cup (220g) caster (superfine) sugar
* 4 x 5cm (2-inch) strips lemon rind
* 3 teaspoons rosewater
* 1 vanilla bean, split, seeds scraped

1 Peel pears, leaving stems intact.
2 Combine sparkling wine, sugar, rind, rosewater, vanilla bean and seeds in a 4.5-litre (18-cup) slow cooker.

3 Lay pears down in cooker to submerge in sparkling wine mixture. Cook, covered, on high, for 4½ hours or until pears are tender.
4 Place 1 cup of the poaching liquid in a small saucepan; bring to the boil. Boil, uncovered, for 7 minutes or until syrup is reduced by half; cool.
5 Place pears in a large deep bowl; add remaining poaching liquid, cool. Serve pears drizzled with syrup.

Not suitable to freeze.

Serving suggestion
Cream, ice-cream or custard.

Tips *We used packham pears in this recipe. Refrigerate any leftover poaching liquid for up to 1 month. Use for poaching more pears or stone fruit.*

Nutritional count per serving *0.2g total fat (0g saturated fat); 1342kJ (321 cal); 61.5g carbohydrate; 0.8g protein; 3.2g fibre*

CARAMEL MUD CAKE

prep + cook time 2 hours 30 minutes (+ cooling) ✱ serves 12

✱ **180g (5½ ounces) white chocolate,
chopped finely**
✱ **60g (2 ounces) unsalted butter,
chopped finely**
✱ **5 eggs, separated**
✱ **2 teaspoons vanilla extract**
✱ **½ cup (60g) ground almonds**
✱ **¼ cup (35g) self-raising flour**
✱ **⅓ cup (75g) firmly packed
dark brown sugar**

CARAMEL ICING
✱ **60g (2 ounces) unsalted butter, chopped**
✱ **½ cup (110g) firmly packed
dark brown sugar**
✱ **½ cup (125ml) milk**
✱ **⅔ cup (110g) icing (confectioners') sugar**

1   Grease a 2-litre (8-cup) pudding steamer; line base with baking paper.
2   Combine chocolate and butter in a medium saucepan; stir over low heat until smooth. Remove from heat; cool 10 minutes. Stir egg yolks and extract, then ground almonds and sifted flour into chocolate mixture.

3   Beat egg whites in a small bowl with an electric mixer until soft peaks form; add sugar and beat until sugar dissolves. Fold egg white mixture into chocolate mixture in two batches. Spoon mixture into steamer.
4   Place steamer, without lid, in a 4.5-litre (18-cup) slow cooker with enough boiling water to come halfway up side of steamer. Cook, covered, on high, for 2 hours or until firm.
5   Remove cake from cooker. Immediately turn onto a baking-paper-lined wire rack; cool cake completely.
6   Make caramel icing. Spread cake with icing.

CARAMEL ICING Melt butter in a small saucepan over medium heat. Add brown sugar and milk; cook, stirring, over medium heat until sugar dissolves. Bring to the boil. Reduce heat; simmer about 1 minute. Remove from heat. Whisk in sifted icing sugar until smooth.

Suitable to freeze
at the end of step 5.

Serving suggestion
*Pouring cream or
ice-cream and berries.*

Nutritional count per serving *18.7g total fat (4g saturated fat); 1353kJ (323 cal); 34.6g carbohydrate; 5.2g protein; 0.6g fibre*

FIG AND CRANBERRY
BREAD PUDDING

prep + cook time 4 hours 20 minutes ✻ serves 6

* 315g (10 ounces) crusty white bread, sliced thickly
* ½ cup (160g) fig jam
* ½ cup (65g) finely chopped dried cranberries
* 2½ cups (625ml) milk
* 600ml pouring cream
* ½ cup (110g) caster (superfine) sugar
* 1 teaspoon vanilla extract
* 6 eggs

1 Grease a 4.5-litre (18-cup) slow cooker. Spread bread with jam. Layer bread, overlapping, in cooker; sprinkle with cranberries.

2 Combine milk, cream, sugar and extract in a medium saucepan; bring to the boil. Whisk eggs in a medium bowl; gradually whisk in hot milk mixture. Pour custard over bread; stand 5 minutes.

3 Cook, covered, on low, about 4 hours.

4 Remove insert from cooker. Stand pudding 5 minutes before serving. Serve pudding dusted with a little sifted icing sugar, if you like.

Not suitable to freeze.

Serving suggestion *Cream or ice-cream.*

Tips *We used a small vienna loaf in this recipe. It's important not to lift the lid during the cooking time as condensation runs down the side of the cooker causing damp patches on the pudding.*

Nutritional count per serving *54.6g total fat (33.2g saturated fat); 3670kJ (878 cal); 78.8g carbohydrate; 17.2g protein; 2.9g fibre*

COFFEE AND
HAZELNUT PUDDING

prep + cook time 3 hours 15 minutes ✳ serves 10

* 4 eggs
* ⅔ cup (150g) firmly packed brown sugar
* 1⅓ cups (160g) ground hazelnuts
* ½ cup (125ml) pouring cream
* ¼ cup (15g) espresso coffee granules
* ⅔ cup (100g) self-raising flour
* 2 cups (500ml) vanilla custard

1 Whisk eggs and sugar in a large bowl until combined. Whisk in ground hazelnuts.
2 Place cream in a small saucepan; bring to the boil then remove from heat. Whisk in coffee granules until dissolved. Whisk coffee mixture into hazelnut mixture. Sift flour over hazelnut mixture; stir to combine.

3 Grease a 2-litre (8-cup) pudding steamer. Spoon mixture into steamer. Top with baking paper and foil; secure with kitchen string. Alternatively, cover with a lid.
4 Place steamer in a 4.5-litre (18-cup) slow cooker with enough boiling water to come halfway up side of steamer. Cook, covered, on high, about 2¾ hours, replenishing with boiling water as necessary to maintain level.
5 Remove pudding from cooker; stand 10 minutes before turning pudding onto a serving plate.
6 Serve pudding with custard.

Suitable to freeze *at the end of step 5.*

Tip *To cover pudding, layer a sheet of foil and baking paper together, large enough to cover the top generously. Fold a vertical pleat; this will give the pudding space to rise.*

Nutritional count per serving *18.2g total fat (5.1g saturated fat); 1350kJ (322 cal); 31.6g carbohydrate; 8.4g protein; 2.3g fibre*

CREAMY RICE PUDDING
WITH CINNAMON SUGAR

prep + cook time 6 hours 10 minutes ✳ serves 6

* 1 cup (200g) white medium-grain rice
* 1.25 litres (5 cups) milk
* ½ cup (110g) caster (superfine) sugar
* 5cm (2-inch) strip orange rind
* 1 vanilla bean, split, seeds scraped
* 2 tablespoons caster (superfine) sugar, extra
* 1 teaspoon ground cinnamon

1 Combine rice, milk, sugar, rind, vanilla bean and seeds in a 4.5-litre (18-cup) slow cooker.
2 Cook, covered, on low, for 6 hours, stirring twice, or until rice is tender. Discard rind.
3 Combine extra sugar and cinnamon in a small bowl, sprinkle over pudding. Remove vanilla bean before serving.

Not suitable to freeze.

Serving suggestion
Stew 150g frozen raspberries with ¼ cup caster sugar and 1 tablespoon water. Serve stewed fruit drizzled with cream.

Tip *The vanilla bean can be reused; wash and dry well, store in an airtight container or add to a container of sugar to make vanilla sugar.*

Nutritional count per serving *8.3g total fat (5.4g saturated fat); 1513kJ (362 cal); 61.5g carbohydrate; 9.3g protein; 0.3g fibre*

LEMON AND LIME
PUDDINGS

prep + cook time 1 hour 30 minutes ✳ makes 4

* **90g (3 ounces) butter, melted**
* **1 teaspoon finely grated lemon rind**
* **½ teaspoon finely grated lime rind**
* **¾ cup (165g) caster (superfine) sugar**
* **2 eggs, separated**
* **⅓ cup (50g) self-raising flour**
* **2 tablespoons lemon juice**
* **1 tablespoon lime juice**
* **1 cup (250ml) milk**

1   Grease four ¾-cup (180ml) deep heatproof dishes.

2   Combine butter, rinds, sugar and egg yolks in a medium bowl. Whisk in sifted flour, then juices. Gradually whisk in milk; batter should be smooth and runny.

3   Beat egg whites in a small bowl with an electric mixer until soft peaks form; fold into batter, in two batches. Divide mixture between dishes.

4   Place dishes in a 4.5-litre (18-cup) slow cooker; pour enough boiling water into cooker to come halfway up sides of dishes. Cook, covered, on high, for 1 hour or until firm. Remove dishes from cooker. Stand puddings 10 minutes before serving.

Not suitable to freeze.

Serving suggestion
Dust with sifted icing (confectioners') sugar and accompany with double cream.

Tip *Ensure the four dishes fit into your slow cooker before you start to cook.*

Nutritional count per serving *23.7g total fat (14.6g saturated fat); 1873kJ (448 cal); 53.8g carbohydrate; 6.9g protein; 0.5g fibre*

VANILLA AND RED WINE
POACHED PEARS

prep + cook time 4 hours 50 minutes (+ cooling) ✱ serves 6

* ✱ 6 medium firm pears (1.4kg)
* ✱ 2 cups (500ml) dry red wine
* ✱ 1½ cups (375ml) water
* ✱ 5cm (2-inch) strip orange rind
* ✱ ½ cup (125ml) orange juice
* ✱ 1 cup (220g) caster (superfine) sugar
* ✱ 1 cinnamon stick
* ✱ 1 vanilla bean, split, seeds scraped

1 Peel pears, leaving stems intact.
2 Combine wine, the water, rind, juice, sugar, cinnamon, vanilla bean and seeds in a 4.5-litre (18-cup) slow cooker.

3 Lay pears down in cooker to cover in wine mixture. Cook, covered, on high, for 4½ hours or until pears are tender.
4 Place 1 cup of the poaching liquid in a small saucepan; bring to the boil. Boil, uncovered, for 7 minutes or until syrup is reduced by half; cool.
5 Place pears in a large deep bowl; add remaining poaching liquid, cool. Serve pears drizzled with syrup.

Not suitable to freeze.

Serving suggestion
Whipped cream or vanilla ice-cream.

Tips *We used packham pears in this recipe. Refrigerate any leftover poaching liquid for up to 1 month. Use for poaching more pears or stone fruit.*

Nutritional count per serving *0.2g total fat (0g saturated fat); 1225kJ (293 cal); 55.9g carbohydrate; 0.8g protein; 3.3g fibre*

CHOCOLATE
SELF-SAUCING PUDDING

prep + cook time 2 hours 50 minutes ✳ serves 6

* 90g (3 ounces) butter
* ¾ cup (180ml) milk
* 1 teaspoon vanilla extract
* 1 cup (220g) caster (superfine) sugar
* 1½ cups (225g) self-raising flour
* 2 tablespoons cocoa powder
* 1 egg, beaten lightly
* 1 cup (220g) firmly packed
light brown sugar
* 2 tablespoons cocoa powder, extra
* 2½ cups (625ml) boiling water

1   Grease a 4.5-litre (18-cup) slow cooker.
2   Melt butter in milk over low heat in a medium saucepan. Remove from heat; cool 5 minutes. Stir in extract and caster sugar, then sifted flour and cocoa, and egg. Spread mixture into cooker.
3   Sift brown sugar and extra cocoa evenly over mixture; gently pour the water over mixture. Cook, covered, on high, for 2½ hours or until centre is firm.
4   Remove insert from cooker. Stand pudding 5 minutes before serving.

Not suitable to freeze.

Serving suggestion
Dust with sifted icing (confectioners') sugar and accompany with cream or ice-cream.

Nutritional count per serving   *15.5g total fat (9.6g saturated fat); 2424kJ (580 cal); 101.3g carbohydrate; 6.9g protein; 1.6g fibre*

PASSIONFRUIT
CRÈME CARAMELS

prep + cook time 2 hours 30 minutes (+ refrigeration) ✳ makes 6

* ½ cup (110g) caster (superfine) sugar
* ¼ cup (60ml) water
* 2 tablespoons passionfruit pulp
* 1 cup (250ml) milk
* ¾ cup (180ml) pouring cream
* 2 x 5cm (2-inch) strips lemon rind
* 3 eggs
* 2 egg yolks
* ⅓ cup (75g) caster (superfine) sugar, extra

1   Stir sugar and the water in a small saucepan over high heat, without boiling, until sugar dissolves; bring to the boil. Boil, uncovered, without stirring, until mixture is deep caramel in colour. Remove from heat; allow bubbles to subside, gently stir in passionfruit pulp. Divide toffee mixture into six greased ½-cup (125ml) metal moulds. Place moulds in a 4.5-litre (18-cup) slow cooker.

2   Meanwhile, combine milk, cream and rind in a medium saucepan; bring to the boil. Whisk eggs, egg yolks and extra sugar in a large bowl until combined; gradually whisk in hot milk mixture. Strain mixture into a large jug; discard rind. Pour mixture into moulds. Pour enough boiling water into cooker to come halfway up sides of moulds.
3   Cook, covered, on low, for 1½ hours or until crème caramels feel firm. Remove moulds from cooker. Cover moulds; refrigerate overnight.
4   Gently ease crème caramels from sides of moulds; invert onto serving plates.

Not suitable to freeze.

Tip *Ensure the six moulds fit into your slow cooker before you start to cook.*

Nutritional count per serving *19.1g total fat (11.1g saturated fat); 1371kJ (328 cal); 34.2g carbohydrate; 6.6g protein; 0.9g fibre*

MANDARIN
AND ALMOND PUDDING

prep + cook time 5 hours 30 minutes ✳ serves 8

* ✳ **4 small mandarins (400g)**
* ✳ **4 eggs**
* ✳ **⅔ cup (150g) caster (superfine) sugar**
* ✳ **1⅓ cups (160g) ground almonds**
* ✳ **⅔ cup (100g) self-raising flour**

1 Place washed unpeeled mandarins in a 4.5-litre (18-cup) slow cooker; cover with hot water. Cook, covered, on high, about 2 hours.

2 Trim ends from mandarins; discard. Halve mandarins; remove and discard seeds. Process mandarins, including rind, until mixture is pulpy.

3 Grease a 2-litre (8-cup) pudding steamer.

4 Beat eggs and sugar in a small bowl with electric mixer until thick and creamy; fold in ground almonds, sifted flour and mandarin pulp. Spoon mixture into steamer. Top with pleated baking paper and foil; secure with kitchen string or lid.

5 Place steamer in cooker with enough boiling water to come halfway up side of steamer. Cook, covered, on high, about 3 hours, replenishing with boiling water as necessary to maintain level. Stand pudding 5 minutes before turning onto a plate.

Not suitable to freeze.

Serving suggestion
Cream, custard or ice-cream.

Tip *The pleat in the baking paper and foil allows the pudding mixture to rise.*

Nutritional count per serving *13.9g total fat (1.6g saturated fat); 1246kJ (298 cal); 32.5g carbohydrate; 9g protein; 3.2g fibre*

NUTTY BAKED APPLES
WITH BUTTERSCOTCH SAUCE

prep + cook time 3 hours 20 minutes * serves 6

* 6 small green apples (780g)
* 90g (3 ounces) butter, chopped finely
* ¼ cup (35g) slivered almonds
* ¼ cup (30g) finely chopped walnuts
* ½ teaspoon ground cinnamon
* 1 cup (220g) firmly packed
light brown sugar
* ¾ cup (180ml) pouring cream
* ½ cup (125ml) apple juice

1   Core unpeeled apples about three-quarters of the way through, making a hole 4cm (1½ inches) in diameter. Use a small sharp knife to score around centre of each apple.

2   Combine one-third of the butter with nuts, cinnamon and ¼ cup of the sugar in a small bowl. Press mixture into apple cavities.
3   Combine cream, juice, remaining butter and sugar in a 4.5-litre (18-cup) slow cooker. Stand apples upright in sauce. Cook, covered, on high, for 2½ hours, turning apples once, or until apples are tender.
4   Remove apples from cooker; cover to keep warm. Drain sauce into a small saucepan; bring to the boil. Boil, uncovered, for 5 minutes or until sauce is thickened slightly.
5   Serve apples drizzled with sauce.

Not suitable to freeze.

Serving suggestion
*Custard, cream or
ice-cream.*

Tip *Make sure the
apples don't touch the
side of the slow cooker.*

Nutritional count per serving *32.1g total fat (17.1g saturated fat); 2107kJ (504 cal); 50.1g carbohydrate; 2.9g protein; 2.8g fibre*

CROISSANT CUSTARD
PUDDING WITH STRAWBERRIES

prep + cook time 3 hours 15 minutes ✳ serves 8

* **4 croissants (200g)**
* **½ cup (160g) strawberry jam**
* **80g (2½ ounces) white eating chocolate, chopped finely**
* **2½ cups (625ml) milk**
* **600ml pouring cream**
* **½ cup (110g) caster (superfine) sugar**
* **1 teaspoon vanilla extract**
* **6 eggs**

MACERATED STRAWBERRIES
* **250g (8 ounces) strawberries, halved**
* **1 tablespoon orange-flavoured liqueur**
* **1 tablespoon icing (confectioners') sugar**

1 Grease a 4.5-litre (18-cup) slow cooker.
2 Split croissants in half; spread cut-sides with jam; sprinkle chocolate over half the croissants, sandwich with remaining croissants. Place croissants in cooker.

3 Combine milk, cream, sugar and extract in a medium saucepan; bring to the boil. Whisk eggs in a large bowl; gradually whisk in hot milk mixture. Pour custard over croissants; stand 10 minutes.
4 Cook, covered, on low, for 2¾ hours or until firm.
5 Meanwhile, make macerated strawberries.
6 Remove insert from cooker. Stand pudding 5 minutes before serving. Serve pudding with macerated strawberries and drizzled with a little extra cream, if you like.

MACERATED STRAWBERRIES Combine ingredients in a medium bowl; stand 30 minutes.

Not suitable to freeze.

Serving suggestion *Ice-cream or cream.*

Tip *It's important not to lift the lid during the cooking time as condensation runs down the side of the cooker causing damp patches on the pudding.*

Nutritional count per serving *44.7g total fat (28.8g saturated fat); 2658kJ (636 cal); 51.4g carbohydrate; 7.9g protein; 1.7g fibre*

CHOCOLATE AND
CHERRY PUDDINGS

prep + cook time 1 hour 45 minutes ✳ makes 4

* ✳ **125g (4 ounces) butter, softened**
* ✳ **¾ cup (165g) caster (superfine) sugar**
* ✳ **1 teaspoon vanilla extract**
* ✳ **2 eggs**
* ✳ **¾ cup (110g) self-raising flour**
* ✳ **½ cup (50g) dutch cocoa**
* ✳ **¼ cup (60ml) milk**
* ✳ **60g (2 ounces) dark (semi-sweet) chocolate, chopped finely**
* ✳ **670g (15 ounces) seeded morello cherries in syrup, drained**
* ✳ **⅓ cup (80ml) thick (double) cream**

1 Grease four 1-cup (250ml) deep heatproof dishes.

2 Beat butter, sugar and extract in a small bowl with an electric mixer until light and fluffy. Beat in eggs, one at a time. Stir in the sifted dry ingredients then milk and chocolate. Fold in half the cherries. Divide mixture between dishes.

3 Place dishes in a 4.5-litre (18-cup) slow cooker. Pour in enough boiling water to come halfway up sides of dishes. Cook, covered, on high, for 1½ hours or until mixture is firm. Remove puddings from cooker; dust with extra cocoa, if you like. Serve with cream and remaining cherries.

Not suitable to freeze.

Tip *Ensure the four dishes fit into your slow cooker before you start to cook.*

Nutritional count per serving *42.3g total fat (23.5g saturated fat); 2971kJ (710 cal); 72.2g carbohydrate; 10.1g protein; 2.5g fibre*

STICKY DATE
AND FIG STEAMED PUDDING

prep + cook time 5 hours 30 minutes ✳ serves 12

✳ 2 cups (300g) finely chopped seeded
dried dates
✳ ½ cup (100g) finely chopped dried figs
✳ 1 cup (250ml) water
✳ 1 cup (220g) firmly packed
light brown sugar
✳ 90g (3 ounces) butter, chopped coarsely
✳ 1 teaspoon bicarbonate of soda
(baking soda)
✳ 2 eggs, beaten lightly
✳ ¾ cup (110g) plain (all-purpose) flour
✳ ¾ cup (110g) self-raising flour

BUTTERSCOTCH SAUCE
✳ ¾ cup (165g) firmly packed
light brown sugar
✳ 1 cup (250ml) pouring cream
✳ 125g (4 ounces) unsalted butter,
chopped coarsely

1 Combine dried fruit, the water, sugar and
butter in a medium saucepan; stir over heat until
butter melts and sugar dissolves. Bring to the boil.
Reduce heat; simmer, uncovered, about 5 minutes.
Transfer mixture to a large heatproof bowl, stir
in soda; cool 10 minutes.

2 Stir eggs and sifted dry ingredients into
fruit mixture.
3 Grease a 2-litre (8-cup) pudding steamer; spoon
mixture into steamer. Top with pleated baking
paper and foil; secure with kitchen string or lid.
4 Place steamer in a 4.5-litre (18-cup) slow
cooker; pour enough boiling water into cooker
to come halfway up side of steamer. Cook,
covered, on high, about 5 hours, replenishing
with boiling water as necessary to maintain level.
5 Remove pudding from cooker. Stand
10 minutes before turning onto plate.
6 Meanwhile, make butterscotch sauce.
7 Serve pudding with sauce, and a dollop of
thick cream, if you like.

BUTTERSCOTCH SAUCE Stir ingredients in
a medium saucepan over heat, without boiling,
until sugar dissolves; bring to the boil. Reduce
heat; simmer, uncovered, about 2 minutes.

Suitable to freeze
at the end of step 5.

Nutritional count per serving *24.9g total fat (15.9g saturated fat); 2174kJ (520 cal); 70.6g carbohydrate; 4.4g protein; 4.3g fibre*

CHOCOLATE FUDGE SAUCE

prep + cook time 15 minutes ✳ makes 1 cup

Stir 20g (¾ ounce) butter and 200g (6½ ounces) coarsely chopped dark (semi-sweet) chocolate in a small heatproof bowl set over a small saucepan of simmering water until smooth. Add ¼ teaspoon vanilla extract and ½ cup pouring cream; stir until combined. Serve sauce warm.

Nutritional count per tablespoon *10.6g total fat (6.7g saturated fat); 585kJ (140 cal); 10.7g carbohydrate; 1.1g protein; 0.2g fibre*

coffee liqueur sauce

crème anglaise

brandy custard

hazelnut cream

See recipes page 470

COFFEE LIQUEUR SAUCE

prep + cook time 20 minutes (+ refrigeration)

✳ **makes 2 cups**

Combine ¼ cup pouring cream and ⅔ cup freshly brewed strong coffee in a small saucepan; stir over heat, without boiling, until hot. Remove from heat; add 250g (8 ounces) coarsely chopped white chocolate, whisk until smooth. Stir in 1 tablespoon coffee-flavoured liqueur. Transfer sauce to a small bowl; cover, refrigerate 30 minutes, stirring occasionally.

Nutritional count per tablespoon *4.5g total fat (2.9g saturated fat); 297kJ (71 cal); 6.2g carbohydrate; 0.8g protein; 0g fibre*

CRÈME ANGLAISE

prep + cook time 30 minutes (+ refrigeration)

✳ **makes 1½ cups**

Split 1 vanilla bean in half lengthways; scrape seeds into a medium saucepan, add bean, 1½ cups milk and 1 tablespoon caster (superfine) sugar. Boil, then strain into a large jug. Discard pod. Whisk 4 egg yolks and ¼ cup caster (superfine) sugar in a medium heatproof bowl set over a medium saucepan of simmering water until thick and creamy; gradually whisk in hot milk mixture. Return custard mixture to pan; stir, over low heat, until mixture is thick enough to coat the back of a spoon. Refrigerate custard 1 hour or until cold.

Nutritional count per tablespoon *2.1g total fat (0.9g saturated fat); 184kJ (44 cal); 5.2g carbohydrate; 1.4g protein; 0g fibre*

BRANDY CUSTARD

prep + cook time 10 minutes ✳ **makes 3½ cups**

Combine 300ml thickened (heavy) cream, 1 tablespoon sifted icing (confectioners') sugar and seeds from 1 vanilla bean in a small bowl; beat with electric mixer until soft peaks form. Stir 500g (1 pound) thick custard and 2 tablespoons brandy in a small saucepan over low heat until warm. Transfer to a large bowl; gently fold cream mixture into warm custard.

Nutritional count per tablespoon *3.1g total fat (2g saturated fat); 167kJ (40 cal); 2.2g carbohydrate; 0.5g protein; 0g fibre*

HAZELNUT CREAM

prep time 20 minutes ✳ **makes 1 cup**

Beat 1 tablespoon hazelnut-flavoured liqueur, ⅔ cup pouring cream and 1 tablespoon caster (superfine) sugar in a small bowl with an electric mixer until soft peaks form; stir in ⅓ cup coarsely chopped roasted hazelnuts.

Nutritional count per tablespoon *8.1g total fat (3.9g saturated fat); 380kJ (91 cal); 2.8g carbohydrate; 0.8g protein; 0.4g fibre*

Pictured on page 469

STRAWBERRY COULIS

prep time 10 minutes ✳ makes 1 cup

Push 300g (9½ ounces) thawed frozen strawberries through a fine sieve into a small bowl; discard seeds.

Stir in 1 tablespoon sifted icing (confectioners') sugar.

Nutritional count per tablespoon *0.3g total fat (0g saturated fat); 42kJ (10 cal); 1.6g carbohydrate; 0.4g protein; 0.6g fibre*

STOCKS

FISH

prep + cook time 30 minutes ✳
makes 2.5 litres (10 cups)

* 1.5kg (3 pounds) white-fleshed fish bones
* 3 litres (12 cups) water
* 1 medium onion (150g), chopped coarsely
* 2 celery stalks (300g), trimmed, chopped coarsely
* 2 bay leaves
* 1 teaspoon black peppercorns

1   Combine ingredients in a large saucepan; simmer gently, uncovered, about 20 minutes. Strain stock through a fine sieve into a large heatproof bowl; discard solids. If not using immediately, cool slightly, then refrigerate to cool completely. Store, refrigerated, for up to 1 week or freeze for up to 1 month. Bring to the boil before using.

VEGETABLE

prep + cook time 1 hour 45 minutes ✳
makes 3.5 litres (14 cups)

* 2 large carrots (360g), chopped coarsely
* 2 large parsnips (700g), chopped coarsely
* 4 medium onions (600g), chopped coarsely
* 10 celery stalks (1.5kg), trimmed, chopped coarsely
* 4 bay leaves
* 2 teaspoons black peppercorns
* 6 litres (24 cups) water

1   Combine ingredients in a large saucepan or stockpot; bring to the boil. Reduce heat; simmer, uncovered, about 1½ hours, skimming surface occasionally. Strain stock through a fine sieve into a large heatproof bowl; discard solids. If not using immediately, cool slightly, then refrigerate to cool completely. Store, refrigerated, for up to 1 week or freeze for up to 1 month.

BEEF

prep + cook time 5 hours 15 minutes ✳
makes 3.5 litres (14 cups)

* 2kg (4 pounds) meaty beef bones
* 2 medium brown onions (300g),
chopped coarsely
* 5.5 litres water (22 cups)
* 2 celery stalks (300g), trimmed,
chopped coarsely
* 2 medium carrots (240g), chopped coarsely
* 3 bay leaves
* 2 teaspoons black peppercorns
* 3 litres water (12 cups), extra

1   Preheat oven to 200°C/400°F.
2   Roast bones for 1 hour or until browned.
3   Transfer bones to a large saucepan or
stockpot. Add onion, the water, vegetables,
bay leaves and peppercorns; bring to the boil.
Reduce heat; simmer, uncovered, about 3 hours,
skimming surface occasionally. Add extra water;
simmer, uncovered, about 1 hour. Strain stock
through a fine sieve into a large heatproof bowl;
discard solids. If not using immediately, cool
slightly, then refrigerate stock to cool completely.
Skim and discard surface fat before using. Store,
refrigerated, for up to 1 week or freeze for up to
1 month. Bring to the boil before using.

CHICKEN

prep + cook time 2 hours 15 minutes ✳
makes 3.5 litres (14 cups)

* 2kg (4 pounds) chicken bones
* 2 medium onions (300g), chopped coarsely
* 2 celery stalks (300g), trimmed,
chopped coarsely
* 2 medium carrots (240g), chopped coarsely
* 3 bay leaves
* 2 teaspoons black peppercorns
* 5 litres (20 cups) water

1   Combine ingredients in a large saucepan or
stockpot; bring to the boil. Reduce heat; simmer,
uncovered, about 2 hours, skimming surface
occasionally. Strain stock through a fine sieve
into a large heatproof bowl; discard solids. If not
using immediately, cool slightly, then refrigerate
stock to cool completely. Skim and discard
surface fat before using. Store, refrigerated, for
up to 1 week or freeze for up to 1 month. Bring
to the boil before using.

GLOSSARY

ALLSPICE
also known as pimento or jamaican pepper; so-named because it tastes like a combination of nutmeg, cumin, clove and cinnamon. Available whole (a dark-brown berry the size of a pea) or ground.

ALMONDS
flat, pointy-tipped nuts with a pitted brown shell enclosing a creamy white kernel which is covered by a brown skin.
blanched brown skins removed.
flaked paper-thin slices.
ground also called almond meal; nuts are powdered to a coarse flour-like texture.
slivered small pieces cut lengthways.

ARTICHOKES
globe large flower-bud member of the thistle family; has tough petal-like leaves, and is edible in part when cooked.
hearts tender centre of the globe artichoke; can be harvested from the plant after the prickly choke is removed. Cooked hearts can be bought from delicatessens or canned in brine.
jerusalem neither from Jerusalem nor an artichoke, this crunchy brown-skinned tuber tastes a bit like a water chestnut and belongs to the sunflower family. Eat raw in salads or cooked like potatoes.

BACON SLICES
also known as bacon rashers; made from cured, smoked pork.

BAKING PAPER
also called parchment paper or baking parchment; a silicone-coated paper that is primarily used for lining baking pans and oven trays so cakes and biscuits won't stick, making removal easy.

BAKING POWDER
a raising agent consisting mainly of two parts cream of tartar to one part bicarbonate of soda (baking soda).

BARLEY
a nutritious grain used in soups and stews. Hulled barley, the least processed, is high in fibre. Pearl barley has had the husk removed then been steamed and polished so that only the 'pearl' of the original grain remains, much the same as white rice.

BASIL
holy also called kra pao or hot basil; different from thai and sweet basil, having an almost hot, spicy flavour similar to clove. Used in many Thai dishes, especially curries; distinguished from thai basil by tiny 'hairs' on its leaves and stems.
sweet the most common type of basil; used extensively in Italian dishes and one of the main ingredients in pesto.
thai also called horapa; different from holy basil and sweet basil in both look and taste, having smaller leaves and purplish stems. It has a slight aniseed taste and is one of the identifying flavours of Thai food.

BAY LEAVES
aromatic leaves from the bay tree available fresh or dried; adds a strong, slightly peppery flavour.

BEANS
black-eyed also called black-eyed peas or cow peas. Mild-flavoured and thin-skinned, so they cook faster than most other beans. Often served in the American south with pork and cornbread.
black turtle also known as black or black kidney beans; an earthy-flavoured dried bean completely different from the better-known chinese black beans (which are fermented soya beans).
borlotti also called roman beans or pink beans, can be eaten fresh or dried. Interchangeable with pinto beans due to their similarity in appearance – pale pink or beige with dark red streaks.
broad (fava) also called windsor and horse beans; available dried, fresh, canned and frozen. Fresh should be peeled twice (discarding both the outer long green pod and the beige-green tough inner shell); the frozen beans have had their pods removed but the beige shell still needs removal.
butter cans labelled butter beans are, in fact, cannellini beans. Confusingly butter is also another name for lima beans, sold both dried and canned; a large beige bean having a mealy texture and mild taste.
cannellini small white bean similar in appearance and flavour to haricot, great northern and navy beans, all of which can be substituted for the other.
green also known as french or string beans (although the tough string they once had has generally been bred out of them), this long thin fresh bean is consumed in its entirety once cooked.
haricot the haricot bean family includes navy beans and cannellini. All are mild-flavoured white beans which are interchangeable.
kidney medium-sized red bean, slightly floury in texture, yet sweet in flavour.
lima large, flat, kidney-shaped, beige dried and canned beans. Also known as butter beans.
snake long (about 40cm/16 inches), thin, round, fresh green bean; Asian in origin with a taste similar to green beans. Are also known as yard-long beans because of their (pre-metric) length.
soy the most nutritious of all legumes; high in protein and low in carbohydrate and the source of products such as tofu, soy milk, soy sauce, tamari and miso. Also available dried and canned.
white a generic term we use for canned or dried cannellini, haricot, navy or great northern beans belonging to the same family, phaseolus vulgaris.

BEEF
blade taken from the shoulder; isn't as tender as other cuts of beef, so it needs slow-roasting to achieve best results.
brisket a cheaper cut from the belly; available with or without bones as a joint for slow-roasting, or for stewing and casseroling as cubes or mince.
cheeks the cheek muscle of a cow. It's a very tough and lean cut of meat and is most often used for braising or slow cooking to produce a tender result.
chuck from the neck and shoulder of the cow; tends to be chewy but flavourful and inexpensive. A good cut for stewing or braising.
corned silverside also known as topside roast; sold vacuum-sealed in brine.
gravy beef also known as beef shin or shank, cut from the lower shin.
osso buco literally meaning 'bone with a hole', osso buco is cut from the shin of the hind leg. It is also known as knuckle.
oxtail a flavourful cut originally from the ox but today more likely to be from any beef cattle; requires long, slow cooking so it is perfect for curries and stews.
sausages seasoned and spiced minced (ground) beef mixed with cereal and packed into casings. Also known as snags or bangers.
shank see gravy beef, above.
short ribs cut from the rib section; usually larger, more tender and meatier than pork spare ribs.

BEETROOT (BEETS)
also known as red beets; firm, round root vegetable.

BICARBONATE OF SODA (BAKING SODA)
a raising agent.

GLOSSARY

BRANDY
a general term for a liqueur distilled from wine grapes (usually white), it is used as the basis for many sweet-to-dry spirits made with fruits. Cognac and Armagnac are two of the finest aged brandies available.

BREAD
brioche French in origin; a rich, yeast-leavened, cake-like bread made with butter and eggs. Available from cake or specialty bread shops.
ciabatta in Italian, the word means slipper, the traditional shape of this popular crisp-crusted, open-textured white sourdough bread.
french stick a long, narrow cylindrical loaf with a crisp brown crust and a light chewy interior. Also called french loaf.
naan the rather thick, leavened bread associated with the tandoori dishes of northern India, where it is baked pressed against the inside wall of a heated tandoor (clay oven). Sold in most supermarkets.
pitta also known as lebanese bread. This wheat-flour pocket bread is sold in large, flat pieces that separate into two thin rounds. Also available in small thick pieces called pocket pitta.
sourdough so-named, not because it's sour in taste, but because it's made by using a small amount of 'starter dough', which contains a yeast culture, mixed into flour and water. Part of the resulting dough is then saved to use as the starter dough next time.
tortilla thin, round unleavened bread; can be made at home or purchased frozen, fresh or vacuum-packed. Two kinds are available, one made from wheat flour and the other from corn.
turkish also called pide. Sold in long (about 45cm/18 inches) flat loaves and individual rounds; made from wheat flour and sprinkled with black onion seeds.

BREADCRUMBS
fresh bread, usually white, processed into crumbs.
packaged prepared fine-textured but crunchy white breadcrumbs; good for coating foods that are to be fried.
panko (japanese breadcrumbs) available in two kinds: larger pieces and fine crumbs; have a lighter texture than Western-style ones. Available from Asian food stores and most supermarkets.
stale crumbs made by grating, blending or processing 1- or 2-day-old bread.

BROCCOLINI
a cross between broccoli and chinese kale; long asparagus-like stems with a long loose floret, both completely edible. Resembles broccoli but is milder and sweeter in taste.

BRUISE
a cooking term to describe the slight crushing given to aromatic ingredients, such as lemon grass and cardamom pods, with the flat side of a heavy knife to release flavour and aroma.

BUK CHOY
also called bok choy, pak choi, chinese white cabbage or chinese chard; has a fresh, mild mustard taste.

BURGHUL
also called bulgar wheat; hulled steamed wheat kernels that, once dried, are crushed into various sized grains. Used in Middle Eastern dishes such as felafel, kibbeh and tabbouleh. Not the same as cracked wheat.

BUTTER
we use salted butter unless stated otherwise; 125g is equal to 1 stick (4 ounces). Unsalted or 'sweet' butter has no salt added and is perhaps the most popular butter among pastry chefs.

BUTTERMILK
originally the term given to the slightly sour liquid left after butter was churned from cream, today it is made from no-fat or low-fat milk to which specific bacterial cultures have neen added. Despite its name, it is actually low in fat.

CAPERBERRIES
olive-sized fruit formed after the buds of the caper bush have flowered; usually sold pickled in a vinegar brine with stalks intact.

CAPERS
grey-green buds of a warm climate (usually Mediterranean) shrub, sold either dried and salted or pickled in a vinegar brine. Capers must be rinsed well before using.
baby capers those picked early; very small, fuller-flavoured and more expensive than the full-size ones.

CAPSICUM (BELL PEPPER)
also called pepper. Comes in many colours: red, green, yellow, orange and purplish-black. Be sure to discard seeds and membranes before use.

CARAWAY SEEDS
the small, half-moon-shaped dried seed from a member of the parsley family; adds a sharp anise flavour when used in both sweet and savoury dishes. Used widely, in foods such as rye bread, harissa and the classic Hungarian fresh cheese, liptauer.

CARDAMOM
a spice native to India and used extensively in its cuisine; can be purchased in pod, seed or ground form. Has a distinctive aromatic, sweetly rich flavour.

CARROTS, BABY
small, sweet and sold in bunches with the tops still attached.

CASHEWS
plump, kidney-shaped, golden-brown nuts having a distinctive sweet, buttery flavour and containing about 48% fat. Because of this high fat content, they should be kept, sealed tightly, in the fridge to avoid becoming rancid. We use roasted unsalted cashews unless stated otherwise; they are available from health-food stores and most major supermarkets. Roasting cashews brings out their intense nutty flavour. See *roasting/toasting*.

CAVOLO NERO
or tuscan cabbage, a staple in Tuscan country cooking. It has long, narrow, wrinkled leaves and a rich and astringent, mild cabbage flavour. It doesn't lose its volume like silver beet or spinach when cooked, but it does need longer cooking.

CELERIAC (CELERY ROOT)
tuberous root with knobbly brown skin, white flesh and a celery-like flavour. Keep peeled celeriac in acidulated water to stop it discolouring. It can be grated and eaten raw in salads; used in soups and stews; boiled and mashed like potatoes; or sliced thinly and deep-fried as chips.

CHEESE
bocconcini from the diminutive of

GLOSSARY

'boccone', meaning mouthful in Italian; walnut-sized, baby mozzarella; a delicate, semi-soft, white cheese traditionally made from buffalo milk. Sold fresh, it spoils rapidly so will only keep, refrigerated in brine, for 1 or 2 days at the most.

cheddar the most common cow's milk 'tasty' cheese; should be aged, hard and have a pronounced bite.

cottage fresh, white, unripened curd cheese with a grainy consistency and a fat content of 15% to 55%.

cream commonly called philadelphia or philly; a soft cow-milk cheese, its fat content ranges from 14% to 33%.

fetta Greek in origin; a crumbly textured goat- or sheep-milk cheese having a sharp, salty taste. Ripened and stored in salted whey; particularly good cubed and tossed into salads.

goat's made from goat's milk, has an earthy, strong taste. Available in soft, crumbly and firm textures, in various shapes and sizes, and sometimes rolled in ash or herbs.

gruyère a hard-rind Swiss cheese with small holes and a nutty, slightly salty flavour. A popular cheese for soufflés.

haloumi a Greek Cypriot cheese with a semi-firm, spongy texture and very salty sweet flavour. Ripened and stored in salted whey; best grilled or fried, it holds its shape well on being heated. Eat while still warm as it becomes tough and rubbery on cooling.

kefalotyri a hard, salty cheese made from sheep and/or goat's milk. Its colour varies from white to yellow depending on the mixture of milk used in the process and its age. It is a great cheese for grating over pasta or salads, it can replace parmesan.

mascarpone an Italian fresh cultured-cream product made in much the same way as yoghurt. Whiteish to creamy yellow in colour, with a buttery-rich, luscious texture. Soft, creamy and spreadable, it is used in Italian desserts and as an accompaniment to fresh fruit.

mozzarella soft, spun-curd cheese originating in southern Italy where it was traditionally made from water-buffalo milk. Now generally made from cow's milk, it is the most popular pizza cheese because of its low melting point and elasticity when heated.

parmesan also called parmigiano; a hard, grainy cow-milk cheese originating in Italy. Reggiano is the best variety.

pecorino the Italian generic name for cheeses made from sheep's milk. This family of hard, white to pale-yellow cheeses, traditionally made in the Italian winter and spring when sheep graze on natural pastures, is matured for 8 to 12 months. They are classified

according to the area in which they were produced – romano from Rome, sardo from Sardinia, siciliano from Sicily and toscano from Tuscany. If you can't find it, use parmesan.

ricotta a soft, sweet, moist, white cow-milk cheese with a low fat content and a slightly grainy texture. The name roughly translates as 'cooked again' and refers to ricotta's manufacture from a whey that is itself a by-product of other cheese making.

romano a hard, sheep- or cow's-milk cheese. Straw-coloured and grainy in texture, it's mainly used for grating. Parmesan can be substituted.

CHERVIL

also called cicily; mildly fennel-flavoured member of the parsley family with curly dark-green leaves. Available fresh and dried but, like all herbs, is best used fresh; like coriander and parsley, its delicate flavour diminishes the longer it's cooked.

CHICKEN

breast fillet breast halved, skinned and boned.

drumsticks leg with skin and bone intact.

maryland leg and thigh still connected in a single piece; bones and skin intact.

small chicken also known as spatchcock or poussin; no more than 6 weeks old, weighing a maximum of 500g (1 pound). Also a cooking term to describe splitting a small chicken open, flattening out then grilling.

thigh skin and bone intact.

thigh cutlets thigh with skin and centre bone intact; sometimes found skinned with bone intact.

thigh fillets skin and bone removed.

CHILLI

available in many types and sizes. Use rubber gloves when seeding and chopping fresh chillies as they can burn your skin. Removing membranes and seeds lessens the heat level.

ancho mild, dried chillies commonly used in Mexican cooking.

cayenne pepper dried, long, thin-fleshed, extremely hot, ground red chilli.

chipotle pronounced cheh-pote-lay. The name used for jalapeño chillies once they've been dried and smoked. With a deep, intensely smoky flavour, rather than a searing heat, chipotles are dark brown, almost black, and wrinkled in appearance.

flakes dried, deep-red, dehydrated chilli slices and whole seeds.

green any unripened chilli; also some particular varieties that are ripe when green, such as jalapeño, habanero, poblano or serrano.

jalapeño pronounced hah-lah-pain-yo. Fairly hot, medium-sized, plump, dark green chilli; available pickled, sold canned or bottled, and fresh, from greengrocers.

long green any unripened chilli.

long red available both fresh and dried; a generic term used for any moderately hot, thin, long (6-8cm/2¼-3¼ inch) chilli.

powder can be used as a substitute for fresh chillies (½ teaspoon ground chilli powder to 1 chopped medium fresh chilli).

thai (serrano) also known as 'scuds'; tiny, very hot and bright red in colour.

CHINESE COOKING WINE (SHAO HSING)

also called chinese rice wine; made from fermented rice, wheat, sugar and salt. Found in Asian food shops; if you can't find it, use mirin or sherry.

CHIVES

related to the onion and leek; has a subtle onion flavour. Used more for flavour than as an ingredient; chopped finely, they're good in sauces, dressings, omelettes or as a garnish.

garlic chives also known as chinese chives; are strongly flavoured, have flat leaves and are eaten as a vegetable, usually in stir-fries.

CHOCOLATE

choc bits also called chocolate chips or chocolate morsels; available in milk, white and dark chocolate. Made of cocoa liquor, cocoa butter, sugar and an emulsifier, these hold their shape in baking and are ideal for decorating.

couverture a term used to describe a fine quality, very rich chocolate high in both cocoa butter and cocoa liquor. This type of chocolate requires tempering when used to coat but not if used in baking, mousses or fillings.

dark (semi-sweet) also called luxury chocolate; made of a high percentage of cocoa liquor and cocoa butter, and little added sugar. Unless stated otherwise, we use dark chocolate in this book as it's ideal for use in desserts and cakes.

melts small discs of compounded milk, white or dark chocolate ideal for melting and moulding.

milk most popular eating chocolate, mild and very sweet; similar in make-up to dark with the difference being the addition of milk solids.

GLOSSARY

white contains no cocoa solids but derives its sweet flavour from cocoa butter. Very sensitive to heat.

CHOY SUM
also known as pakaukeo or flowering cabbage, a member of the buk choy family; easy to identify with its long stems, light green leaves and yellow flowers. Stems and leaves are both edible, steamed or stir-fried.

CINNAMON
available in pieces (called sticks or quills) and ground into powder; one of the world's most common spices, used as a sweet, fragrant flavouring for both sweet and savoury foods.

CLOVES
dried flower buds of a tropical tree; can be used whole or in ground form. They have a strong scent and taste so should be used sparingly.

COCOA POWDER
also known as unsweetened cocoa; cocoa beans (cacao seeds) that have been fermented, roasted, shelled, ground into powder then cleared of most of the fat content. Unsweetened cocoa is used in hot chocolate drink mixtures; milk powder and sugar are added to the ground product.
dutch cocoa treated with an alkali to neutralize its acids. It has a reddish-brown colour, mild flavour, and is easy to dissolve in liquids.

COCONUT
cream obtained commercially from the first pressing of the coconut flesh alone, without the addition of water; the second pressing (less rich) is sold as coconut milk. Available in cans and cartons at most supermarkets.
desiccated concentrated, dried, unsweetened and finely shredded coconut flesh.
flaked dried flaked coconut flesh.
milk not the liquid found inside the fruit (coconut water), but the diluted liquid from the second pressing of the white flesh of a mature coconut (the first pressing produces coconut cream). Available in cans and cartons at most supermarkets.
shredded unsweetened thin strips of dried coconut flesh.

CORIANDER (CILANTRO)
also called pak chee or chinese parsley; bright-green-leafed herb with a pungent flavour. The leaves, stems and roots of coriander are also used. Wash under cold water, removing any dirt clinging to the roots; scrape the roots with a small flat knife to remove some of the outer fibrous skin. Chop roots and stems together to obtain the amount specified. Also available ground or as seeds; these should not be substituted for fresh coriander as the tastes are completely different.

CORNFLOUR (CORNSTARCH)
available made from corn or wheat (wheaten cornflour, gluten-free, gives a lighter texture in cakes); used as a thickening agent in cooking.

COUSCOUS
a fine, dehydrated, grain-like cereal product made from semolina; it swells to three or four times its original size when liquid is added. It is eaten like rice with a tagine, as a side dish or salad ingredient.

CRANBERRIES
available dried and frozen; have a rich, astringent flavour and can be used in cooking sweet and savoury dishes. The dried version can usually be substituted for or with other dried fruit.

CREAM
pouring also known as pure or fresh cream. It has no additives and contains a minimum fat content of 35%.
sour a thick, commercially-cultured sour cream with a minimum fat content of 35%.
thick (double) a dolloping cream with a minimum fat content of 45%.
thickened (heavy) a whipping cream that contains a thickener. It has a minimum fat content of 35%.

CREAM OF TARTAR
the acid ingredient in baking powder; added to confectionery mixtures to help prevent sugar from crystallising. Keeps frostings creamy and improves volume when beating egg whites.

CRÈME FRAÎCHE
a mature, naturally fermented cream (minimum fat content 35%) having a velvety texture and slightly tangy, nutty flavour. Crème fraîche, a French variation of sour cream, can boil without curdling and be used in sweet and savoury dishes.

CUCUMBER, LEBANESE
short, slender and thin-skinned cucumber. Probably the most popular variety because of its tender, edible skin, tiny, yielding seeds, and sweet, fresh and flavoursome taste.

CUMIN
also known as zeera or comino; resembling caraway in size, cumin is the dried seed of a plant related to the parsley family. Its spicy, almost curry-like flavour is essential to the traditional foods of Mexico, India, North Africa and the Middle East. Available dried as seeds or ground.

CURRY LEAVES
available fresh or dried and have a mild curry flavour; use like bay leaves.

CURRY PASTES
some recipes in this book call for commercially prepared pastes of varying strengths and flavours. Use whichever one you feel best suits your spice-level tolerance.
green hottest of the traditional thai pastes; particularly good in chicken and vegetable curries, and a great addition to stir-fry and noodle dishes.
korma a mix of mostly heat-free spices; forms the base of a mild, slightly nutty-tasting, slow-cooked curry.
massaman has a rich, spicy flavour reminiscent of Middle Eastern cooking; favoured by southern Thai cooks for use in hot and sour stew-like curries and satay sauces.
panang based on the curries of Penang, an island off the north-west coast of Malaysia, close to the Thai border. A complex, sweet and milder variation of red curry paste; good with seafood and for adding to soups and salad dressings.
red a popular curry paste; a hot blend of red chilli, garlic, shallot, lemon grass, salt, galangal, shrimp paste, kaffir lime peel, coriander, cumin and paprika. It is milder than the hotter thai green curry paste.
rogan josh a medium-hot blend that is a specialty of Kashmir in northern India. It contains tomatoes, fenugreek, coriander, paprika and cumin.
tikka in Indian cooking, the word 'masala' loosely translates as paste and the word 'tikka' means a bite-sized

piece of meat, poultry or fish, or sometimes a cutlet. Tikka paste is any maker's choice of spices and oils, mixed into a mild paste, frequently coloured red. Used for marinating or for brushing over meat, seafood or poultry, before or during cooking instead of as an ingredient.
vindaloo a Goan combination of vinegar, tomatoes, pepper and other spices that exemplifies the Portuguese influence on that part of India's coast.
yellow one of the mildest thai pastes; it is similar in appearance to Indian curries as they both include yellow chilli and fresh turmeric. Good blended with coconut in vegetable, rice and noodle dishes.

CURRY POWDER
a blend of ground spices used for making Indian and some South-East Asian dishes. Consists of dried chilli, cumin, cinnamon, coriander, fennel, mace, fenugreek, cardamom and turmeric. Available mild or hot.

CUSTARD POWDER
instant mixture used to make pouring custard; similar to North American instant pudding mixes.

DATES
fruit of the date palm tree, eaten fresh or dried, on their own or in dishes. About 4-6cm (1½-2¼ inches) in length, oval and plump, thin-skinned, with a honey-sweet flavour and sticky texture.

DILL
also called dill weed; used fresh or dried, in seed form or ground. Its anise/celery sweetness flavours the food of the Scandinavian countries, and Germany and Greece. Its feathery, frond-like fresh leaves are grassier and more subtle than the dried version or the seeds (which slightly resemble caraway in flavour). Use dill leaves with smoked salmon and sour cream, poached fish or roast chicken; use the seeds with simply cooked vegetables, or home-baked dark breads.

DRIED CURRANTS
dried tiny, almost black raisins so named from the grape type native to Corinth, Greece; most often used in jams, jellies and sauces (the best-known of which is the English cumberland sauce). These are not the same as fresh currants,

which are the fruit of a plant in the gooseberry family.

DUCK
we use whole ducks in some recipes; available from specialty chicken shops, markets and some supermarkets.
breast fillets boneless whole breasts, with the skin on.
chinese barbecued traditionally, in China, cooked in special ovens; dipped into and brushed during roasting with a sticky sweet coating made from soy sauce, sherry, ginger, five-spice, star anise and hoisin sauce. Available from Asian food shops as well as dedicated Chinese barbecued meat shops.
maryland thigh and drumstick still connected, skin on.

DUKKAH
an Egyptian specialty spice mixture made up of roasted nuts, seeds and an array of aromatic spices.

EGGPLANT
also known as aubergine. Ranging in size from tiny to very large and in colour from pale green to deep purple. Can also be purchased char-grilled, packed in oil, in jars.
baby also known as finger or japanese eggplant; very small and slender so can be used without disgorging.
thai also known as makeua prao, golf ball-sized eggplants available in different colours but most commonly green traced in off-white; crisper than the common purple variety, they have bitter seeds that must be removed before using.

EGGS
we use large chicken eggs weighing an average of 60g (2 ounces). If a recipe calls for raw or barely cooked eggs, exercise caution if there is a salmonella problem in your area, particularly in food eaten by children and pregnant women.

FENNEL
also called finocchio or anise; a crunchy green vegetable slightly resembling celery that's eaten raw in salads; fried as an accompaniment; or used as an ingredient in soups and sauces. Also the name given to the dried seeds of the plant which have a stronger licorice flavour.

FENUGREEK
a member of the pea family, the seeds

have a bitter taste; the ground seeds are used in Indian curries, powders and pastes.

FIGS
best eaten in peak season, at the height of summer. Vary in skin and flesh colour according to type not ripeness. When ripe, figs should be unblemished and bursting with flesh; nectar beads at the base indicate when a fig is at its best. Figs are also glacéd, dried or canned in sugar syrup; these are usually sold at health-food stores, Middle Eastern food shops or specialty cheese counters.

FIVE-SPICE POWDER (CHINESE FIVE-SPICE)
a fragrant mixture of ground cinnamon, cloves, star anise, sichuan pepper and fennel seeds.

FLOUR
plain (all-purpose) unbleached wheat flour, the best for baking: the gluten content ensures a strong dough, for a light result.
rice very fine, almost powdery, gluten-free flour; made from ground white rice. Used in baking, as a thickener, and in some Asian noodles and desserts. Another variety, made from glutinous sweet rice, is used for chinese dumplings and rice paper.
self-raising all-purpose plain or wholemeal flour with baking powder and salt added; make at home in the proportion of 1 cup plain or wholemeal flour to 2 teaspoons baking powder.
wholemeal also known as wholewheat flour; milled with the wheat germ so is higher in fibre and more nutritional than plain flour.

GAI LAN
also known as chinese broccoli, gai larn, kanah, gai lum and chinese kale; appreciated more for its stems than its coarse leaves.

GALANGAL
a rhizome with a hot ginger-citrusy flavour; used similarly to ginger and garlic. Use fresh ginger if unavailable.

GARAM MASALA
a blend of spices including cardamom, cinnamon, cloves, coriander, fennel and cumin, roasted and ground together.

Black pepper and chilli can be added for a hotter version.

GHEE
a type of clarified butter where the milk solids are cooked until they are a golden brown, which imparts a nutty flavour and sweet aroma; this fat has a high smoking point so can be heated to a high temperature without burning. Used as a cooking medium in most Indian recipes. Available from many Indian supermarkets. Replace with clarified butter, if you can't find it.

GINGER
fresh also called green or root ginger; the thick gnarled root of a tropical plant.
ground also called powdered ginger; used as a flavouring in baking but cannot be substituted for fresh ginger.

GRAVY POWDER
an instant gravy mix made with browned flour. Plain flour can be used instead for thickening. Available from supermarkets in a variety of flavours.

GREASING/OILING PANS
use butter or margarine (for sweet baking), oil or cooking-oil spray (for savoury baking) to grease baking pans; overgreasing pans can cause food to overbrown. Use paper towel or a pastry brush to spread the oil or butter over the pan. Try covering your hand with a small plastic bag then swiping it into the butter or margarine.

HARISSA
a Moroccan sauce or paste that's made from dried chillies, cumin, garlic, oil and caraway seeds. The paste, available in a tube, is extremely hot and should not be used in large amounts; bottled harissa sauce is more mild. Available from Middle-Eastern food shops and some supermarkets.

HAZELNUTS
also known as filberts; plump, grape-sized, rich, sweet nut having a brown skin that is removed by rubbing heated nuts together vigorously in a tea-towel.
ground made by grounding hazelnuts to a coarse flour texture for use in baking or as a thickening agent.

HONEY
the variety sold in a squeezable container is not suitable for the recipes in this book.

HORSERADISH
a root vegetable with edible green leaves but mainly grown for its long, pungent white root. Used more often as a condiment than as an actual vegetable. It has a very hot spicy flavour that lends itself to meat dishes. Occasionally found fresh in specialty greengrocers and some Asian food shops, but commonly purchased in bottles at the supermarket as horseradish cream and prepared horseradish. These cannot be substituted one for the other in cooking but both can be used as table condiments.
cream a paste of grated horseradish, mustard seeds, oil and sugar.
prepared preserved grated horseradish.

HUMMUS
a Middle Eastern salad or dip made from softened dried chickpeas, garlic, lemon juice and tahini; can be purchased ready-made from most delicatessens and supermarkets. Also the Arabic word for chickpeas.

KAFFIR LIME
also known as magrood, leech lime or jeruk purut. The wrinkled, bumpy-skinned green fruit of a small citrus tree originally grown in South Africa and South-East Asia. As a rule, only the rind and leaves are used.
kaffir lime leaves also known as bai magrood, sold fresh, dried or frozen; looks like two glossy dark green leaves joined end to end, forming a rounded hourglass shape. A strip of fresh lime peel may be substituted for each kaffir lime leaf.

KITCHEN STRING
made of a natural product such as cotton or hemp so that it neither affects the flavour of the food it's tied around nor melts when heated.

KUMARA
Polynesian name of an orange-fleshed sweet potato often confused with yam.

LAMB
chump cut from just above the hind legs to the mid-loin section; can be used as a piece for roasting or cut into chops.
cutlet small, tender rib chop; sometimes

sold french-trimmed, with all the fat and gristle at the narrow end of the bone removed.
forequarter chops cut from the shoulder.
leg cut from the hindquarter; can be boned, butterflied, rolled and tied, or diced.
rolled shoulder boneless section of the forequarter, rolled and secured with string or netting.
sausage, merguez small, spicy sausage believed to have originated in Tunisia but eaten in North Africa, France and Spain; traditionally made with lamb and easily recognised because of its chilli-red colour. Can be fried, grilled or roasted; available from many butchers, delis and specialty sausage stores.
shank forequarter leg; sometimes sold as drumsticks or frenched shanks if the gristle and narrow end of the bone are discarded and the remaining meat trimmed.
shoulder large, tasty piece having much connective tissue so is best pot-roasted or braised. Makes the best mince.

LEEK
a member of the onion family, the leek resembles a green onion but is much larger and more subtle in flavour. Tender baby or pencil leeks are essentially young, slender leeks; available early in the season, they can be cooked and eaten whole like asparagus with minimal cooking. Adult leeks are usually trimmed of most of the green tops then chopped or sliced and cooked as an ingredient in stews, casseroles and soups.

LEMON GRASS
also known as takrai, serai or serah. A tall, clumping, lemon-smelling and tasting, sharp-edged aromatic tropical grass; the white lower part of the stem is used, finely chopped, in many South-East Asian dishes. Can be found fresh, dried, powdered and frozen, in supermarkets, greengrocers and Asian food shops.

LENTILS (RED, BROWN, YELLOW)
dried pulses often identified by and named after their colour. Eaten by cultures all over the world, most famously perhaps in the dhals of India.
French-style a local cousin to the famous (and very expensive) French lentils du puy; green-blue, tiny lentils with a nutty, earthy flavour and a hardy nature that allows them to be rapidly cooked without disintegrating.

LIQUEUR, ORANGE-FLAVOURED

such as curaçao, Grand Marnier or Cointreau.

MACADAMIAS

native to Australia; fairly large, slightly soft, buttery rich nut. Should always be stored in the fridge to prevent their high oil content turning them rancid.

MANGO

tropical fruit originally from India and South-East Asia. With skin colour ranging from green to yellow and deep red; fragrant, deep yellow flesh surrounds a large flat seed. Slicing off the cheeks, cross-hatching them with a knife then turning them inside out shows the sweet, juicy flesh at its best. Mangoes can also be used in curries and salsas, or pureed for ice-cream, smoothies or mousse.

MAPLE-FLAVOURED SYRUP

also called golden or pancake syrup; made from sugar cane. It is not a substitute for pure maple syrup.

MAPLE SYRUP

also called pure maple syrup; distilled from the sap of sugar maple trees found only in Canada and the USA. Maple-flavoured syrup or pancake syrup is not an adequate substitute for the real thing.

MARJORAM

closely related to and similar in flavour to oregano, but milder and sweeter. Delicious in herb mixtures for omelettes, stuffings, herb scones and herb and cream cheese sandwiches. As with oregano, many chefs prefer dried marjoram to fresh.

MARSALA

a sweet, fortified Italian wine to which additional alcohol has been added, most commonly in the form of brandy. Produced in the region surrounding the Sicilian city of Marsala and recognisable by its intense amber colour and complex aroma, it is available in a range of styles, from sweet to dry. Often used in cooking, especially in sauces, risottos and desserts.

MAYONNAISE, WHOLE-EGG

commercial mayonnaise of high quality made with whole eggs and labelled as such; some prepared mayonnaises

substitute emulsifiers such as food starch, cellulose gel or other thickeners to mimic the same thick and creamy consistency but never achieve the same rich flavour. Must be refrigerated once opened.

MINT

the most commonly used variety of mint is spearmint; it has pointed, bright-green leaves and a fresh flavour.

MIRIN

a Japanese champagne-coloured cooking wine, made of glutinous rice and alcohol. It is used just for cooking and should not be confused with sake. A seasoned sweet mirin, manjo mirin, made of water, rice, corn syrup and alcohol, is used in dipping sauces.

MIXED DRIED FRUIT

a mix of sultanas, raisins, currants, mixed peel and cherries.

MIXED SALAD LEAVES

also called mesclun; a salad mix of young lettuce and other green leaves, including baby spinach leaves, mizuna and curly endive.

MIXED SPICE

a classic spice mixture generally containing caraway, allspice, coriander, cumin, nutmeg and ginger, although cinnamon and other spices can be added. It is used with fruit and in cakes.

MOLASSES

a thick, dark brown syrup, the residue from the refining of sugar; available in light, dark and blackstrap varieties. Its slightly bitter taste is an essential ingredient in American cooking, found in foods such as gingerbread, shoofly pie and boston baked beans.

MOROCCAN SEASONING

available from most Middle-Eastern food stores, spice shops and major supermarkets. A blend of turmeric, cinnamon and cumin adds a Moroccan flavour to cooking.

MORTAR AND PESTLE

a cooking tool whose design has remained the same over the centuries: the mortar is a bowl-shaped container and the pestle a rounded, bat-shaped

tool. Together, they grind and pulverise spices, herbs and other foods. The pestle is pressed against the mortar and rotated, grinding the ingredient between the two surfaces. Essential for curry pastes and crushing spices.

MUSHROOMS

button small, cultivated white mushrooms with a mild flavour.
dried porcini also known as cèpes; the richest-flavoured mushrooms. Expensive, but because they're so strongly flavoured, only a small amount is required.
enoki cultivated mushrooms also called enokitake; tiny long-stemmed, pale mushrooms that grow and are sold in clusters, and can be used that way or separated by slicing off the base. They have a mild fruity flavour and are slightly crisp in texture.
flat large, flat mushrooms with a rich earthy flavour, ideal for filling and barbecuing. They are sometimes misnamed field mushrooms which are wild mushrooms.
oyster also called abalone; grey-white mushrooms shaped like a fan. Prized for their smooth texture and subtle, oyster-like flavour. Also available in pink.
portobello mature, fully opened swiss browns; large, dark brown mushrooms with full-bodied flavour; ideal for filling or barbecuing.
shiitake when fresh are also known as chinese black, forest or golden oak mushrooms. Large, meaty and, although cultivated, have the earthiness and taste of wild mushrooms. When dried, they are known as donko or dried chinese mushrooms; rehydrate before use.
swiss brown also known as roman or cremini. Light to dark brown mushrooms with full-bodied flavour; suited for use in casseroles or being stuffed and baked.

MUSLIN

inexpensive, undyed, finely woven cotton fabric called for in cooking to strain stocks and sauces; if unavailable, use a clean chux or linen tea towel.

MUSTARD

dijon pale brown, distinctively flavoured, fairly mild-tasting french mustard.
seeds, black also called brown mustard seeds; more pungent than the yellow (or white) seeds used in prepared mustards.
wholegrain also known as seeded. A french-style coarse-grain mustard made from crushed mustard seeds and dijon-style french mustard.

NOODLES

dried rice also called rice stick noodles. Made from rice flour and water, available flat and wide or very thin (vermicelli). Must be soaked in boiling water to soften.
fresh rice also called ho fun, khao pun, sen yau, pho or kway tiau, depending on the country of manufacture; the most common form of noodle used in Thailand. Can be purchased in strands of various widths or large sheets of about 500g (1 pound) which are to be cut into the desired size. Chewy and pure white, they do not need pre-cooking before use.
rice stick also called sen lek, ho fun or kway teow; especially popular South-East Asian dried rice noodles. They come in different widths (thin used in soups, wide in stir-fries), but all should be soaked in hot water to soften. The traditional noodle used in pad thai which, before soaking, measures about 5mm in width.
rice vermicelli also called sen mee, mei fun or bee hoon. Used throughout Asia in spring rolls and cold salads; similar to bean threads, only longer and made with rice flour instead of mung bean starch. Before using, soak the dried noodles in hot water until softened, boil them briefly then rinse with hot water.

NUTMEG

a strong and pungent spice ground from the dried nut of an evergreen tree native to Indonesia. Usually found ground but the flavour is more intense from a whole nut, available from spice shops, so it's best to grate your own.

OIL

cooking spray we use a cholesterol-free cooking spray made from canola oil.
olive made from ripened olives. Extra virgin and virgin are the first and second press, respectively, of the olives and are therefore considered the best; 'light' refers to taste not fat levels.
peanut pressed from ground peanuts; most commonly used oil in Asian cooking because of its high smoke point (capacity to handle high heat without burning).
sesame roasted, crushed, white sesame seeds; a flavouring rather than a cooking medium.
vegetable oils sourced from plant rather than animal fats.

OKRA

also called bamia or lady fingers. A green, ridged, oblong pod with a furry skin. Native to Africa, this vegetable is used in Indian, Middle Eastern and South American cooking. Can be eaten on its own; as part of a casserole, curry or gumbo; used to thicken stews or gravies.

OLIVES

black have a richer and more mellow flavour than the green ones and are softer in texture. Sold either plain or in a piquant marinade.
green those harvested before fully ripened and are, as a rule, denser and more bitter than the black variety.

ONIONS

baby also called pickling and cocktail onions; are baby brown onions but are larger than shallots. To peel, cover with boiling water and stand for 2 minutes, then drain. The skins will slip off easily.
brown and white interchangeable; white onions have a more pungent flesh.
green (scallions) also called, incorrectly, shallot; an immature onion picked before the bulb has formed, has a long, bright-green edible stalk.
red also known as spanish, red spanish or bermuda onion; a sweet-flavoured, large, purple-red onion.
shallots also called french or golden shallots or eschalots; small and elongated with a brown skin.
spring an onion with a small white bulb and long, narrow green-leafed tops.

ORANGE FLOWER WATER

concentrated flavouring made from orange blossoms.

OREGANO

a herb, also known as wild marjoram; has a woody stalk and clumps of tiny, dark-green leaves. Has a pungent, peppery flavour.

PAPRIKA

ground, dried, sweet red capsicum (bell pepper); there are many grades and types available, including sweet, hot, mild and smoked.

PARSLEY

a versatile herb with a fresh, earthy flavour. There are about 30 varieties of curly parsley; the flat-leaf variety (also called continental or italian parsley) is stronger in flavour and darker in colour.

PARSNIP

their nutty sweetness is especially good when steamed and dressed with a garlic and cream sauce or in a curried parsnip soup, or simply baked. Can be substituted for potatoes. Available all year but the cold develops their sweet/savoury flavour in winter.

PASTA

fettuccine fresh or dried ribbon pasta made from durum wheat, semolina and egg. Also available plain or flavoured.
fresh lasagne sheets thinly rolled wide sheets of plain or flavoured pasta; they do not need par-boiling before being used in cooking.
gnocchi Italian 'dumplings' made of potatoes, semolina or flour; can be cooked in boiling water or baked with sauce.
macaroni tube-shaped pasta available in various sizes; made from semolina and water; does not contain eggs.
pappardelle from the Italian verb pappare, meaning 'to gobble up', pappardelle are broad, flat or frilly, ribbons of pasta. Goes well with red meat sauces (rabbit is a Tuscan favourite), chunky tomato and mushroom sauces as in pappardelle boscaiola, or with cream.
penne Italian for 'pen', this dried pasta resembles a quill, and has angled ends and ridges to hold chunky sauces. Penne are also available in a smooth variety to complement finer sauces.
risoni small rice-shape pasta; very similar to orzo, another small pasta.
spaghetti long, thin solid strands of pasta.
tagliatelle long, flat strips of wheat pasta, slightly narrower and thinner than fettuccine.

PATTY-PAN SQUASH

also known as crookneck or custard marrow pumpkins; a round, slightly flat summer squash that is yellow to pale-green in colour and has a scalloped edge. Has a firm white flesh and a distinct flavour.

PEANUTS

also called groundnut, not in fact a nut but the pod of a legume. We mainly use raw (unroasted) or unsalted roasted peanuts.

PEAS

green also known as garden peas, must be shelled and their pods never eaten. Peas in the pod will yield just under half their weight of shelled peas; 1kg (2 pounds) will serve 4. Peas in the pod are available fresh and shelled peas are available frozen.

snow also called mangetout; a variety of garden pea, eaten pod and all (although you may need to string them). Used in stir-fries or eaten raw in salads. Snow pea sprouts are available from supermarkets or greengrocers and are usually eaten raw in salads or sandwiches.
sugar snap also called honey snap peas; fresh small pea which can be eaten, whole, pod and all, similarly to snow peas.

PECANS
native to the US and now grown locally; pecans are golden brown, buttery and rich. Good in savoury as well as sweet dishes; walnuts are a good substitute.

PEPITAS (PUMPKIN SEEDS)
the pale green kernels of dried pumpkin seeds; they can be bought plain or salted.

PEPPERCORNS
black picked when the berry is not quite ripe, then dried until it shrivels and the skin turns dark brown/black. It's the strongest flavoured of the three (white, green and black) – slightly hot with a hint of sweetness.
green soft, unripe berry of the pepper plant, usually sold packed in brine (occasionally found dried, packed in salt). Has a distinctive fresh taste.
pepper medley a mixture of black, white, green and pink peppercorns, coriander seeds and allspice, sold in disposable grinders in supermarkets.
pink a dried berry from a type of rose plant grown in Madagascar, usually sold packed in brine (occasionally found freeze-dried); they possess a distinctive pungently sweet taste.
sichuan also known as szechuan or chinese pepper, native to the Sichuan province of China. A mildly-hot spice that comes from the prickly ash tree. Although not related to the peppercorn family, its small, red-brown aromatic berries look like black peppercorns and have a distinctive peppery-lemon flavour and aroma. They should always be dry-roasted to bring out the flavour.
white less pungent; has been allowed to ripen, after which the skin is removed and the berry is dried. The result is a smaller, smoother-skinned, light-tan berry with a milder flavour.

PINE NUTS
also called pignoli; not a nut but a small, cream-coloured kernel from pine cones. They are best roasted before use to bring out the flavour.

PISTACHIOS
green, delicately flavoured nuts inside hard off-white shells. Available salted or unsalted in their shells; you can also buy them shelled. We use the weight of shelled nuts in our recipes.

POACH
a cooking term to describe gentle simmering of food in liquid (generally water or stock); spices or herbs can be added to impart their flavour.

POLENTA
also known as cornmeal; a ground, flour-like cereal made of dried corn (maize) sold in several different textures. Also the name of the dish made from it.

POMEGRANATE
dark-red, leathery-skinned fresh fruit about the size of an orange filled with hundreds of seeds, each wrapped in an edible lucent-crimson pulp having a unique tangy sweet-sour flavour.

POPPY SEEDS
small, dried, bluish-grey seeds of the poppy plant, with a crunchy texture and a nutty flavour. Can be purchased whole or ground from most supermarkets and delicatessens.

PORK
American-style spare ribs usually sold in long slabs or racks of 10 to 12 ribs, trimmed so little fat remains; slather with barbecue sauce before cooking.
belly fatty cut sold in rashers or in a piece, with or without rind or bone.
cutlets cut from ribs.
ham hock the lower portion of the leg; includes the meat, fat and bone. Most have been cured, smoked or both, but fresh hocks are sometimes available.
hand of pickled pork the 'hand' is a portion of leg and breast. You may need to order this from the butcher in advance.
loin chops or roasting cut from the loin.
neck sometimes called pork scotch fillet; a boneless cut from the foreloin.
pancetta an Italian unsmoked bacon; pork belly cured in salt and spices then rolled into a sausage shape and dried for several weeks. Used, sliced or chopped, as an ingredient rather than eaten on its own.
prosciutto a kind of unsmoked Italian ham; salted, air-cured and aged, it is usually eaten uncooked.
sausage, chorizo of Spanish origin, made from coarsely minced (ground) smoked pork and highly seasoned with garlic, chilli powder and other spices.
sausage, italian pork available as both sweet, which is flavoured with garlic and fennel seeds, and hot, which has chilli added.
scotch fillet sometimes called neck; a boneless cut from the foreloin.
shoulder joint sold with the bone in or out.

POTATOES
baby also called chats; not a separate variety but an early harvest with very thin skin; good unpeeled steamed and eaten, hot or cold, in salads.
coliban round, smooth white skin and flesh; good for baking and mashing.
desiree oval, smooth and pink-skinned, waxy yellow flesh; good in salads, boiled and roasted.
idaho also known as russet burbank; russet in colour, delicious baked.
king edward slightly plump and rosy; great mashed.
lasoda round, red skin with deep eyes, white flesh; good for mashing or roasting.
pink-eye small, off-white skin, deep purple eyes; good steamed and boiled, great baked.
pontiac large, red skin, deep eyes, white flesh; good grated, boiled and baked.
sebago white skin, oval; good fried, mashed and baked.
spunta large, long, yellow flesh, floury; great mashed and fried.

PRESERVED LEMON RIND
a North African specialty; lemons are quartered and preserved in salt and lemon juice or water. To use, remove and discard pulp. Squeeze juice from rind, then rinse well and slice thinly. Sold in delicatessens and major supermarkets.

QUINCE
yellow-skinned fruit with hard texture and astringent, tart taste; eaten cooked or as a preserve. Long, slow cooking makes the flesh a deep rose pink.
quince paste a thick quince preserve which is sliceable; served on a cheese platter; goes well with cheeses such as brie and camembert. Available from most supermarkets and delicatessens.

RADICCHIO
a red-leafed Italian chicory with a refreshing bitter taste that's eaten raw and grilled. Comes in varieties named

after their places of origin, such as round-headed Verona or long-headed Treviso.

RAISINS
dried sweet grapes (traditionally muscatel grapes).

RAITA
a minted yoghurt and cucumber dish served as a cooling accompaniment to fiery curries.

RAS EL HANOUT
a classic spice blend used in Moroccan cooking. The name means 'top of the shop' and is the very best spice blend a spice merchant has to offer. Most versions contain over a dozen spices, including cardamom, nutmeg, mace, cinnamon and ground chilli.

RHUBARB
a plant with long, green-red stalks; becomes sweet and edible when cooked.

RICE
arborio small, round grain rice well-suited to absorb a large amount of liquid; the high level of starch makes it especially suitable for risottos for its classic creaminess.
basmati a white, fragrant long grain rice; the grains fluff up when cooked. Wash several times before cooking.
brown retains the high-fibre, nutritious bran coating that's removed from white rice when hulled. It takes longer to cook than white rice and has a chewier texture. Once cooked, the long grains stay separate, while the short grains are soft and stickier.
jasmine a long grain white rice recognised around the world as having a perfumed aromatic quality; moist in texture, it clings together after cooking. Sometimes substituted for basmati rice.
medium grain previously sold as calrose rice; extremely versatile rice that can be substituted for short or long grain rices if necessary.
wild not a member of the rice family but the seed of an aquatic grass native to the cold regions of North America. Wild rice has a strong nutty taste and can be expensive, so is best combined with brown and white rices in pulaos, stuffings and salads.
wild rice blend a packaged blend of white long grain rice and wild rice. With its dark brown, almost black grains, crunchy, resilient texture and smokey-like flavour,

wild rice contrasts nicely with mild-tasting white rice. Perfect with fish, lentils, in pulaos or added to soups.

ROASTING/TOASTING
nuts and dried coconut can be roasted in the oven to restore their fresh flavour and release their aromatic essential oils. Spread them evenly onto an oven tray then roast in a moderate oven for about 5 minutes. Desiccated coconut, pine nuts and sesame seeds roast more evenly if stirred over low heat in a heavy-based frying pan; their natural oils will help turn them golden brown.

ROCKET (ARUGULA)
also called rugula and rucola; peppery green leaf eaten raw in salads or used in cooking. Baby rocket leaves are smaller and less peppery.

ROSEMARY
pungent herb with long, thin pointy leaves; use large and small sprigs, and finely chop leaves.

SAFFRON
stigma of a member of the crocus family, available ground or in strands; imparts a yellow-orange colour to food once infused. The quality can vary greatly; the best is the most expensive spice in the world. Should be stored in the freezer.

SAGE
pungent herb with narrow, grey-green leaves; slightly bitter with a slightly musty mint aroma. Refrigerate fresh sage wrapped in paper towel and sealed in a plastic bag for up to 4 days. Dried sage comes whole, crumbled or ground. It should be stored in a cool, dark place for no more than three months.

SAKE
also known as Japanese cooking rice wine and ryori shu. Made from alcohol (about 14%), rice, salt and corn syrup; often used in marinades for meat and fish. In cooking, it is often used to add body and flavour to various tsuyu (soup stock) and sauces, or to make nimono (simmered dishes) and yakimono (grilled dishes).

SAMBAL OELEK
also called ulek or olek; an Indonesian

salty paste made from ground chillies and vinegar.

SAUCES
char siu a Chinese barbecue sauce made from sugar, water, salt, fermented soya bean paste, honey, soy sauce, malt syrup and spices. Found at most supermarkets.
fish also called nam pla or nuoc nam; made from pulverised salted fermented fish, most often anchovies. Has a very pungent smell and strong taste, so use according to your taste level.
hoisin barbecue sauce made from salted fermented soybeans, onions and garlic; used as a marinade or baste, or to accentuate stir-fries and barbecued or roasted foods. Available from Asian food shops and supermarkets.
oyster Asian in origin, this rich, brown sauce is made from oysters and their brine, cooked with salt and soy sauce, and thickened with starches.
soy also known as sieu; made from fermented soya beans. Several variations are available in most supermarkets and Asian food stores. We use a mild Japanese variety in our recipes.
dark deep brown, almost black in colour; rich, with a thicker consistency than other types. Pungent but not particularly salty; good for marinating.
japanese an all-purpose low-sodium soy sauce made with more wheat content than its Chinese counterparts; fermented in barrels and aged. Possibly the best table soy and the one to choose if you only want one variety.
light fairly thin in consistency and, while paler than the others, the saltiest tasting; used in dishes in which the natural colour of the ingredients is to be maintained. Not to be confused with salt-reduced or low-sodium soy sauces.
Tabasco brand name of an extremely fiery sauce made from vinegar, thai red chillies and salt.
tamari a thick, dark soy sauce made mainly from soya beans without the wheat used in standard soy sauces.
tomato pasta made from a blend of tomatoes, herbs and spices.
worcestershire this dark-coloured condiment is made from garlic, lime, soy sauce, tamarind, onions, molasses, anchovies, vinegar and seasonings.

SEAFOOD
blue swimmer crab also known as sand crab, blue manna crab, bluey, sand crab or sandy. Substitute with lobster, balmain or moreton bay bugs.
fish fillet, firm white includes bream, flathead, whiting, snapper, dhufish,

redfish and ling.

mussels must be tightly closed when bought, indicating they are alive. Before cooking, scrub the shells with a strong brush and remove the 'beards'. Some mussels might not open – you do not have to discard these, just open with a knife and cook a little more if you wish. Varieties include black and green-lip.

ocean trout a farmed fish with pink, soft flesh. From the same family as the atlantic salmon; one can be substituted for the other.

octopus usually tenderised before you buy them; both octopus and squid require either long slow cooking (usually for the large molluscs) or quick cooking over high heat (usually for the small molluscs) – anything in between will make the octopus tough and rubbery.

prawns (shrimp) varieties include, school, king, royal red, sydney harbour, tiger. Can be bought uncooked (green) or cooked, with or without shells.

salmon red-pink firm flesh with few bones; moist delicate flavour.

SEMOLINA

coarsely ground flour milled from durum wheat; the flour used in making gnocchi, pasta and couscous.

SESAME SEEDS

black and white are the most common of this small oval seed, however there are also red and brown varieties. The seeds are used in cuisines the world over as an ingredient and as a condiment. Roast the seeds in a heavy-based frying pan over low heat.

SHERRY

fortified wine consumed as an aperitif or used in cooking. Sherries differ in colour and flavour; sold as fino (light, dry), amontillado (medium sweet, dark) and oloroso (full-bodied, very dark).

SILVER BEET (SWISS CHARD)

also called, incorrectly, spinach; has fleshy stalks and large leaves and can be prepared as for spinach.

SPINACH

also called english spinach and incorrectly, silver beet. Baby spinach leaves are best eaten raw in salads; the larger leaves should be added last to soups, stews and stir-fries, and should be cooked until barely wilted.

SPLIT PEAS

a variety of yellow or green pea grown specifically for drying. When dried, the peas usually split along a natural seam. Whole and split dried peas are available packaged in supermarkets and in bulk in health-food stores.

STAR ANISE

dried star-shaped pod with an astringent aniseed flavour; used to flavour stocks and marinades. Available whole and ground, it is an essential ingredient in five-spice powder.

SUGAR

caster (superfine) finely granulated table sugar.

brown a soft, finely granulated sugar retaining molasses for its characteristic colour and flavour.

dark brown a moist, dark brown sugar with a rich, distinctive full flavour from molasses syrup.

light brown a very soft, finely granulated sugar that retains molasses for its colour and flavour.

demerara small-grained golden-coloured crystal sugar.

icing (confectioners') also known as powdered sugar; pulverised granulated sugar crushed together with a small amount of cornflour (cornstarch).

palm also called nam tan pip, jaggery, jawa or gula melaka; made from the sap of the sugar palm tree. Light brown to black in colour and usually sold in rock-hard cakes; use light brown sugar if unavailable.

pure icing (confectioners') also known as powdered sugar.

raw natural brown granulated sugar.

vanilla available in supermarkets, usually among the spices. Or, you can make your own by putting a couple of vanilla beans in a jar of caster (superfine) sugar.

white (granulated) coarse, granulated table sugar, also known as crystal sugar.

yellow rock available from Asian supermarkets. It's mainly used in braises and sauces as it gives them a lustre and glaze.

SULTANAS

also called golden raisins; dried seedless white grapes.

SUMAC

a purple-red, astringent spice ground from berries growing on shrubs that flourish wild around the Mediterranean; adds a tart, lemony flavour to dips and dressings and goes well with barbecued meat. Can be found in Middle Eastern food stores.

SWEDE

so-named in England and Australia, the hard, slightly yellow root vegetable that slightly resembles a large dried turnip is called a neep in Scotland and rutabaga in the United States. Because this vegetable thrives in the cold, it has always been popular in Scandinavia, especially in Sweden, hence the name. The swede is a great tasting vegetable with a delicate sweetness and flavour that hints of the freshness of cabbage and turnip.

TAMARIND

the tamarind tree produces clusters of hairy brown pods, each of which is filled with seeds and a viscous pulp, that are dried and pressed into the blocks of tamarind found in Asian food shops. Gives a sweet-sour, slightly astringent taste to marinades, pastes, sauces and dressings.

TAMARIND CONCENTRATE (OR PASTE)

the distillation of tamarind pulp into a condensed compacted paste with a sweet-sour, slightly astringent taste. Thick and purple-black, it requires no soaking. Found in Asian food stores.

TARRAGON

french tarragon, with its subtle aniseed flavour, complements chicken, eggs and veal, and is perfect in a béarnaise sauce. It is also one of the herbs that make up the French *fines herbs*. Russian and Mexican tarragons are slightly coarser in taste.

THYME

a basic herb of French cuisine widely used in Mediterranean countries to flavour meats and sauces. A member of the mint family, it has tiny grey-green leaves that give off a pungent minty, light-lemon aroma. Dried thyme comes in both leaf and powder form. Dried thyme should be stored in a cool, dark place for no more than three months. Fresh thyme should be stored in the refrigerator, wrapped in a damp paper towel and placed in a sealed bag for no more than a few days.

TOFU

also known as bean curd, an off-white, custard-like product made from the 'milk' of crushed soya beans; comes fresh as soft or firm. Leftover fresh tofu can be refrigerated in water (which is changed daily) for up to 4 days.
silken tofu refers to the method by which it is made – where it is strained through silk.

TOMATOES

bottled pasta sauce a prepared sauce; a blend of tomatoes, herbs and spices.
canned whole peeled tomatoes in natural juices; available crushed, chopped or diced. Use undrained.
cherry also called tiny tim or tom thumb tomatoes; small and round.
egg also called plum or roma; these are smallish, oval-shaped tomatoes much used in Italian cooking or salads.
paste triple-concentrated tomato puree used to flavour soups, stews and sauces.
puree canned pureed tomatoes.
roma (egg) also called plum; these are smallish, oval-shaped tomatoes much used in Italian cooking or salads.
semi-dried partially dried tomato pieces in olive oil; softer and juicier than sun-dried, these are not a preserve thus do not keep as long as sun-dried.
sun-dried tomato pieces that have been dried with salt; this dehydrates the tomato and concentrates the flavour. We use sun-dried tomatoes packaged in oil, unless stated otherwise.
truss small vine-ripened tomatoes with vine still attached.

TREACLE

thick, dark syrup not unlike molasses; a by-product of the sugar refining process.

TURMERIC

also called kamin; a rhizome related to galangal and ginger. Must be grated or pounded to release its acrid aroma and pungent flavour. Known for the golden colour it imparts, fresh turmeric can be substituted with the more commonly found dried powder, in the proportion of 1 teaspoon ground turmeric for every 20g (¾ ounce) fresh turmeric. Be aware that fresh turmeric stains your hands and plastic utensils such as chopping boards and spatulas.
ground turmeric fresh turmeric root is dried and ground, resulting in the rich yellow powder that gives many Indian dishes their characteristic yellow colour. It is intensely pungent in taste but not hot.

VANILLA

bean dried, long, thin pod from a tropical golden orchid; the minuscule black seeds inside the bean impart a luscious flavour in baking and desserts. Place a whole bean in a jar of sugar to make vanilla sugar; a bean can be used three or four times.
extract obtained from vanilla beans infused in water; a non-alcoholic version of essence.
paste made from vanilla beans and contains real seeds. Highly concentrated: 1 teaspoon replaces a whole vanilla bean. Found in most supermarkets in the baking section.

VEAL

osso buco also called veal shin, usually cut into 3-5cm (1¼-2-inch) thick slices and used in the famous Italian slow-cooked casserole of the same name.
rack row of small chops or cutlets.
scaloppine a piece of lean steak hammered with a meat mallet until almost see-through; cook over high heat for as little time as possible.
schnitzel thinly sliced steak.

VIETNAMESE MINT

not a mint at all, but a pungent and peppery narrow-leafed member of the buckwheat family. Not confined to Vietnam, it is also known as cambodian mint, pak pai (Thailand), laksa leaf (Indonesia), daun kesom (Singapore) and rau ram in Vietnam. It is a common ingredient in Thai foods, particularly soups, salads and stir-fries.

VINEGAR

balsamic originally from Modena, Italy, there are now many balsamic vinegars on the market ranging in pungency and quality depending on how, and for how long, they have been aged. Made from the juice of Trebbiano grapes; it is a deep rich brown colour with a sweet and sour flavour. Quality can be determined up to a point by price; use the most expensive sparingly.
white balsamic a clear and lighter version of balsamic vinegar; it has a fresh, sweet, clean taste.
brown malt made from fermented malt and beech shavings.
cider (apple cider) made from crushed fermented apples.
rice a colourless vinegar made from fermented rice and flavoured with sugar and salt. Sherry can be substituted.
white made from the spirit of cane sugar.

white wine made from a blend of white wines.

WALNUTS

a rich, flavourful nut. Should be plump and firm, not shrivelled or soft. Has a high oil content, so store in the fridge. Pecans can be substituted.

WATERCRESS

one of the cress family, a large group of peppery greens used raw in salads, dips and sandwiches, or cooked in soups. Highly perishable, so it must be used as soon as possible after purchase.

WHITE SWEET POTATO

less sweet than kumara; has an earthy flavour and a purple flesh beneath its white skin; best baked.

WITLOF

also known as belgian endive; related to and confused with chicory. A versatile vegetable, it tastes as good cooked as it does eaten raw. Grown in darkness like white asparagus to prevent it becoming green; looks somewhat like a tightly furled, cream to very light-green cigar. The leaves can be removed and used to hold a canapé filling; the whole vegetable can be opened up, stuffed then baked or casseroled; and the leaves can be tossed in a salad with other vegetables.

WOMBOK (NAPA CABBAGE)

also called chinese cabbage or peking cabbage; elongated in shape with pale green, crinkly leaves. The most common cabbage in South-East Asia. Can be shredded or chopped and eaten raw or braised, steamed or stir-fried.

YOGHURT, GREEK-STYLE

often made from sheep milk that is strained in a cloth (traditionally muslin) to remove the whey and to give it a thick, smooth, creamy consistency, almost like whipped cream.

ZUCCHINI

also known as courgette; small green, yellow or white vegetable belonging to the squash family. When harvested young, its edible flowers can be stuffed then deep-fried or oven-baked.

487
CONVERSION CHART

MEASURES

One Australian metric measuring cup holds approximately 250ml; one Australian metric tablespoon holds 20ml; one Australian metric teaspoon holds 5ml. The difference between one country's measuring cups and another's is within a two- or three-teaspoon variance, and will not affect your cooking results. North America, New Zealand and the United Kingdom use 15ml tablespoons.
All cup and spoon measurements are level.
The most accurate way of measuring dry ingredients is to weigh them. When measuring liquids, use a clear glass or plastic jug with the metric markings.
We use large eggs with an average weight of 60g.

DRY MEASURES

METRIC	IMPERIAL
15g	½ oz
30g	1oz
60g	2oz
90g	3oz
125g	4oz (¼ lb)
155g	5oz
185g	6oz
220g	7oz
250g	8oz (½ lb)
280g	9oz
315g	10oz
345g	11oz
375g	12oz (¾ lb)
410g	13oz
440g	14oz
470g	15oz
500g	16oz (1lb)
750g	24oz (1½ lb)
1kg	32oz (2lb)

LIQUID MEASURES

METRIC	IMPERIAL
30ml	1 fluid oz
60ml	2 fluid oz
100ml	3 fluid oz
125ml	4 fluid oz
150ml	5 fluid oz
190ml	6 fluid oz
250ml	8 fluid oz
300ml	10 fluid oz
500ml	16 fluid oz
600ml	20 fluid oz
1000ml	1¾ pints

LENGTH MEASURES

METRIC	IMPERIAL
3mm	in
6mm	¼ in
1cm	½ in
2cm	¾ in
2.5cm	1in
5cm	2in
6cm	2½ in
8cm	3in
10cm	4in
13cm	5in
15cm	6in
18cm	7in
20cm	8in
23cm	9in
25cm	10in
28cm	11in
30cm	12in (1ft)

OVEN TEMPERATURES

The oven temperatures in this book are for conventional ovens; if you have a fan-forced oven, decrease the temperature by 10-20 degrees.

	°C (CELSIUS)	°F (FAHRENHEIT)
Very slow	120	250
Slow	150	300
Moderately slow	160	325
Moderate	180	350
Moderately hot	200	400
Hot	220	425
Very hot	240	475

S

This book is first published in 2018 by Octopus Publishing Group Limited based on materials licensed to it
by Bauer Media Books, Australia.

Bauer Media Books is a division of Bauer Media Pty Limited, 54 Park St, Sydney; GPO Box 4088, Sydney, NSW 2001, Australia

phone (+61) 2 9282 8618; fax (+61) 2 9126 3702 www.awwcookbooks.com.au

BAUER MEDIA BOOKS
Publisher Jo Runciman
Editorial & food director Sophia Young
Director of sales, marketing & rights Brian Cearnes
Editorial director-at-large Pamela Clark
Senior designer Hieu Nguyen
Designer Bernhard Schmitz
Junior editor Amy Bayliss
Operations manager David Scotto

Published and distributed in the United Kingdom by
Octopus Publishing Group Ltd
Carmelite House
50 Victoria Embankment
London, EC4Y 0DZ
United Kingdom
info@octopus-publishing.co.uk;
www.octopusbooks.co.uk

Printed in china by Leo Paper Products Ltd.

International foreign language rights
Brian Cearnes, Bauer Media Books
bcearnes@bauer-media.com.au

A catalogue record for this book is available from
the National Library of Australia.
ISBN: 978 1 74245 676 8 (hardback)

© Bauer Media Pty Limited 2016
ABN 18 053 273 546

This publication is copyright. No part of it may be
reproduced or transmitted in any form without the
written permission of the Publisher.